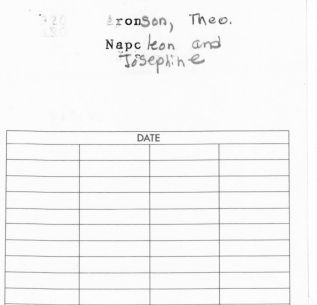

Aronson, Theo.
Napoleon and
Josephine

Napoleon and Josephine

NAPOLEON

AND

JOSEPHINE

A Love Story

THEO ARONSON

ST. MARTIN'S PRESS
NEW YORK

Library of Congress Cataloging-in-Publication Data

Aronson, Theo.
    Napoleon and Josephine : a love story / by Theo Aronson.
        p.   cm.
    "A Thomas Dunne book."
    ISBN 0-312-05135-2
    1. Napoleon I, Emperor of the French, 1769–1821. 2. Josephine, Consort of
Napoleon I, Emperor of the French, 1763–1814. 3. France—History—Consulate and
Empire, 1799–1815.   4. France—Kings and rulers—Biography.   5. France—Empresses—
Biography.   I. Title.
    DC203.A78   1990
    944.05'0922—dc20
    [B]   90-37252

First published in Great Britain by John Murray Publishers Ltd.

First U.S. Edition
10 9 8 7 6 5 4 3 2 1

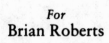

For
Brian Roberts

Contents

———

Illustrations

Author's Note

———————————

THIS book is the result of a life-long fascination with the Napoleonic saga. Ever since, in my early twenties, I visited Napoleon's first grave on the island of Saint Helena, I have been obsessed with the turbulent story of the Bonaparte family. It would not be too much to claim that the sight of that simple grave in Geranium Valley served as a turning point in my life. I became a writer because of my interest in, initially, the exile and death of Napoleon and then in the chequered history of his dynasty.

In the years following the first of my three visits to Saint Helena, I have seen almost all the places connected with the Napoleonic saga: birthplaces, palaces, places of captivity, houses of exile, battlefields, tombs and monuments. I have researched and studied the subject extensively. My first published book was *The Golden Bees: The Story of the Bonapartes*; since then I have written two more books on the dynasty: *The Fall of the Third Napoleon* and *Queen Victoria and the Bonapartes*. So, in writing this book on Napoleon and Josephine, I am returning, after having written many biographies on other royal subjects, to my first love.

Surprisingly, there has been no recent book published in English devoted entirely to the relationship between Napoleon and Josephine. There have, of course, been individual biographies on them but it is over twenty-five years since the publication of Frances Mossiker's *Napoleon and Josephine*; while Margaret Laing's *Josephine and Napoleon*, published seventeen years ago, is more in the nature of a short biography of the Empress. Neither of these books is in print. On the premise that every generation thrills again to the Napoleonic story, I have decided that the time is ripe for a fresh look at one of the most fascinating aspects of that story.

In writing the book, I have kept the two principals firmly centre-stage. What I am presenting is domestic history: the great political, economic and military events of the period are heard dimly, as 'noises off'. Only where these events directly affect the relationship between Napoleon and Josephine are they dealt with in any detail; otherwise they are simply mentioned *en passant*. With Napoleon in his many-faceted role as soldier, administrator, politician and empire-builder, I have not concerned myself. There is no shortage of books covering these aspects of his career. This book is the biography of a marriage; in it I have gone, in the words of that talented Bonaparte biographer, Dormer Creston, 'in search of two characters'.

In researching this book I have made use, wherever possible, of contemporary sources. However, several of the memoirs, on which biographers of Napoleon and Josephine usually rely, must be treated with extreme caution. Most of these books were published after the fall of Napoleon's empire at a time when it was, to say the least, inadvisable to speak favourably of him. For this or for other reasons, such as self-justification, self-aggrandisement or simply sensationalism, few of these memoirs can be regarded as accurate or impartial. The accounts of people like Josephine's ladies-in-waiting, Claire de Rémusat and Georgette Ducrest, her friend Laure Junot, her maid Mademoiselle Avrillon, her ex-lover Barras, Napoleon's secretary Bourrienne and his valet Constant, are all suspect to a greater or lesser degree. Where they are valuable, however, is in evoking the flavour of the period and in providing information which they had no reason to distort.

On the other hand, there are many other far more reliable memoirs which can be used with confidence. The most trustworthy of contemporary material is, of course, the letters. In addition to the massive, thirty-two volume *Correspondance de Napoleon 1er*, which includes letters to his family, there are hundreds of letters between Napoleon, Josephine and her two children Eugène and Hortense. There are also her recently discovered love letters to Hippolyte Charles. These published letters, as well as all other books consulted, are listed in the Bibliography.

I am indebted to the Archives Nationales, the Bibliothèque

Author's Note

Nationale and the *Fonds Masson* in the Bibliothèque Thiers, Paris; the British Library, London; the Bristol Reference Library; the 'Napoleon Collection' at the Bath Reference Library; and, as always, to Mrs S. Bane and the staff of the Frome Library for their helpfulness.

I must also thank, in alphabetical order, those many people who, to a greater or lesser extent, have helped me in the researching and writing of this book. They are: Dr Anna Benna, Miss E. H. Berridge, M. Pierre Blanchard, Mr André Bothner, Mr Mervyn Clingan, Mr Ronald Duff, M. Louis Durand, M. Paul du Toit, Mlle Louise Duval, Mr David Griffiths and Mrs Angela Griffiths, Miss A. T. Hadley, Mrs Phyllis Huie, Miss Sue Manby and Mrs Betty Ross. As always, my chief thanks go to Mr Brian Roberts who has not only endured but encouraged my Napoleonic obsession for over thirty years.

Malmaison

THE time to see Malmaison is in late September. This season seems to capture, more than any other, something of the bitter-sweet quality of the story of Napoleon and Josephine. On the one hand, Josephine's famous rose gardens still retain some of their summer opulence; on the other, the leaves of the chestnut trees are already turning brown. There is, in spite of the sunshine, a slight melancholy in the air, a presage of winter to come.

The Château of Malmaison, far more than the palaces of the Tuileries, Saint-Cloud or Fontainebleau, was the setting of some of the couple's happiest, most intimate times together. It also saw them in periods of their deepest *tristesse*. Josephine bought the little manor house not long after their marriage; both during the Consulate and the Empire it represented the only place in which they were able to live a life relatively free of the constraints and formalities of their position. It was the one spot that they could call their own; it was their only real home. After their divorce, Josephine spent most of her time at Malmaison; she died there, in her gilded swan bed, four and a half years later. Napoleon enjoyed his last days as a free man at Malmaison, roaming through the gardens and expecting, as he put it, to see Josephine come gliding along its paths at any moment. 'Wouldn't it be delightful', he sighed, if he 'could remain here forever?'[1]

Much has changed at Malmaison since those days. For almost a century after the fall of the First Empire, the house suffered from either neglect or insensitive restoration. The huge park has been whittled away by the spread of suburbia; only a fragment of those leafy grounds remains. Josephine's romantically landscaped 'English' garden is a faint echo of what it once was. Her famous picture gallery has gone; her matchless conservatories are empty; most of her treasures have been dispersed. Only in the twentieth century has a costly, conscientious and continuing programme of restoration been undertaken. It has now become possible to recapture something of the look and spirit of the place as it was at the time of Napoleon and Josephine.

Malmaison is unlike any other royal, or imperial, home in France. Built of silvery-grey stone and rising from a gravelled forecourt set with clipped bay trees in tubs, it has a lightness and a simplicity lacking in the great French palaces. And once inside the house, all feelings of melancholy disappear. Its air is redolent of new beginnings: of a new century, a new regime, a new way of life. In contrast to the overwhelming sumptuousness and traditionalism of the palaces of the former kings of France, Malmaison is decorated in the then fashionable neo-classical and Empire styles. Everything – from the striped fabrics of the tented rooms to the Roman-like busts of the members of Napoleon's family (looking more dignified in marble than ever they did in the flesh) – reflects an elegant, contemporary taste. It reflects, also, the youth of its owners; for even in the last year of his fourteen-year-long marriage to Josephine, Napoleon was still only in his thirties.

There is no trace, in these light-flooded rooms, of any ownership previous, or subsequent, to theirs. The house bears the indelible imprint of their taste; it is impregnated by their personalities. The Emperor's study is the room of an industrious, serious-minded man; his bedroom suggests, if somewhat artfully, the spartan simplicity of a soldier. The salons are perfect manifestations of the Empress's grace and chic; her crimson and gold bedroom is that of a *femme du monde*.

The rooms abound in portraits of the celebrated couple: of Napoleon because they were a form of propaganda and an affirmation of how high he had risen in the world; of Josephine because they rendered permanent the transient art of self-adornment to which she devoted so much of her time – and Napoleon's money. The Emperor's Italianate features are shown amidst swirling cloaks and drifting smoke in the battle scenes, and looking suitably imperious in official portraits. But the Empress's likenesses

2

are less evocative. She always looks stiff, guarded, enigmatic, for few artists could capture her allure. Josephine's was essentially a beauty of expression and mobility. She was, as Napoleon said on revisiting Malmaison after her death, 'the most enchanting being I have ever known. She was a woman in every sense of the word, vivid, vivacious and so tender-hearted...'[2] Few of her portraits convey this.

At Malmaison, then, is to be found the very essence of the story of Napoleon and Josephine. Although the scenes of their lives, apart and together, were played out against a variety of backgrounds, from the humblest to the most palatial, it is at Malmaison that they are most frequently seen in close-up. It remains the most enduring monument not, admittedly, to Napoleon's stupendous career but to his life with Josephine; a monument to a romance which is still one of the most intriguing, tempestuous and touching in history. For the story of Napoleon and Josephine is, quite simply, one of the greatest love stories in the world.

Part One

BUONAPARTE AND BEAUHARNAIS

1

The Corsican

THEY were an oddly assorted couple. 'Nature,' as Napoleon once put it to Josephine, 'has given me a strong and resolute character; she has made you of lace and gauze.'[1] And although Napoleon might sometimes be driven to near distraction by her gossamer qualities – her pliability, her nonchalance, her indiscriminating generosity – they were the very qualities which made her so attractive to him.

Her frothiness served as a foil to his own steeliness. Where he could offend by his brusqueness, she could captivate by her charm; where he could be brutal, she was ineffably sweet-natured. No day was long enough for the myriad things he had to do; she could, marvelled one of her friends, 'idle away her days doing nothing and yet never be bored with it.'[2] He was intense, incisive, interested in everything; she was superficial, apathetic, lacking in application. He had an almost bourgeois concern for the value of money; she was recklessly extravagant. He created an atmosphere that was tense and electric; she wove a dulcet and harmonious spell. His imperial emblem was the all-powerful eagle, hers the graceful swan. He was a genius; she could not even be called clever. In short, and in almost every way, theirs was an attraction of opposites.

Yet the celebrated couple did have some things in common; not least in the circumstances of their early days. By a curious coincidence, neither Napoleon nor Josephine – the future Emperor and Empress of the French – was born in France. Equally curious is the fact that they were both born on islands: he on Corsica, she on Martinique. Indeed, Corsica could only just be regarded as French as it was not until May 1769, a mere three months before Napoleon was born, that France, having finally conquered those Corsican patriots fighting for their independence, took possession of the island. By this precarious margin of time did the future Emperor of the French succeed in actually being born French.

Culturally, linguistically and historically, Corsica was Italian. Only in the year before Napoleon's birth had the republic of Genoa ceded Corsica to France. Italian was the young Napoleon's native tongue; he was nine before he began to learn French. To some words, in fact, he was always to give Italian pronunciation. And, throughout his youth and young manhood, he spelt his name in the Italian fashion: Napoleone Buonaparte.

Martinique, too, had only just come under French control at the time of Josephine's birth, in 1763. It had been captured by the British the year before; not until March, less than four months before Josephine was born, was it restored to France. And lying in the West Indies, over four thousand miles and several weeks' sailing from mainland France, the island was even more remote than Corsica from the day-to-day life of the mother country. The young Josephine was regarded as a Creole, the name given to those European colonists born and bred in the tropics, and for the rest of her life there was a certain Creole quality, a mellifluous drawl, to her spoken French. Where Napoleon was nine before he set foot in France, Josephine was sixteen.

But the two islands – the Mediterranean island of Corsica and the Caribbean island of Martinique – bequeathed more than just peculiarities of French pronunciation to Napoleon and Josephine. The atmosphere of these two dissimilar places seemed to have permeated their very natures. In Napoleon was personified something of the harsh, masculine, unforgiving character of his native land. He had been conceived and carried in embryo in the throes of a violent guerrilla war, for his parents had spent many months fighting alongside their fellow Corsican patriots against the French.

Josephine, on the other hand, seemed to epitomise all the grace, insouciance and seductiveness of Martinique. She retained always the warmth and langour that are usually associated with tropical islands. Even the name of the group to which Martinique belonged – the Windward Islands, Les Iles du

Vent – captures something of the capriciousness of Josephine's personality.

But, of course, not too much should be made of any of this. Napoleon's elder brother Joseph, born on the same island of Corsica in the same turbulent period of its history, developed into one of the most urbane, irresolute and peace-loving of men; a male version of Josephine, almost. And there can be no doubt that Martinique, for all its balmy atmosphere and luxuriant beauty, had its share of tyrants.

The social standing of the families into which Napoleon and Josephine were born was, in both cases, somewhat equivocal. Although it is true that, on Corsica, the Bonapartes were regarded as noble, it was a nobility of a particularly meaningless variety. Unlike the nobility of the rest of Europe, Corsican nobles were neither rich nor privileged. Their way of life was hardly better than that of their peasant neighbours; they lived equally close to the soil. There was no sign, on Corsica, of those powdered, scented, beauty-spotted aristocrats who clustered around the monarch at Versailles.

Josephine's forebears had hardly been top-ranking aristocrats either. They had belonged to the ancient gentry of France, the *gentilshommes de province*. Later, on Martinique, where her grandfather settled, her family formed part of the lower stratum of the *grand blancs* – the local aristocracy. On mainland France, Creoles were generally regarded as ill-educated, unsophisticated, provincial. They remained colonials.

It was, perhaps, this shared ambiguity of status – outsiders, islanders, not quite French and yet not foreign, not quite noble and yet not bourgeois – that allowed both Napoleon and Josephine one day to adopt, and play to such perfection, their new imperial roles.

During the years that Napoleon was master of Europe, and since, dedicated Bonapartists have been tireless in their attempts to trace his elevated origins. By tortuous genealogical calculation he has been linked to the various ruling dynasties of Europe, including the Bourbons, the Brunswicks and the 'old Kings of the North'. There have even been some fawning references to his descent from the emperors of Byzantium and Trebizond. It is to Napoleon's credit that he – who was not above a little invention when necessary – had no time for this particular form of flattery. He was the Rudolf of his race, Napoleon once told the Emperor of Austria, referring to Rudolf, founder of the Hapsburg dynasty. And on another occasion he silenced some sycophantic genealogist by claiming that his patent dated back to the *coup d'état* by which he won the mastery of France, and no further.

His ancestors, Napoleon once admitted, had been *condottieri* – 'little gentleman adventurers'. But even that, writes one of his biographers, was 'hitting slightly above the mark'.[3] It is generally agreed, though, that both his father and mother – Carlo-Maria Buonaparte and Letizia Ramolino – were descended from patrician Italian families in northern Italy. In time, this tenuous descent enabled Carlo Buonaparte to claim, or at least to convince Corsica's new French masters that he had a right to claim, noble status.

Born on 15 August 1769, Napoleon was Carlo and Letizia Buonaparte's second surviving child. Recent research has revealed the generally accepted view of Napoleon's parents to be a somewhat mistaken one.[4] The marriage, in 1764, of these two exceptionally good-looking young people was not, as previously believed, a love match: Carlo seems to have been talked into it. Nor, apparently, were they married in the cathedral at Ajaccio; their wedding, at the home of the bride, might not even have been a religious ceremony at all.

Far from having the bland, aristocratic features of his posthumous portraits, Carlo Buonoparte had a sharp, sensuous, very Italian face. Nor was he quite the idle, profligate ne'er-do-well of popular legend: charming and pleasure-loving he might have been, but he was also shrewd, socially ambitious and dedicated to the improvement of his family's fortunes. A lawyer, of questionable qualifications, Carlo Buonaparte expended much of his energy on often unsuccessful litigation and invariably fruitless financial schemes.

But if he never achieved the heights of his ambitions, Carlo's life was not entirely unfulfilled. Within a couple of years of Napoleon's birth, by turning his back on his pro-Corsican, anti-French past and by taking advantage of the opportunities offered by the new regime, Carlo Buonaparte was able to improve his lot to a considerable extent. He wangled an appointment as an assistant judge, or *assesseur*. He won official recognition of his noble status. He was elected as a deputy to the Corsican Estate. He ingratiated himself with the Comte de Marbeuf, commander-in-chief of the French forces on Corsica.

Letizia Buonaparte, too, was not always the long-suffering, tight-lipped drudge of popular belief. As a young woman (she was only fourteen when she married Carlo) she was very beautiful, and, while her husband was alive, fond of clothes and entertaining. As much as Carlo, Letizia knew the value of keeping up appearances. It has even been suggested that, in order to support her husband in his social aspirations, Letizia became Marbeuf's mistress. True or not, there is no doubt that, as a woman of considerable spirit and forceful personality, Letizia Buonaparte was no less ready than her husband to take advantage of anything the new French masters – Marbeuf included – had to offer.

Although the marriage of Carlo Buonaparte and Letizia Ramolino might have been arranged, it developed into a very successful one. In their twenty years of married life Letizia bore her husband thirteen children, eight of whom survived. Their upbringing was entirely in her hands. Whenever the softer hearted Carlo tried to temper the severity of her regime, she would tell him not to interfere. It was her business, she would say, not his, to look after the children. She was the dominant figure in their lives. 'To the manner in which she formed me at an early age,' Napoleon later claimed, 'I principally owe my subsequent elevation.'[5]

The couple lived in Ajaccio, in a large, shuttered stone house which they shared with several other members of the Buonaparte family. In addition, they owned a small house in the countryside, a couple of vineyards, an olive grove and some other arable land. They were not rich but they were self-sufficient. 'In my family,' Napoleon was to claim in later life, 'it was a matter of principle with us not to spend money. We never bought anything except what was strictly necessary, such as clothes and furniture. But we spent practically nothing on food.'[6] Food, he went on to explain, was accepted from the neighbours as payment for the use of the communal mill and bakehouse owned by his family.

Napoleon's picture might have been accurate but it was slightly misleading. By the time he was growing up, his father had begun to move up in the world. Carlo was able to improve the house, to entertain more lavishly and to spend more on the clothes by which he set such store. By the standards of the French aristocracy the family might have lived very modestly, but by Corsican standards they were able to cut something of a dash.

To the characteristics inherited from his parents – the love of display and the determination to make a mark from his father, and the driving energy and craving to domineer from his mother – Napoleon added some of his own. In infancy he revealed himself as an assertive, combative little bully; as he grew older, so did he develop that methodical, analytical mind that was to be yet another facet of his many-faceted personality.

In short, there could hardly have been a greater contrast between the ambitious, orderly and overbearing Napoleon growing up on Corsica and the pliable, indolent and good-natured Josephine growing up on Martinique.

Another legacy from Napoleon's Corsican beginnings that was to have a profound effect on the life of Josephine was the clannishness, the almost primitive sense of kinship which was so characteristic of the island. In late eighteenth-century Corsica, the population was still rigidly divided into clans; it was an island of fierce family loyalties, of burning family pride, of bloody vendettas that gathered strength from generation to generation. Any slight, real or imagined, had to be avenged. Men would grow their beards until they had had their revenge on whoever had insulted a member of their family, no matter how distantly related that member might be. The *barbe di vendetta* was a great feature of the island's male population.

In later life Napoleon boasted that whenever his grandmother needed support in some local misunderstanding, she could be sure of between two and three hundred armed clansmen hurrying unquestioningly to her aid.

Napoleon shared this sense of family solidarity to the full. It caused him to elevate his relations far beyond their capabilities and contributed, in no small measure, to his downfall. It also caused these relations, who bickered ceaselessly amongst themselves, to unite in the face of any threat to the family. One of the greatest of these threats, they were one day to decide, was their brother's wife, Josephine. From the day that she married Napoleon, Josephine would be obliged to battle against the typically Corsican machinations of the Buonaparte clan.

One of the most important advantages of Carlo Buonaparte's newly-won status as a member of the nobility was that it enabled him – as a still far from wealthy man – to apply for scholarships at leading French schools for his children. He and Letizia decided that their eldest son, the mild-mannered Joseph, should eventually enter the Church while their second, the fiery Napoleon, must make a career in the Army. With the boys' scholarships to the college at Autun being granted, Carlo, late in 1778, accompanied the ten-year-old Joseph and the nine-year-old Napoleon to France to begin their schooling.

Carlo's journey was to serve another purpose as well. Much to his delight, he had been chosen as a member of a deputation representing the nobility of Corsica; the deputation was to go to Versailles to pay its respects to the new sovereigns, King Louis XVI and Queen Marie Antoinette.

Once among the splendours of Versailles, Carlo's always romantic imagination took wing. He could see himself developing into a courtier-politician, being rewarded by a grateful monarch, perhaps even being granted a title. At Versailles, with its crystal chandeliers being reflected into infinity in the mirrored walls, its fountains flinging their illuminated jets high into the night sky, its swarms of courtiers in their silks, satins and velvets, its wealth of painting and statuary and furniture, Carlo could dream – if only for a few days – that he was part of this enchanted and privileged world.

Never, in his wildest dreams, would Carlo have imagined that his second son would one day hold sway over a regime even grander, more powerful than this. One can appreciate why Napoleon, dressed in splendour for his coronation twenty-six years later, should have turned to his brother Joseph, as they set out for Notre-Dame, to say, 'If only our father could see us now.'[7]

13

2

The Creole

IN 1779, the year after the nine-year-old Napoleon left Corsica for France, the sixteen-year-old Josephine set sail from Martinique. Where he had come to be educated, she had come to be married.

Born on 23 June 1763 and baptized Marie-Josephe-Rose Tascher de la Pagerie (she was known as Rose until renamed by Napoleon), she was the daughter of Joseph-Gaspard Tascher de la Pagerie, whose father had emigrated from France in 1726 in the hope of making his fortune in the New World. He had not succeeded. Nor had his son – Josephine's father – proved any more successful. In fact, Joseph-Gaspard's only worthwhile achievement was his marriage to a woman of nobler blood, much stronger character and considerably more in the way of tangible assets. For with his bride came the sugar plantation of Les Trois-Ilets, lying about twenty miles across the bay from the island's capital, Fort-Royal.

But for neither sugar planting nor family life did Joseph-Gaspard Tascher de la Pagerie show the slightest aptitude. A feckless philanderer, he was happiest amongst the somewhat provincial delights of Fort-Royal society. The birth of three daughters, of whom Josephine was the eldest, did little to anchor him to his home. In any case, that home, a large wooden house, was swept away by a hurricane when Josephine was three; from that time on, the family lived in a converted upper floor of the plantation's sugar refinery, the *sucerie*. Worse still, from Joseph-Gaspard's

14

point of view, was the fact that when his father-in-law died, he left, not the expected fortune but a mountain of debts. It was bad enough having no son, but to be landed with three daughters without dowries was little short of disastrous.

Yet life for the young Josephine was anything but frugal. Compared to the Buonapartes, the Taschers lived in an almost luxurious style. The plantation teemed with slaves, the house was furnished with a certain faded elegance, they moved in the best island society and Martinique itself was something of a paradise. Josephine was never to forget the physical delights of her island home: the warm climate, the lush vegetation, the sweet-scented flowers, the brilliantly plumaged birds. As Empress of the French, she would import its blooms for her conservatories and its birds for her aviaries.

Josephine's education, at the hands of the nuns of Les Dames de la Providence, can only be described as undemanding. There was nothing in that curriculum of deportment, writing, drawing, embroidery, dancing and music to stimulate the intellect. 'Her voice is sweet, she plucks prettily at the guitar and, showing a general aptitude for music, she could with proper instruction perfect her singing, playing and dancing',[1] reads her father's somewhat desperate catalogue of his eldest daughter's accomplishments. It was regrettable, he went on to say, that she did not have the advantages of a French education.

While she remained on Martinique, this hardly mattered. It was well known in France that Creole ladies, no matter how elevated their status, could barely read or write. It was enough that Josephine appear well-bred and behave decorously. Her only goal was marriage. That feathery education over, Josephine returned home to Les Trois-Ilets to spend her days in pleasurable idleness: swaying in a hammock, chatting to the house slaves, listening to the gossip on some shady verandah and plucking prettily at that guitar. Her physical advantages at this early stage were her chestnut hair and her large hazel eyes; her most notable characteristic was her sweet nature. For even in girlhood, Josephine was remarkable for her goodness and her generosity.

It must have been, then, with considerable scepticism, that this kindly, passive, ill-educated and unambitious girl one day found herself listening to the predictions of a mulatto fortune teller. She would marry young; she would be unhappy; she would be widowed; she would marry again; and she would become 'more than a Queen' in France. On Martinique, in those apparently secure days of the *ancien régime*, with King Louis XVI and Queen Marie Antoinette having recently ascended the throne, it must all have sounded like so much nonsense.

Indeed, Josephine might well have remained on Martinique, to become the wife of a planter or an officer had it not been for the machinations of her father's sister, her Aunt Edmée, Madame Renaudin. The resourceful Aunt Edmée, having at one stage joined the household of the governor of the island, the Marquis de Beauharnais, went on to become his mistress. Ignoring both the governor's wife and her own husband, Aunt Edmée accompanied the Marquis de Beauharnais on his return to Paris and there set up home with him.

In an effort, perhaps, to link herself even more closely to her lover, Madame Renaudin then suggested that his younger son, Alexandre de Beauharnais, born in 1760, marry one of her three Tascher nieces. Alexandre, at seventeen, seemed willing enough. The only unresolved question (questions and answers criss-crossed the Atlantic for months) was which of the three girls he should choose. With Josephine, at fifteen, being considered too old and Marie-Françoise, at eleven, too young, Alexandre plumped for the middle girl, Catherine-Desirée.

But her sudden death before the arrival of the letter indicating Alexandre's choice, re-opened the whole business. In the end, the Beauharnais ménage left the choice to the Taschers. 'Bring us whichever daughter you consider most likely to suit my son,'[2] ran the Marquis de Beauharnais's offhand instructions to Joseph-Gaspard. In the accompanying marriage document, the space for the name of the bride was left blank.

As the younger had no wish to leave her mother while the elder, according to her father, was 'all eagerness to go', it was Josephine who was chosen. Father and daughter set sail for France late in the summer of 1779.

The affianced couple first set eyes on each other at Brest, on 27 October. If the nineteen-year-old Alexandre, Vicomte de Beauharnais, was disappointed at the sight of his sixteen-year-old bride-to-be, he did not make too much of it. She was, he admitted to his father, rather less pretty than they had been led to expect but the sweetness of her nature more than made up for this. Josephine, on the other hand, must have been overwhelmed. In her naïve eyes, Alexandre de Beauharnais was everything that a girl could hope for. With his powdered hair and his dashing white and silver infantry uniform, he seemed the very epitome of the handsome, debonair, cultivated young aristocrat of the day. Only later would she discover something about his less attractive qualities: his egotism, his snobbery and, above all, his licentiousness.

Why this elegant young aristocrat should have been so willing to marry a gauche and penniless Creole is something of a mystery. It has been suggested that Alexandre's motives were entirely mercenary: that marriage would allow him to gain control of the estate bequeathed him by his mother for which he would otherwise have had to wait until he came of age.

Whatever the reason, the couple were married on 13 December 1779. The marriage was to last for fifteen years, and was to be, as predicted by that fortune teller on Martinique, unhappy.

Hardly had Josephine married Alexandre de Beauharnais than the marriage began falling apart. He found that he had saddled himself with a wife who could not possibly match up to his exacting standards of culture, conversation, or literacy even. In letter after letter – for he was seldom home – he nagged her to improve herself. She was, he complained, too indolent, too ill-read, too incurious. He could not even think of showing her off in those smart salons in which he himself shone so brightly.

Josephine, on the other hand, found herself married to a tireless philanderer. Not only did her new husband resume relations with the mistress who had first seduced him at seventeen but he made what he listed as 'conquests' in whatever garrison town his military duties happened to take him. 'Instead of spending my time at home with a creature with whom I can find nothing in common,' he explained to his former tutor, 'I have to a great extent resumed my bachelor life.'[3]

On at least two occasions, though, Alexandre spent enough time in his wife's bed for her to conceive. Their son, Eugène, was born on 3 September 1781; their daughter, Hortense, on 10 April 1783. And whereas Alexandre did happen to be at home for his son's birth, he was half-way across the world at the time that his daughter was born.

For suddenly, one night in September 1782, without a word

to Josephine, he left for Martinique. He had decided to apply for the post of aide-de-camp to the governor. With him sailed his recently widowed mistress, Madame de Longpré.

It was Madame de Longpré who dealt the already tottering marriage the final blow. When news reached Martinique of the birth of Hortense, Madame de Longpré assured Alexandre that he could not possibly be the girl's father, on the curious grounds that whereas babies could be born late, they could never be born early. Hortense, apparently, had been born twelve days before the date on which she was due. Having planted this poisoned dart, Madame de Longpré left her incensed lover to scour the island for proof of Josephine's girlhood depravities (he unearthed none that withstood investigation) and sailed back to France to get married again. One of her first duties on reaching Paris was to deliver a violent letter of denunciation from Alexandre to Josephine.

Such was the measure of Josephine's good-heartedness that twenty-five years later, as Empress, she arranged for the malicious Madame de Longpré, who had just been widowed for a second time, to be granted a pension. The lady, she explained, was by now 'very infirm'.[4]

From this point on, Alexandre, blithely ignoring his own well-known infidelities, railed against his wife's imagined ones to anyone who was prepared to listen. As very few were, for the very good reason that they did not believe him, he was obliged to resort to a more drastic course of action. He insisted that Josephine leave their home and enter a convent. Such were the conventions of the time that she was forced to comply. But as – in these circumstances – a convent was merely a place in which ladies of fashion who found themselves in temporary domestic difficulties could rent apartments, Alexandre's punishment was not quite as draconian as might be imagined.

Josephine acting, one may be sure, on the advice of her redoubtable Aunt Edmée, Madame Renaudin (who was still the mistress of the Marquis de Beauharnais), chose the most fashionable of these retreats – the convent of Penthemont in the Rue de Grenelle. With her was her two-year-old son Eugène; the baby Hortense had had to be left with a wet-nurse. Within weeks of her arrival, Josephine had applied for a legal separation from her husband who had, by now, returned to France. As not one of Alexandre's wild accusations could stand up to investigation, he was obliged to agree to her terms. These included custody of

Eugène until he reached the age of five, after which his father would have control of his education; permanent custody of Hortense; and a handsome annual allowance.

Josephine's two-year-long stay at the Penthemont did more, though, than just give her time to sort out her marital affairs. It saw her final transition from awkward provincial to woman of fashion: from an ugly duckling to the swan which was to be – in the imperial years that lay ahead – her emblem.

What did Josephine look like as she prepared to leave the Penthemont at the age of twenty-two? She was not really a beauty. Official descriptions, in these days before she became celebrated, tell one very little. She was about five feet, four inches tall, and slender; her hair was chestnut brown; her long-lashed eyes, which were probably her best feature, were so variable in colour as to appear sometimes green, sometimes amber; to hide her already discoloured teeth, she perfected a sweet, tight-lipped, provocative smile.

Yet Josephine de Beauharnais was one of those women who, without actually being beautiful, give an illusion of beauty. In the six years between her arrival in Paris and her departure from the convent, she learned how to make the most of herself. Like many another not particularly intelligent woman, her appearance was one of her chief preoccupations. She knew exactly what to wear, how to do her hair, how to paint her face. To this studied elegance was added a natural grace. There was something fluid, seductive, almost abandoned about her movements.

The father of one of her legal advisers, accompanying his son on a visit to the Vicomtesse de Beauharnais at her convent, came away enchanted. She was 'a fascinating young person', runs his enthusiastic report, 'a lady of distinction and elegance, perfect of manner, endowed with a multitude of graces, and with the loveliest of speaking voices.'[5]

This charm of appearance and manner was greatly enhanced, during her stay at Penthemont, by her absorption of the cultivated atmosphere in which she found herself. For the convent was full of aristocratic women, members of some of France's most illustrious families, all thoroughly at home in the mannered world of the *ancien régime*. A poor originator but a skilled imitator, Josephine soon mastered the complicated patterns by which they lived their lives. Indeed, instead of keeping her at home, Alexandre de Beauharnais would have done better to have introduced Josephine into society; she was the type who learned by listening and looking, not by reading or studying. How ironic that Alexandre's official break with Josephine should coincide with the very time that she was emerging as the sort of woman he had always wanted her to be: stylish, attractive and, if not intellectual, certainly socially accomplished.

A spell with her Aunt Edmée and her father-in-law in their Fontainebleau house – during which she is rumoured to have attracted a host of aristocratic admirers – further accustomed her to the company of the rich and the fashionable. It also brought her close to, if not exactly into, the highly artificial world surrounding the monarchs, Louis XVI and Marie Antoinette.

It was during this period, too, that Josephine was afterwards accused of having given birth to a daughter. Why else, it was asked, had both she and her Aunt Edmée taken such an interest in a baby born in Paris in 1786? Madame Renaudin left the girl something in her will and Josephine not only negotiated her marriage but provided her with a dowry. The most likely explanation (and the one believed by the young woman's descendants) is that Josephine's estranged husband, the licentious Alexandre, had fathered the child and that as he had refused to accept responsibility for her, she had been taken under the wings of the worldly Madame Renaudin and the soft-hearted Josephine.

In 1788, when Josephine was twenty-five, she decided to visit her parents on Martinique. Accompanied by her little daughter Hortense, she spent over two years on the island. Once again, the decorative and attractive young vicomtesse was caught up in a social melée and, before long, was sending to Paris for some of those '*décolleté* and diaphanous' ball gowns which she always wore to such effect.

Her stay on Martinique gave rise to yet another of the many rumours which proliferated after the falls of the First and Second Empires, about her having given birth to a child not fathered by Alexandre. Her mother was said to have taken particular interest in a baby girl born on the plantation at about this time, and it was claimed that Josephine, when Empress, provided the young woman with a dowry. The story was finally rebutted, over a century later, by the discovery of the child's birth certificate: she had been born in 1786, two years before Josephine's arrival on Martinique.

Josephine was still on the island when news of the outbreak

of the French Revolution reached Martinique. With the news came encouragement for those islanders – negro slaves, mulattos and underprivileged whites – who felt that they, too, were being oppressed by their aristocratic masters. Insurrection broke out and one evening, while Josephine and Hortense were guests at Government House at Fort-Royal, the town was attacked by what Hortense called 'mutineers'. Never a brave woman, Josephine decided that they must get off the island as soon as possible. She was not to know that by jumping out of the frying pan of revolutionary Martinique, she was to land herself in the fire of revolutionary France.

A ship, commanded by one of her many admirers, was in port. Dodging the insurgents' cannon fire, mother and daughter dashed across the Savane – the public square – and boarded the vessel. They set sail the next day, just as the town fell to the revolutionaries.

In the square across which Josephine scurried on that wild September night in 1790 there now stands a larger than lifesize marble statue of her, in her full splendour as Empress of the French.

During that pre-Revolutionary period in which Josephine was being transformed from a gauche Creole into a soignée gentle-woman, Napoleon was changing from a thin-skinned Corsican boy into a serious-minded young French officer.

From his arrival in France in 1778 until the outbreak of the French Revolution eleven years later, Napoleon had been pursuing an apparently conventional military career. After a few months at the college at Autun, he moved on to the military academy at Brienne. His five-and-a-half-year period of training over, he entered the Ecole Militaire in Paris. Here his progress was so good that he passed out after only one year; at sixteen Napoleon was an officer. Commissioned in the artillery, he joined a regiment stationed first at Valence and then at Auxonne.

The nineteen-year-old Lieutenant Buonaparte was still at Auxonne when the Bastille, that hated symbol of the *ancien régime*, was stormed in July 1789.

Napoleon's personal progress, during these years, was any-thing but conventional. Gradually he developed, from an unhappy, taciturn, solitary youngster, deeply conscious of his humble

Corsican origins and resentful of his dependence on the charity of the King of France, into a talented artillery officer: diligent, intelligent, with an incisive mind and a strong sense of responsibility. He read voraciously. Mathematics was his favourite subject for, as he once significantly declared, in mathematics 'all is resolved by logic, all is rational'.[6] But there were few subjects in which he was not interested. That already formidable mind could focus itself, with equal concentration, on almost any topic. He made copious notes, he wrote innumerable papers. In view of his future career, his opinion on the monarchy in the year before the Revolution is instructive. The King, he decided, had become too powerful; what was needed was a constitution which would ensure that the monarch acted in the interests of the French people as a whole.

Napoleon's burgeoning self-importance was greatly encouraged by the death of his father, Carlo Buonaparte, of cancer of the stomach early in 1785. Even before then, the youth had begun to oust his elder brother Joseph from first place among the eight Buonaparte children. With extraordinary precocity, Napoleon had taken it upon himself to shape his brother's career. With his father's death, he assumed full responsibility, not only for Joseph, but for those other Buonaparte children who were being educated in France. While at Brienne he was joined by his hot-headed brother Lucien; at Auxonne, he took his more pliable brother Louis under his wing. His sister Elisa was a pupil at the famous girls' school of Saint-Cyr in Paris. There could be no doubt that, by the age of seventeen, Napoleon was head of the family.

Widowhood, in the meantime, was revealing all the strength of Letizia Buonaparte's character. Having lost her husband when she was thirty-five, she turned her back on the sexual side of life and devoted herself entirely to her duties as a mother. During the days that Carlo had been friendly with the new French masters of Corsica, the family had been moderately wealthy but his death had brought a return to the impecuniousness of their early married life. Uncomplainingly, Letizia set about making ends meet. So weighed down was she with household duties that she had to ask her confessor for a dispensation from churchgoing. 'Losses, privations, fatigues, she sustained and faced them all,' remembered Napoleon. 'She had the head of a man on the body of a woman.'[7]

These lessons in drudgery and poverty were never lost on Letizia Buonaparte. Her thrift was to turn to miserliness, her miserliness to avarice. When, in years to come, Napoleon would chide her for her penny-pinching, she would answer, in that quiet, cynical way, 'If ever all of you fall on my hands again, you will thank me for what I am doing now.'[8] Time was to prove her right. *Pourvue que cela doure* – provided that it lasts – remained Letizia Buonaparte's wry comment on her son's glittering empire.

Napoleon's adult responsibilities (for much of the time he was obliged to support his entire family on his meagre army pay) were not, however, turning him into a confident man of the world. On the contrary, his growing self-importance was not mirrored in his manner or appearance. He looked, at first glance, quite insignificant. He has been described, during his time at Valence, as 'small, beardless, pale, thin...his shoulders looked so narrow in his uniform which hung loosely as he moved, about his neck a huge pleated cravat, long, straight hanging locks hid his temples, his cheeks were hollow, his mouth had an air of seriousness as if pursed up with care, his eyes were alert and observant...'.

In short, the observer goes on to say, 'his whole aspect was that of a meditative and reserved young man, little given to conversation, defiant yet shy.'[9]

The truth was that despite his exceptional mental qualities, the young Napoleon was ill at ease in general company. He remained awkward, provincial, Corsican. Although he was always too arrogant to feel inferior, Napoleon bitterly resented the obvious wealth and social superiority of others. At the Ecole Militaire, he, who was being educated at the King's expense, had fumed against his rich fellow cadets with their valets, their horses, their dandified clothes and their aristocratic airs. He had railed, not so much against the unfairness of it all, as against the fact that he stood humiliated before them. Why, when his mother could not even afford to send him his home-made clothes before he had sent her the money for the postage, should these dandies with their lordly voices and self-confident manners enjoy so much luxury?

To mask his social inadequacies, Napoleon took refuge in truculence. He criticised constantly, he spoke little and briefly, he developed a carapace of chilly hostility. Extraordinarily thin-skinned, he never forgot an insult. Even a good-humoured laugh at his expense was stored away in that unforgiving mind.

There is, for instance, the story which Laure Permon tells about the day on which Napoleon, as a newly commissioned sub-lieutenant, first put on his new uniform. Although Laure Permon (afterwards Madame Junot and then the Duchess d'Abrantès) is not always to be trusted as a chronicler, her anecdote serves as an illustration of the touchiness noted by many of the young Napoleon's contemporaries.

In his new uniform – high collar, button-back revers, tight breeches and top boots – Napoleon presented himself at the home of the only people he knew in Paris, the Permons. Madam Permon, Corsican-born like himself, was a friend of his mother. The sight of Napoleon's spindly legs in his bulky military boots was too much for the two Permon daughters: the little girls burst into uncontrollable laughter. Napoleon was furious. He became more furious still when Cecile, the elder girl, called him a 'Puss in Boots'.

A few days later Napoleon arrived at the Permons with presents for each of the girls: for Cecile a beautifully bound copy of the story of Puss in Boots, and for Laure, the younger, an especially made toy 'Puss in Boots'. Madame Permon, who was no fool, appreciated that these expensive gifts from the almost penniless young officer were an indication, not of his sense of humour, but of his wounded pride.

But the real significance of the incident emerged years later, at the time when Napoleon was First Consul. On meeting the by now important Napoleon after a long time, Laure Permon made some passing reference to the Puss in Boots toy he had once given her. 'I shall never forget the First Consul's face,' she writes. Pinching her nose so brutally that she cried out, Napoleon growled, 'You're witty, you little pest, but you're malicious. Don't be that. A woman who is feared has no charm.'[10]

Over ten years had passed since Laure had first laughed at him in his boots. He had forgotten, and forgiven, nothing.

The outbreak of the French Revolution, which was to sweep Napoleon to the very pinnacle of power, affected him little at first. Auxonne, where he was stationed, was, in all respects, a long way from Paris. Nevertheless, Napoleon's sympathies were with the revolutionaries. He joined various revolutionary clubs and societies; he supported the measures taken against priests and nobles; he welcomed, and unhesitatingly gave his allegiance to, the new constitution which limited the powers of the monarchy. This, after all, is what he had wanted for some years.

In time, his initial enthusiasm was somewhat tempered by

some of the excesses of the Revolution. He happened to be in Paris when, in August 1792, a mob stormed the Tuileries and butchered Louis XVI's Swiss Guard. The sight of this rampaging and blood-thirsty crowd left Napoleon with a lifelong disgust for the common man in action. It also strengthened his belief in resolute leadership. 'If Louis XVI had mounted his horse, the victory would have been his,'[11] he claimed in a letter to his brother Joseph.

Napoleon was still in Paris when an even worse outrage took place: the famous September Massacres, when a mob broke into the prisons and killed hundreds of innocent priests and aristocrats. By that stage Napoleon had already decided to take his sister Elisa – a pupil at the aristocratic school of Saint-Cyr – back to the safety of Corsica. On their way south, the stage coach in which brother and sister were travelling was frequently stopped by groups of revolutionaries demanding their passports and insisting on their shouting 'Vive la nation!' It was a cry which Napoleon could still echo with enthusiasm. In any case, as a soldier in uniform, he was spared too much harassment; it was Elisa, with her Saint-Cyr accent and manners, who aroused suspicion.

When, on reaching Marseilles, she exchanged her simple Saint-Cyr head-dress for a feathered hat, the watching crowd was convinced that she was an aristocrat. 'We are no more aristocrats than you are!' shouted Napoleon and, snatching the hat from his sister's head, flung it into the cheering crowd. They reached Corsica, unharmed, in October 1792.

It was, in fact, with Corsica that Napoleon's fortunes were chiefly bound up during the four years following the outbreak of the Revolution. Always conscious of his Corsican origins, he hoped that, from out of this gigantic upheaval, something could be gained for his native land. While, in Paris, the Revolution was going through its successive and increasingly bloody stages – the meeting of the new Estates General, the storming of the Bastille, the introduction of a new constitution, the abolition of the monarchy and the declaration of a republic, the execution of Louis XVI and the Reign of Terror – Napoleon was chiefly concerned with the situation on Corsica. In the course of a series of exceptionally long leaves of absence from his regiment, he plunged into the island's political mêlée.

His attempts, as a member of the Corsican National Guard, to bring the benefits of the new Revolutionary regime to Corsica were vigorously opposed by those Corsican patriots who saw, in the Revolution, an opportunity to win their independence from France. Eventually, with the island split into two warring factions, Napoleon was declared an outlaw and the entire Buonaparte family was forced to flee to France.

They landed in Toulon on 14 June 1793: a bedraggled, penniless, homeless, provincial family, with almost nothing in the way of future prospects.

3

The Reign of Terror

JOSEPHINE'S fortunes had been far more directly bound up in the excesses of the Revolution.

She and her little daughter Hortense had returned to France, after their two-year stay on Martinique, towards the end of 1790. They had found the country in turmoil. Yet, curiously enough, it was a turmoil out of which Josephine's estranged husband, Alexandre de Beauharnais, had risen to prominence. Always something of a drawing-room liberal, ready to defend the Rights of Man in the smartest salons in the land, Alexandre had proved as good as his words. He had thrown in his lot with the reformers. Like many another young nobleman, the Vicomte de Beauharnais declared himself ready to renounce feudalism and to embrace liberty, equality and fraternity.

'Beneath this air and this habit of frivolity,' as one of his friends put it, 'M. de Beauharnais possessed energy, a stubbornness of disposition, a depth of intelligence, a longing to win fame and an overpowering ambition.'[1]

Combined, these qualities now lifted Alexandre, briefly, into one of the most powerful positions in the land. Taking advantage of the tumultuous times through which he was living, he rose to become President of the Constituent Assembly, at that stage busily converting France into a constitutional monarchy. It was Alexandre who organised the arrest and return of the royal family after they had attempted to flee the country and who acted as regent during that confused period when France was without a head. It was no wonder that his son, the ten-year-old Eugène, could claim, with forgivable exaggeration, that his father was '*le premier personnage de France*' and that the boy should swell with pride on being greeted, in the streets, with cries of '*Voilà le Dauphin!*'[2]

From this surge of family glory, Josephine de Beauharnais derived very little benefit. The only aspect of her husband's career in which the apolitical Josephine was remotely interested was its financial rewards. For, although separated from him, she still depended on him for her support. But whatever his rewards may or may not have been, a very small proportion of them reached Josephine – and then only sporadically. Yet never one to let a lack of funds cut her off from life's luxuries, Josephine resumed – as far as was still possible during this uncertain period – her inconsequential social life. First in an apartment in Paris and then, as the situation in the capital deteriorated, in a house in Croissy on the Seine, she lived through the increasingly frightening stages of the Revolution. Eventually even she, superficial and pleasure-loving though she might have been, could not close her mind to the tumultuous events taking place.

Although Josephine might never have moved in the highest circles in France, her world had always been a privileged one and now, stage by stage, that world was collapsing around her. In the spring of 1792 the invasion of France by the monarchist armies of Austria and Prussia caused a violent anti-royalist reaction. That August, the Palace of the Tuileries was mobbed, the King's Swiss Guard butchered and Louis XVI imprisoned in the Temple. The proclamation of a republic the following month was followed by the bloodthirsty September Massacres. On 21 January 1793, King Louis XVI was guillotined. Nine months later, Queen Marie Antoinette followed him to the scaffold. By then, the Convention had passed the terrifying Law of Suspects by which all aristocrats stood in danger of being arrested, imprisoned and guillotined. This led, inevitably, to the infamous Reign of Terror.

Josephine's chief concern during this period was for the safety of herself and her children. For this she was quite ready to bend with the republican wind. The former Vicomtesse de Beauharnais now re-emerged as *citoyenne* Beauharnais. Eugène and Hortense were obliged, like all good republican children, to learn a trade: he was apprenticed to a carpenter, she to a seamstress. (That the 'seamstress' happened to be Hortense's governess was something that Josephine omitted to mention.) In her letters to the authorities,

Josephine was quick to claim that hers was a 'republican house-hold', that her children had always been 'indistinguishable from the *sans-culottes*' and that she herself was – as 'an American' – a 'genuine *sans-culotte*'.[3]

Those who afterwards accused Josephine of opportunism, of switching, with indecent ease, from monarchism to republicanism (and on to imperialism) show little appreciation, either of her character or of the times through which she was living. Far from being devious or calculating, she was simply taking – as she would always take – the line of least resistance. She had no strong political convictions. Her social background had always been too brittle. A Creole, a colonist or what she, with understandable inaccuracy, called 'an American', Josephine had never been wholly identified with the monarchist and aristocratic society of the *ancien régime*. She was just as capable of taking on the colour of those well-born liberals, reformers and revolutionaries with whom her husband had allied himself. Perhaps by now, in her easily influenced way, she really imagined that she was 'a good republican'. In any case, as there was no cause about which she felt strongly enough to die for, she saw no reason why she should not do whatever was necessary to keep herself and her children alive. Self-preservation was an art which Josephine – often in curiously negative ways – was to practise with considerable success.

But by the spring of 1794 it looked as though all her efforts had been in vain. The Reign of Terror, presided over by the fanatical Robespierre, was reaching its climax. The guillotine, standing starkly in the Place de la Revolution, was proving insatiable; the only answer to the troubles besetting France, appar-ently, was the lopping off of yet more aristocratic heads. Almost daily Josephine heard of the arrest, imprisonment and execution of either relatives or friends. And then in March came the news that her husband had been arrested.

Alexandre de Beauharnais's fall from favour had been as swift as his rise. From President of the Constituent Assembly he had gone on to become Commander-in-Chief of the Army of the Rhine. His military achievements were hardly spectacular. General Beauharnais, read one commissioner's report, 'made a fool of himself at Strasbourg by chasing after whores all day and giving balls for them at night.'[4] Eventually his failure to relieve the besieged city of Mainz (and he knew what happened to aristocratic commanders who failed) caused him to resign his commission.

But neither this nor his unflagging speechmaking in favour of republican principles, could save him. He was denounced as 'a friend of tyranny and an enemy of liberty' and imprisoned.

By one of history's ironies, Alexandre's order of arrest was signed by, among others, the revolutionary artist Jacques-Louis David. A decade later David was to paint a vast canvas depicting the imperial coronation of Napoleon and Josephine. Would David have remembered, as he chatted to the erstwhile *citoyenne* Beauharnais as she sat for him, that he had signed what was, in effect, her first husband's death warrant?

Five weeks later – on 21 April 1794 – Josephine herself was arrested. An anonymous denunciation ('Beware of the former vicomtesse, wife of Alexandre Beauharnais, who has many connections in the offices of the ministeries...'[5]) had led to a search of her Paris apartment. What was found there was judged incriminating. She was taken away to the Carmes, the prison in which Alexandre was also confined.

Her last thoughts on being taken from her home that night were for her two beloved children. 'Let them sleep,' she whispered to their governess. 'I could not bear to see them cry. I would not have the strength to leave them.'[6]

The old convent of the Carmelites in which both Josephine and Alexandre were confined, was the most sinister of the revolutionary prisons. The stone walls were still bloodstained from the September Massacres; the cells were dark and damp; the corridors, in which the inmates were fed, were crowded with slop pails and crawling with rats and mice. Over two hundred prisoners, men and women, were jammed into this depressing place, often sleeping eighteen to a cell. Yet so ingrained were the snobberies of the period that one English prisoner, a Mrs Elliot – who faced the guillotine just as surely as did any of the others – could take comfort from the fact that she was being confined with 'so many delightful, so many great ladies'.[7]

The extraordinary composure – or mask of composure – exhibited by these great ladies, did not apply to Josephine. Although many of her fellow prisoners speak of her graceful bearing, charming manners and kind heart, not one of them mentions her courage. For the truth was that Josephine spent much of her time in tears. If some of the others could console themselves with the thought that they were about to be executed for some noble, monarchist cause (one fellow prisoner criticised Josephine for being a 'constitutionalist' as opposed to an upholder of the doctrine of the Divine Right of Kings), all she was interested in was her own fate. 'The other prisoners were resigned,' reported one of them, 'but she continued hoping against hope.'[8]

Although Josephine could not take much comfort from her husband's presence in the prison (in any case, a womaniser to the end, he was conducting a passionate love affair with a prisoner named Delphine de Custine), she was greatly cheered by the letters from her two children. When these were stopped by the authorities, Eugène and Hortense found other ways of keeping in touch. One of the most successful was the use of Josephine's little pug dog, Fortuné. With a message fastened under his collar, Fortuné would dash past the guards, find his way to his mistress, wait for her reply to be attached and then dash back to the children.

It was claimed, years later, that while she was in the Carmes, Josephine had a love affair with the dashing, twenty-six-year-old General Lazare Hoche. Physically, this would have been quite possible. Alexandre de Beauharnais was not the only one to be conducting a romance in these unlikely surroundings. The bravery of many of these aristocratic prisoners, all facing the possibility of death on the scaffold, was matched only by their lustfulness. They found ways, at dead of night, of making love with an abandon that astonished their fellows. Whether or not Madame Beauharnais and General Hoche were among their number cannot be conclusively proved. But it would have been perfectly under-standable if this frail and frightened young woman, facing possible execution, had sought love and reassurance in the arms of this self-confident man.

In June 1794, the newly passed Law of 22 Prairial, which allowed the 'enemies of the people' to be sentenced to death without even the customary mock trial, ushered in the bloodiest period of the Terror. During the following seven weeks, 1,366 heads went tumbling into the baskets beneath the guillotine. One of them belonged to Alexandre de Beauharnais. He was executed on 24 July 1794.

There now seemed very little doubt that Josephine would follow him to the scaffold. Indeed, a few days later a jailer came into her cell. He had come, he explained, to take away her bed to give to another prisoner. Did that mean, asked one of her companions, that she would be getting a better one?

'It means she'll not be needing one of any kind,' he chuckled. 'It means they're coming to take her to the Conciergerie and from there to the guillotine.'

That Josephine was not, in fact, taken to the guillotine was said to have been due to the fact that her dossier had disappeared. It had disappeared, not in some bureaucratic muddle but – quite literally – down the throat of an employee of the dreaded Committee of Public Safety named Delperch de la Bussière. This one-time actor made a practice of removing the dossiers of certain of his favourites and of getting rid of them by the only possible method in the circumstances: that is, by eating them.

Certainly, a decade later, when a benefit performance was being staged on behalf of the, by then, penniless actor, Napoleon and Josephine attended it in state, with Josephine sending the actor a purse of a thousand francs, marked 'in grateful remembrance'.

In later years Josephine would regale her ladies-in-waiting with a somewhat fanciful version of how she had learned that she was not to be executed. She would describe how, on the very day that the jailer had removed her bed, she happened to look out of her cell window. In the street below she saw a woman making incomprehensible signs to her. The woman kept pointing to her dress. When Josephine called out '*Robe?*' ('Dress?') she nodded her head vigorously. She then picked up a stone and held it up '*Pierre?*' ('Stone?') asked Josephine. Again the woman nodded. Then, holding up her dress and the stone together, the woman made signs of slitting her throat. Suddenly Josephine realised what she was trying to convey. Robespierre had been guillotined.

She was right. Afraid for their own throats, several of Robespierre's fellow Jacobins had turned on him. On 28 July, four days after Alexandre de Beauharnais had been guillotined, Robespierre and his little group of zealots were likewise executed. The excesses of the Reign of Terror were over.

That night they brought back Josephine's bed. On it she enjoyed, she says, 'the soundest night's sleep of my life.'

And just before going to bed, in a moment of joyous near-delirium, Josephine said jokingly to her companions, 'You see, I have not been guillotined, and I shall yet be crowned Queen of France.'[9]

She was released ten days later.

*   *   *

Hardly had Josephine been released from prison than Napoleon was put under arrest. In those confused days, when it was advisable not to be too closely associated with any of France's short-lived regimes, he was regarded, briefly, as a protégé of Robespierre. When Robespierre fell from power, Napoleon was arrested on a charge of conspiracy. But the charge could not be sustained and, on 20 August 1794, after a fortnight's imprisonment, Napoleon was released.

At that stage, just over a year after the fleeing Buonaparte family had struggled ashore at Toulon from Corsica, Napoleon was still in the south of France. During that year one of his chief concerns had been for the welfare of his impoverished family. With his elder brother Joseph, who had studied law in Italy, not having the necessary degree to practise in France, Napoleon was obliged to support the entire family – his widowed mother and the seven other children – on his soldier's pay. He had established them as cheaply as he could in a house in Marseilles and had rejoined his regiment.

In the months that followed, he found himself becoming more and more sickened by having to take part in what was virtually civil war in France. It was France's enemies – those invading monarchist armies – and not Frenchmen, that he wanted to fight. Napoleon put his feelings into words during the summer of 1793 when he wrote a political pamphlet entitled *Le Souper de Beaucaire*. In the form of a dialogue, it was a skilfully written denunciation of the folly of civil war. In it, for the first time, the author showed signs of the spare, striking and highly individual style that was to characterise the bulletins and proclamations of his years of power. He had the pamphlet published at his own expense and ensured that it was distributed in influential circles.

A more rewarding opportunity to strike a blow at what Napoleon considered to be the real enemy came towards the end of that year. The city of Toulon, still stubbornly royalist, had called on the British for help. Reinforced by not only the British but the Spanish, Toulon was successfully withstanding a siege by the French government forces. As luck would have it (and luck was to play a considerable part in his career), Napoleon happened to be on his way to join the army of Italy when the officer commanding the artillery at the siege of Toulon was wounded. Through the influence of a fellow Corsican, a political commissioner in Nice, Napoleon was appointed to replace him.

With luck and influence having given him the opening, Napoleon's energy and professionalism did the rest. In no time, he had sized up the strategic essentials. On the night of 17 December 1793, and in spite of being wounded in the thigh, Napoleon carried out a brilliant attack against the enemy; the daylight found the British ships fleeing towards the open sea. Toulon surrendered.

'I lack words to convey Buonaparte's merit to you,' reported General du Teil to the Minister of War in Paris. 'Much knowledge, equal intelligence and too much bravery; that is but a feeble sketch of this rare officer's virtues....'[10]

'From that date,' one of Napoleon's disciples was afterwards to declare, 'history took him up.'[11] The twenty-four-year-old Napoleon was promoted to brigadier-general and, equally important, his pay greatly increased. This allowed him to move his family from the degrading poverty of their Marseilles house to the comparative luxury of a villa near Antibes (where the redoubtable Letizia, in spite of servants, insisted on doing the laundry herself in a stream in the garden) and to busy himself with the careers of three of his brothers.

The eldest, the good-natured Joseph, did his bit towards easing Napoleon's financial burden by getting married in August 1794. His bride, Julie Clary, was the daughter of a textile merchant in Marseilles. Her homely face and slightly misshapen body were more than offset, in the eyes of the handsome, graceful Joseph, by her considerable fortune. Letizia was delighted with the match. Not only was Julie rich but she was a sensible, sweet-natured girl who would love her husband devotedly.

Napoleon was equally delighted. In fact, the thought of Joseph's successful marriage to Julie would sometimes engulf the younger Napoleon in a wave of bitter-sweet envy. 'How lucky he is, *ce coquin de Joseph*,'[12] he would sigh.

In these early days, Napoleon was still genuinely fond of his brother Joseph. Exasperation with his failure to fulfil Napoleon's grandiose expectations of him would come later. 'In whatever position fortune may place you,' he wrote to him during this period, 'you know well, *mon ami*, that you could not have a better friend than myself, one to whom you are dearer, and who wishes more sincerely for your happiness. Life is a slight dream that vanishes. If you go away and think it will be for some time, send me your portrait; we have lived so many years together, so closely united, that our hearts are mingled, and you know better than anyone how entirely mine is yours....'[13]

With his brother Lucien, there was no such mingling of hearts. Six years younger than Napoleon, Lucien was a hot-headed, argumentative, undisciplined creature who had early on developed a strong antipathy towards the equally headstrong Napoleon. He bitterly resented his brother's dictatorial attitude.

Lucien's marriage, which took place in the same year as Joseph's, considerably worsened his relationship with Napoleon. For Lucien's bride was as much a liability to the family as Joseph's was an asset. Her name was Christine Boyer. An inn-keeper's daughter, dark and pretty, she was two years older than Lucien, completely illiterate and very poor. With characteristic impulsiveness, Lucien had faked his birth certificate (he was still a minor at the time) and had married her without bothering to inform his family. In his memoirs Lucien claimed that he had felt morally obliged to marry Christine as, after a particularly eloquent speech on the subject of equality, made of course by himself, her father had stood up and, in front of a large audience, had tackled him on the subject of his daughter. If, heckled M. Boyer, we were all equal, why did Lucien, who was pressing his attentions on her, not marry her?

When Napoleon heard of Lucien's marriage, he was furious. But Letizia, on meeting the modest, well-meaning girl, resigned herself to the match. Lucien was, and always would be, her favourite son. The quicksilver quality of his mind and his infectious eloquence appealed to the strong vein of romanticism running through her otherwise practical nature. He was so like what his father had been at the same age.

With his brother Louis, fifteen years old in 1794, Napoleon was better satisfied. The two of them had already spent a great deal of time together. For, while stationed at Auxonne, Napoleon had undertaken the boy's education and supported him out of his own pay. The two of them had lived in a wretchedly furnished little room, sleeping on hard mattresses and eating very little other than broth cooked by the older brother.

Louis, Napoleon now wrote on seeing him again in the family's new home in Antibes, 'has just the qualities I like: warmth, good health, talent, precision in his dealings, and kindness.'[14]

Unlike his rebellious brother Lucien, Louis was very grateful for Napoleon's goodness towards him. Indeed, he worshipped him. The fact that Louis, so alert and affectionate in these days, was to become so embittered in later life, might well have had something to do with this early passion he harboured for Napoleon. Louis loved his brother, the Empress Josephine was to say in later years, as a lover loves his mistress.

Napoleon's three sisters – Elisa, Pauline and Caroline – and his remaining brother Jerome were still too young, at this stage, to cause him any lasting concern. That would come later, and in abundance.

The flame of self-satisfaction, ignited by his brilliant contribution to the fall of Toulon, was snuffed out in August 1794. For this was when, because of his slight association with the brother of the now discredited Robespierre, Napoleon was put under house arrest for a short period.

His release and a move to Paris brought very little improvement in his prospects. For over a year, Napoleon lived in a state of frustration. In spite of, or perhaps because of, his considerable military reputation, he was offered no satisfactory command. Indeed, he was given a desk job in the *bureau topographique* which was, in effect, a military planning centre. As much of his pay went towards supporting his family, and as Paris was so expensive, Napoleon was obliged to live in a cheap Left Bank hotel. For entertainment, he went for dreary walks in the Jardin des Plantes. He even, at one stage, toyed with the idea of offering his services to the Sultan of Turkey.

'I hardly care what happens to me. I watch life almost indifferently . . . ,' he wrote one day in deep disillusion to his brother Joseph. 'If this continues, I shall end by not stepping aside when a carriage rushes past.'[15]

His opportunity came suddenly in the autumn of 1795. Yet another turn in the revolutionary wheel brought a new constitution, to be headed by a Directory of five members. The introduction of this new constitution was violently opposed, not only by the royalists but by various disaffected elements. On 5 October (or 13 Vendémiaire, according to the new republican calendar) this opposition came to a head: the rebels prepared to attack the seat of government – the Palace of the Tuileries.

Paul Barras, as Commander-in-Chief of the Army of the Interior, was advised to delegate to Napoleon – who had acquitted himself so well at Toulon – the task of crushing the expected revolt. On the night before the uprising Napoleon was summoned to Barras's headquarters. Was Napoleon, asked Barras, prepared to defend the Constitution? He was. Setting to work immediately, Napoleon ordered troops and guns to be brought into Paris and, by the morning of 13 Vendémiaire, had deployed his force.

The attack came that afternoon. Within a few minutes it was all over. The advancing insurgents had simply been mown down by skilfully directed gun fire. Two hundred men had been killed or wounded and the rebels had retreated.

Although the success of 13 Vendémiaire had not been due to Napoleon alone (other generals had been involved), it was he who reaped the greatest benefits. For the famous 'whiff of grapeshot' had not only saved the Republic; it had flung open the door to Napoleon's own spectacular future. With Barras being chosen as one of the five new directors, Napoleon was appointed to succeed him as Commander-in-Chief of the Army of the Interior. Quite literally overnight, Napoleon had become both rich and powerful.

His first thoughts were for the welfare of his family. His mother and three sisters were showered with gifts. He saw that Joseph was awarded a consulship; that Lucien was appointed commissioner with the Army of the North; that Louis was made a lieutenant and his aide-de-camp; and that Jerome, the youngest, was packed off to a good school in Paris.

'Luck,' as he reported to Joseph, 'is on my side.'[16] It was indeed. And it is significant that this change in his luck should have coincided with his meeting with Josephine; for his luck was to hold for as long as he was married to her.

4

Napoleon and Love

SEXUAL love, the earnest young Napoleon had once written
in one of his many notebooks, was 'harmful to society and
to the individual happiness of men.'[1] It was the result of
weakness and loneliness; it closed one's ears to reason; it deprived
one of the control of one's actions. Therefore, in order to fulfil
one's patriotic duty, one must know how to master one's soul and
close it to love.

Until the day that he met Josephine, Napoleon had been able
to abide by this somewhat cheerless theory. His love affairs – such
as they were – had been matters of the mind and the body,
rather than of the heart. For all the romanticism of his character,
Napoleon had never been swept away on a tide of passion.

His first emotional involvement seems to have been, naturally
enough, with a fellow pupil at the military school at Brienne.
Notorious for his inability to make friends, the fourteen-year-old
Napoleon none the less befriended a boy by the name of Pierre
François Laugier de Bellecour. For a while the two adolescents –
the truculent Corsican and the aristocrat with the pretty face –
enjoyed a close and apparently chaste relationship. But gradually
Pierre François, who had been born, aptly, in Nancy, began to
show signs of becoming, in Brienne slang, a 'nymph'. Disturbed,
Napoleon tackled his friend about it.

'You're mixing with a crowd I don't approve of. Your new
friends are corrupting you,' he lectured. 'So make a choice between
them and me.'

'I haven't changed,' replied Pierre François, 'and I consider you my best friend.'

Napoleon was satisfied and the close friendship continued.

But when the two boys moved on to the Ecole Militaire in Paris, where the surroundings were more luxurious and the atmosphere more worldly, the effeminate Pierre François was quickly drawn into overtly homosexual circles. Deeply disturbed, Napoleon broke off the friendship. 'Monsieur,' he declared with all the priggishness of a fifteen-year-old, 'you have scorned my advice, and so you have renounced my friendship. Never speak to me again.'[2]

Not content with this break, Napoleon sat down to write a memorandum to the Minister of War in which he suggested that 'the rigours of Spartan youth' were an example that should be followed in French academies. He sent a draft of this self-righteous essay to one of his old masters at Brienne who, very wisely, advised him to let the matter drop.

Napoleon's reaction, or over-reaction, to his friend Pierre François's homosexuality is interesting. As he was to admit in later life, Napoleon quite often felt himself drawn physically towards good-looking young men. Was it because of his personal experience of homosexual urges that he was so anxious to see them discouraged?

Napoleon's next emotional entanglement was more conventional. During his first posting, to Valence in 1785, the sixteen-year-old Second Lieutenant Buonaparte became friendly with a local family by the name of Colombiers. Madame du Colombiers was one of those charming, warm-hearted women who so often fulfil a mother's role for young men far from home. Giving Madame du Colombiers an added attraction in Napoleon's eyes was the fact that she had a daughter, a demure and pretty girl named Caroline. Inevitably the two young people – the bony, tongue-tied soldier and the shy, fresh-complexioned girl – were drawn together, and, during the course of the summer of 1786, their adolescent romance blossomed.

'No one could have been more innocent than we were,' remembered Napoleon on Saint Helena. 'We often used to arrange little assignations and I recollect one in particular, which took place at daybreak one morning in the middle of summer. It may not be believed but our sole delight on that occasion consisted of eating cherries together.'[3]

This blameless youthful idyll was to have an interesting sequel. Twenty years later the couple met again. Caroline was married by then and Napoleon, of course, was the all-powerful Emperor of the French. Their meeting was the result of a letter she had written him and it took place at Lyons, as Napoleon was passing through the town on his way to Milan to be crowned King of Italy. To see this once gauche, lank-haired soldier now transformed into a celebrated and self-assured monarch was a revelation to the still provincial Caroline.

'She watched his every movement,' noted a member of the Emperor's entourage, 'her eye following him with an attention which seemed to emanate from her very soul.'4

Napoleon, apparently, was considerably less impressed. He could hardly recognise in this plump, housewifely woman the pretty girl with whom he had once gobbled cherries in the summer dawn. But, in memory of those far-off days, he granted her husband an official government post, her brother a lieutenancy and appointed Caroline as a lady-in-waiting to his mother, who was by then rejoicing in the title of Madame Mère. In time, Caroline's husband was created Baron of the Empire.

Napoleon's first sexual experience seems to have occurred late the following year, 1787, when he was eighteen. With characteristic precision, he made careful note of the encounter in one of his notebooks. He was in Paris at the time, on leave from the army and busily badgering some government department for a sum of money due to his family – at that stage still living on Corsica. One chilly November evening he went for a walk under the arcades of the Palais Royal. He was in search, he seems to have convinced himself, of *'une expérience philosophique.'*

There he met a frail young prostitute who, apparently accustomed to inexperienced young men pretending to be on a research assignment, answered all his questions with touching honesty, engaging modesty and commendable patience. In reply to the usual query as to why a pretty girl like her should have resorted to prostitution, she explained that she had to make a living. Her answer to his equally predictable question, as to how she had 'lost her virtue', was even more conventional. She, a simple country girl from Brittany, had been seduced by one officer, flung out of her home by her irate mother, taken to Paris by a second officer, deserted by him, set up by a third who, in turn, had cleared off to London, leaving her to fend for herself as best she could.

Not wanting to waste any more valuable time in unprofitable conversation, the girl suggested that she go home with Napoleon.

'But what will we do there?' he asked.

'Come on,' she answered briskly, 'we'll get warm and you'll have your fill of pleasure.'

And this is what they did. Napoleon had had his first 'philosophical experience'.[5]

His next relationship – the only one, before his meeting with Josephine, which can possibly be described as an affair of the heart – was with Désirée Clary, the sister of his brother Joseph's wife, Julie.

Napoleon, by the summer of 1794, was going through a time of deep frustration: that two-year-long trough between his twin triumphs – the capture of Toulon and 13 Vendémiaire. It was during this period that the twenty-five-year-old Napoleon met the sixteen-year-old Désirée Clary. Like all the women with whom he was to become emotionally involved, Désirée was intensely feminine: dark-haired, small and slight, with a sweet smile and a tender nature. Her voice was soft and she had those other attributes which, to Napoleon, were inseparable from true beauty – small hands and feet. An added attraction was the fact that she, no less than her sister Julie, was the daughter of a very rich man: François Clary, the textile merchant in Marseilles.

Having met, the two corresponded, with Napoleon writing in the style of a mentor rather than a lover, and using always her first name – Eugénie – rather than the more generally used Désirée. On returning to Marseilles in the spring of 1795, after a nine-month-long separation, Napoleon – either imagining himself in love or attracted by her dowry – raised the question of marriage with her mother. Madame Clary was having none of it. With her eldest daughter Julie already married to the penniless Joseph, one Buonaparte, she decided, was enough.

But Napoleon was not put off. From Paris, he bombarded Désirée with affectionate letters. In one of his pockets he kept a locket containing a twist of her dark hair. He even wrote a flowery story, *Clisson et Eugénie*, which apparently mirrored his attitude towards their love affair. How much this was a true expression of his feelings or how much the result of the deep depression into which he was plunged during these uncertain, pre-Vendémiaire

41

days, one does not know; from a squalid, Left Bank hotel room in Paris, the thought of the wealthy, sweet-natured Désirée Clary living in the sunshine of the south of France must have been very alluring. Indeed, throughout Napoleon's romance with Désirée distance tended to lend enchantment; there was always something unreal about their relationship. It was a love affair conducted on paper.

In the end, time and a gradual improvement in Napoleon's circumstances (even before the triumph of 13 Vendémiaire things had begun to look up) weakened his feelings towards Désirée. By the autumn of 1795 he was writing to tell her, as gently as possible, that things were no longer what they had once been. In the time-honoured fashion of the one who is doing the jilting, he put the onus of ending the relationship on her. Her feelings towards him, he assured her, would change; knowing this, he could not possibly accept her promise of eternal love; the day that she no longer loved him, she must feel free to tell him so; if she fell in love with someone else, she must yield to these feelings.

For a man who, in later life, was to be accused of callousness towards women, it was a kind and tactfully phrased letter. Equally gracefully worded was a subsequent letter in which he made the final break.

Désirée Clary went on to marry another up and coming soldier, Jean Baptiste Bernadotte, and eventually to become – so full of opportunities were the times through which they were all living – a queen, when Bernadotte ascended the Swedish throne. Her descendants sit on it still.

Napoleon, conscience-stricken perhaps about the way he had rejected Désirée, was always to treat her with great kindness. On Saint Helena he would refer to her as his 'first love'.

'At that time,' as Laure Permon was afterwards to say, 'Bonaparte had a heart capable of devotion.'[6] She was in a position to know for she was intimately involved in Napoleon's last, and most curious emotional adventure, before he finally fell in love with Josephine de Beauharnais.

For many years, whenever he was in Paris, Napoleon had visited the Permon family. After the austerity of his Corsican home and his various military quarters, the Permons' apartment – with its Aubusson carpets, draped curtains and vases of fresh flowers –

struck Napoleon as the height of elegance. It made a perfect setting for the hostess, for Madame Permon was a woman who loved to entertain.

A friend and contemporary of Napoleon's mother, Madame Permon was still extremely good-looking. Superficial and frivolous she might have been (her boast was that she had read only one book in her life) but she had a highly developed social sense. She was charming, amusing, gregarious. No one, claims Napoleon (who was, frankly, in no position to judge), could rival her in the art of 'holding a salon'. She certainly proved a valuable friend for the awkward young officer. She could coax him out of his depression; she could laugh him out of his pedantry; she could charm him out of his tempers.

Her daughter Laure has left a vivid pen-picture of Napoleon as he appeared in 1794 – the year before 13 Vendémiaire – when he was twenty-five. She could never forget, she afterwards wrote, the sight of him as he crossed the courtyard towards their home. A shabby round hat was crammed over his eyes; his hair hung lank and badly powdered over the collar of his greatcoat; his complexion was sallow, his features angular, his expression belligerent; his hands were ungloved (gloves, he would scowl, were a 'useless luxury'); his boots were badly made and unpolished. All in all, in this haggard and untidy young man, Laure Permon could see nothing of the handsome and sensuous-looking monarch of a later period.

During his earlier visits to the Permons, his hosts had frequently to contend with his violent outbursts against the wealth, privilege and self-confidence of those aristocratic young officers with whom he was obliged to associate. Even now, many years later, he could become so incensed by the sight of an *Incroyable* – one of those foppish young exquisites who had surfaced after the worst of the Revolutionary excesses were over – that the poor Permons were obliged to sit through yet more tirades.

But there were times when Napoleon revealed an altogether more agreeable side to his nature. His smile, Laure Permon admitted, had always been winning; it was to remain one of his chief attractions. He was capable of great kindness. Time and again, in gestures that ranged from the presenting of posies of violets to Madame Permon to dashing out in the pouring rain to fetch a doctor for Monsieur Permon, he gave evidence of this generosity of spirit. There were even occasions when he could be positively light-hearted, almost skittish. Often, while Cecile thumped out a tune on the piano, Napoleon and Laure would dance the *Monaco* or *Les Deux Coqs*.

One of Madame Permon's main attractions, in Napoleon's eyes, was the fact that she was a fellow Corsican. Sometimes, after a good dinner, the young soldier would seat himself in front of the roaring fire, arms crossed over his chest and legs stretched out towards the hearth, and say to his hostess, 'Let us talk of Corsica, let us talk of Signora Letizia.' Then the two of them would drift away in happy reminiscence of the rocky mountainsides and grey-green olive groves of their native land, until the acrid smell of Napoleon's muddy boots, slowly roasting before the flames, would force Madame Permon to leave the room.

There was, to the young Napoleon, yet another side of which not even the sympathetic Permons were aware. This was the dreamy, romantic, almost mystical side. It was best captured in his autobiographical story *Clisson et Eugénie* where, allowing for cliché and over-writing, there is evidence of a highly sensitive mind at work. 'Sometimes,' writes Napoleon of Clisson, 'on banks silvered by the star of love, he would give himself up to the desires and throbbings of his heart. He could not tear himself away from the sweet and melancholy spectacle of the night, lit by the moon. He would remain there until she disappeared, till darkness effaced his reverie.... He would spend entire hours meditating in the depths of a wood, and in the evening he would remain there until midnight, lost in reveries by the light of the silver star of love.'[7]

One really cannot imagine the average young army officer sitting down to write anything like this.

As was only to be expected, it was to the Permons' home that Napoleon hurried soon after his triumph of 13 Vendémiaire. But his glow of self-satisfaction faded as he realised that Monsieur Permon, who had been ill for some time, was dying, and that his condition had been considerably worsened by the very street fighting in which Napoleon had played so brilliant a part. 'He behaved wonderfully to my mother during these moments of grief,' testifies Laure. 'He was himself in a position that must have made all other interests seem unimportant. Well, all I can say is, he behaved like a son, a brother.'

On 17 Vendémiaire, or 9 October 1795, Monsieur Permon died.

After her husband's death, Madame Permon, with her son

Albert and her daughter Laure, went to live in a small house in the fashionable Chaussée d'Antin. In no time Madame Permon, who remained as feckless with money and as fond of company as ever, had furnished it in her usual sumptuous style and was entertaining on an only slightly less lavish scale. One of her most constant visitors was Napoleon. Since 13 Vendémiaire, though, there had been a considerable change, not only in his status but in his attitude and appearance. As Commander-in-Chief of the Army of the Interior, he had moved out of his humble hotel room into a house in the Rue des Capucines; he had his own carriage, a smart new uniform and was invariably accompanied by a posse of aides. The days of muddy boots, as Laure Permon puts it, were over.

One Saturday morning Napoleon arrived unaccompanied and, finding the widowed Madame Permon alone, announced that he had a proposal to put to her. He would very much like to unite the Buonaparte and Permon families and, to this end, he suggested that her son Albert marry his pretty sister Pauline. Albert, replied Madame Permon, was his own master; it was up to him to decide so serious a matter; she would do nothing to influence him.

Undeterred, Napoleon then went on to suggest that her daughter Laure marry his brother Jerome. As Laure was then only eleven and Jerome even younger, Madame Permon burst out laughing.'Really, Napoleon! You are playing the high priest today,' she exclaimed. 'You're marrying everyone, even children.'

But she had not heard the last of him yet. To her stupefaction, Napoleon went on to suggest that this matrimonial merry-go-round begin with his own marriage to her. He was prepared to wait, he assured her, until *les convenances* of her widowhood allowed it.

She could hardly believe her ears. 'My dear Napoleon,' she said gently, 'let us talk sensibly. You fancy you know my age. The truth is, you know nothing about it. And I shall not tell you. That is my secret. But I am old enough to be your mother. Do spare me this kind of joke; it distresses me, coming from you.'[8]

But Napoleon assured her that it was no joke. A woman's age mattered to him not at all, he declared, provided she looked no more than thirty. When not even this compliment (Madame Permon was well over forty) could change her mind, Napoleon left abruptly. He was never again to pay an intimate call on Madame Permon.

Napoleon's extraordinary proposal to the Corsican-born Madame Permon marked his last attempt to anchor himself to his past: to the familiar, bourgeois, tribal world of his youth.

5

The Widow Beauharnais

JOSEPHINE, by now the Widow Beauharnais, had emerged from prison into a very different age. Although the end of the Reign of Terror did not mean the end of all revolutionary upheaval, it did usher in a less frightening, more carefree period. Gradually the more savage Revolutionary legislation was repealed: the austerities of 'Republican virtue' were replaced by an almost feverish pursuit of pleasure. Instead of the unsmiling Robespierrists, opportunists and fixers now took over the government of the country. While a great many Frenchmen lived as desperately as ever they had done under the monarchy, fortunes were being made by a new breed of man: the contractors, the speculators, the black marketeers, the war profiteers. It was the age of the *arriviste*.

Fashion was highly exaggerated. Foppish young men – the *jeunesse dorée* – sported skin-tight trousers, shoulder-length hair and huge, snowy, mouth-concealing neckerchiefs. The women – *les merveilleuses* – topped their brightly painted faces with outsize bonnets, festooned their elaborate dresses with jewels and trinkets, and trailed small, preferably mongrel, dogs on – for some obscure reason – green ribbons. The greatest craze was for dancing. Paris alone boasted over six hundred dance halls. The most exclusive, and macabre, of these dances was the *Bal à la Victime* to which only the relatives of those who had been guillotined were invited. Women came coiffured *à la guillotine* (their hair cropped or pinned up to expose the neck) and about their throats they wore a thin, blood-red ribbon.

It was in this gimcrack society that the thirty-one-year-old Widow Beauharnais was obliged to make her way. Her problem was, quite simply, one of survival. She had nothing. With her husband's arrest and execution, her annual allowance had ceased. His property had long since been sequestered. Nor could she expect any help from her Aunt Edmée; both the ageing Madame Renaudin and her even older lover, Josephine's father-in-law, the Marquis de Beauharnais, were in an equally impecunious position. And as if keeping herself afloat were not difficult enough, Josephine had her two children, Eugène and Hortense, to support.

She solved the problem of the thirteen-year-old Eugène by entrusting him to her fellow prisoner and probable lover, General Hoche, who had also been released after the fall of Robespierre. The boy joined the General's staff as a junior ordnance officer. To support Hortense and herself, Josephine borrowed money. Much of it came – and, indeed, had been coming for several years – from the Dunkirk banker, Jean Emmery, who acted as the Taschers' European agent. Time and again, against the promise of long-delayed remittances from Martinique, Emmery had forwarded Josephine money. To her widowed mother she wrote anguished letters, begging her to transfer funds.

'I know your tender heart too well to doubt that you will make all possible haste to provide me with the means to live and to pay back the sums I owe,'[1] she wrote in January 1795. Madame Tascher de la Pagerie, poor and widowed herself, was in no position to help.

But the pleasure- and luxury-loving Josephine was simply not prepared to live – as so many other dispossessed aristocrats were obliged to live – a life of genteel poverty. She was determined to enjoy herself. Her loveless marriage, her years of insecurity, her brush with death, her lack of prospects, even the fact that she was already in her thirties convinced her that she must live life to the full. The money which she had borrowed with such desperation, she squandered with merry abandon. It went, for the most part, on inessentials: on carriage hire, on exotic food, on furnishing fabrics, on fashionable clothes, even on flowers. And when there was no money, she bought what she wanted anyway. Her bills, says one of her biographers, 'fluttered in her wake like confetti.'[2]

Making use of the one asset she had in abundance – her charm – Josephine talked what influential friends she had into getting the authorities to return her confiscated property. The seals on her Paris apartment were removed, thus allowing her access to her jewels, clothes and furnishings. The contents of her late husband's château at La Ferté were also released and she was generously compensated for such of his books, silver and furniture as had already been sold. Emboldened by all this, she asked to be supplied with a carriage and pair in compensation for the horses and equipment which General Beauharnais had abandoned on giving up his command of the Army of the Rhine. This, too, was granted.

But, as there were limits to the patience of her creditors and to the co-operation of the authorities, Josephine – in order to live her extravagant life – was obliged to find other means of support. There was only one sure way in which a woman of her generous physical attractions could do this and, understandably, Josephine chose it. That there is any truth in the rumours that she gave herself to all and sundry at this period is doubtful, but there is no doubt that she became the mistress of one of the leading members of the government, Paul Barras.

Josephine was introduced into government circles by Thérèse de Fontenay who, like Josephine, had been imprisoned during the Terror. The daughter of a Spanish banker, Thérèse de Fontenay was richly typical of the sort of beautiful, stylish, amoral woman who flourished during this hedonistic period. She was referred to, with good reason, as 'government property'. In quick succession, Thérèse became the mistress of two leading members of the government – Jean Tallien (to whom she was afterwards married for a while) and Paul Barras – and of the financier, Gabriel Ouvard. When Barras tired of Thérèse, he turned to her equally delectable friend, Madame de Beauharnais.

An ex-nobleman and an ex-officer of the *ancien régime*, Paul Barras had thrown in his lot with the revolutionaries. His strong instinct for survival had kept him afloat in the churning waters in which so many others of similar background had drowned. Now that those waters were subsiding, he was to be found high and dry on the shore: a shore crowded with fellow adventurers, intriguers and trimmers. With Robespierre gone, Barras – who had helped get rid of him – became the most important man in the government. But whereas power had been what Robespierre coveted most, luxury was what Barras cared most about. His Paris home (in time he was to move into the Luxembourg Palace) was as lavishly furnished as any pre-Revolutionary salon. Barras lived, unashamedly, for pleasure. He had all the tastes, noted one colleague, 'of an opulent, extravagant, magnificent and dissipated prince.'[3]

As such, he suited Josephine beautifully. And as he was a physically attractive man (although unattractive in almost every other way), she had no hesitation in becoming his mistress. For this, Josephine was always to be roundly condemned by her contemporaries. It was not so much that they minded (or were in any position to mind) her sexual immorality; what they resented was the fact that she had allied herself to so unprincipled and debauched a man who, in turn, presided over so disreputable and raffish a regime.

But to Josephine, in the year 1795, things looked very different. To a woman whose own background had always been irregular – a father who had been a philanderer, an aunt who was the mistress of her father-in-law, a husband who had been a tireless adulterer – there was nothing so unusual about becoming a man's mistress. And in comparison to those bloodstained figures of the Terror who had arrested and imprisoned her, Barras was an easy-going man: approachable, understanding, sybaritic. He was also extremely generous. Josephine had had her share of life's uncertainties; now she wanted to enjoy its pleasures.

It was curious that the unambitious and apolitical Josephine should, with so little effort on her own part, have been linked to three men who were, in turn and for a time, the most important figures in France: her first husband who became President of the Constituent Assembly, Barras who became the most important member of the Directory and Napoleon who became Emperor of the French.

As Barras's mistress, Josephine now became the queen of his tinselly court. First in his town house and then at the Luxembourg, she acted as his hostess. From La Chaumière, his picturesque retreat near the Rond-Point of the Champs-Elysées, she sent out invitations in her own name. Often, she would entertain him at her home at Croissy (whose rent he obligingly paid) and this would entail – to the fascination of her neighbours – a flurry of preparations. From early in the morning baskets of luxuries would arrive from Paris, to be followed first by a detachment of mounted police and then by Barras and a great company of friends.

'As is so often the case with Creoles,' writes one of Josephine's long-suffering neighbours, 'Madame de Beauharnais's house boasted a certain luxury of appointments, one in which all the superfluities were present and only the essentials lacking. Fowl, wild game and rare fruits were stacked high in the kitchen, and yet there was a shortage of saucepans, plates and glasses, which she had to borrow from our modest household.'[4]

In her new position, Josephine was able to improve her own standard of living. Her son Eugène was sent to the College Irlandais at Saint-Germain, and Hortense to the Institut National de Saint-Germain-en-Laye – that smartest of girls' schools run by the remarkable Madame Campan who had once been *femme de chambre* to Queen Marie Antoinette. It was some indication of the topsy-turvy times through which they were all living that a mere two years after Marie Antoinette had been guillotined, her former lady-in-waiting should be instilling the old standards of ladylike behaviour into a new, post-Revolutionary generation.

In October 1795 Josephine moved into a new home. This was number 6, Rue Chantereine. It was soon to become famous, not only as the house in which Napoleon and Josephine started their married life but as the place in which the conspiracy, which was to make him master of France, was hatched. From here, Josephine would leave to take up residence as consort of the master of France, first in the Luxembourg and then in the Palace of the Tuileries.

Today, no trace of the house remains. The name of the street was changed to the Rue de la Victoire in honour of Napoleon's early triumphs and the house itself was demolished in 1859 in the course of the spectacular remodelling of Paris by Josephine's grandson, the Emperor Napoleon III.

By all accounts, 6 Rue Chantereine was charming. Secluded, set in a wooded garden, more of a pavilion than a house, it was transformed by Josephine into a jewel of a home. Every room reflected both contemporary fashion and her own good taste. Marble busts and terracotta coloured walls proclaimed the neo-classicism of the day; a bedroom ceiling painted with swans gliding in a sea of pink roses, and a dressing room entirely lined with mirrors emphasised her femininity; and, once Josephine had married Napoleon, a bedroom decorated like a soldier's tent, and with stools disguised as regimental drums, paid tribute to his military career.

To run this establishment, Josephine employed a personal maid, a chambermaid, a cook, a manservant and a coachman. That she could barely manage to pay their wages, let alone the bills for all her fashionable furniture and fabrics, was something which Josephine did not allow to bother her unduly.

Into this elegant setting, Josephine fitted perfectly. For by now she had established herself as one of the best-dressed women in Paris. The setting up of the new government, the Directory of five members, towards the end of 1795, ushered in the *directoire* fashion for women: a neo-classical style based on the draped marble figures of ancient Greece. With her slender, seductive figure and her short, riotously curling chestnut hair, Josephine suited those high-waisted, flimsy, softly-flowing garments beautifully. Although she never went quite as far as one member of her circle, Madame Hamelin, who walked down the Champs-Elysées naked to the waist, Josephine was ready enough to adopt most of the extravagances of the fashion: bare arms, near-naked bosoms, flesh-coloured body-stockings, diamond-studded circlets around the thigh.

Yet for all the casualness of her morals and the daring of her dress, Josephine was never a hard-hearted *femme du monde* in the mould of someone like her friend Thérèse Tallien. Trans-cendentally smart she might have been but she retained always a softness, a gentleness, and a generosity. Someone who knew her at this time speaks of her as 'naturally and invariably gracious, ingratiating, the most congenial and sympathetic companion, with an ineffable sweetness not only in her expression but in the very sound of her voice. And there was a certain intriguing air of languorousness about her – a Creole characteristic – apparent in her attitudes of repose as well as in her movements.... All these qualities lent her a charm which more than offset the dazzling beauty of her rivals....'[5]

For if it was Josephine's chic and sophistication that first attracted General Buonaparte, it was her femininity that held him.

'Women,' wrote Napoleon to his brother from Paris at about this time, 'are everywhere – applauding in the theatre, strolling in the parks, reading in the bookshops. You will find these lovely creatures even in the savant's study. Here is the only place in the world where they deserve to steer the ship of state. The men are mad about them, think of nothing else, and live only for them . . . ."[6]

But he was not one of them. Not, that is, until after his triumph of Vendémiaire. Then, with his promotion to Commander-in-Chief of the Army of the Interior and his name on everyone's lips, the twenty-six-year-old General Buonaparte suddenly had access to the most fashionable salons and the loveliest creatures in Paris. His name has since been linked, usually unconvincingly, with several of them.

One of these creatures (an un-named young woman quoted by Stendhal), having met General Buonaparte three or four times, began to see more than just a haggard-looking, awkwardly mannered and disconcertingly quiet young man. 'Buonaparte had magnificent eyes that lighted up when he talked,' she remembered. 'If he had not been so painfully thin – so emaciated as to give the impression of ill-health – one might have noticed his fine features. The contour of his mouth was especially comely. A student of David's, a painter who frequented the salon of Monsieur N., where I met the General, described his features as "Grecian", which was enough to make me admire the strange man...You would never have guessed him to be a military man; there was nothing dashing about him, no swagger, no bluster, nothing rough . . . .'[7]

There is some doubt as to when Napoleon and Josephine first set eyes on each other (he may well have glimpsed her at one of Barras's receptions) but there is no reason to disbelieve the generally accepted account of their first real meeting. After all, the story was told, with only minor discrepancies, by two people directly involved: Napoleon, and Josephine's son, Eugène de Beauharnais.

A few days after 13 Vendémiaire an order went out that all unauthorised weapons in private hands, in certain troubled sections of the city, had to be handed in to the authorities. When the commissioner visited 6 Rue Chantereine to enforce the order, Josephine's fourteen-year-old son protested at having to relinquish the only weapon in the house: the sword which had once belonged to his late father, Alexandre de Beauharnais, when he had been a general in the Republican army. The sympathetic commissioner advised him to ask the commanding general in Paris for permission to keep the sword. Hurrying to headquarters, Eugène came face to face with General Buonaparte. He pleaded to be allowed to keep his father's sword. Napoleon, a good son himself, was touched by this show of filial devotion. He agreed to the boy's request.

On the following day the boy's mother, Madame de Beauharnais – moved, one imagines, both by gratitude and by curiosity to meet this new man of the hour – came to thank the general. One does not know what her initial impressions of Napoleon were. The worldly Josephine, who had been the wife of one handsome man and the reputed mistress of at least two others – the dashing General Hoche and the self-assured Barras – would not have been particularly impressed by this small, slight, lank-haired soldier with the brusque bearing. But we know what he thought of her. He was struck, of course, by her poise and her decorativeness and by the ease with which she made conversation, but what impressed him most, Napoleon afterwards admitted, were her gentler qualities: 'her extraordinary grace and her irresistibly sweet manner.'[8]

Emboldened by her friendliness, Napoleon asked if he could call on her. Josephine, who would have appreciated that there was more to this little general than met the eye and who sensed, perhaps, that he was a man with a future, granted permission. She invited him to one of her regular Thursday receptions.

It would be tempting to claim that a great love was born during that first meeting between Napoleon and Josephine. In truth, several weeks were to pass before Napoleon found himself hopelessly besotted by the glamorous Creole, and longer than that before Josephine felt able to return that overwhelming love.

During the first days of their association, the gauche, twenty-six-year-old soldier might well have felt diffident in the company, not only of his thirty-two-year-old hostess but of her circle. He was still, in spite of his brilliant intellect and his military successes, socially insecure. He felt tongue-tied in the presence of those actors and playrights, contractors and stock-jobbers who made up her circle. He was intimidated by those brazen beauties like Thérèse Tallien and Juliette Récamier.

'I was not indifferent to the charms of women, but up to this time they had not spoiled me,' he once claimed, 'and my disposition made me shy in their company.'[9]

Josephine was the first woman, he admitted, who gave him 'reassurance'. Yet, in spite of her flattering attentiveness and irresistible charm, he would have felt slightly wary of her. His basically bourgeois instincts would have been disturbed by her way of life: by her undisguised pursuit of pleasure, by her unpaid bills, by her *outré* clothes. What she spent on food, flowers and decorations for one of her evening parties would have kept his Corsican-born family for weeks.

And he would have known, of course, about her relationship with Barras. 'Bonaparte was as well acquainted with all of the lady's adventures as we were; I knew he knew, because he heard the stories in my presence . . . ,' wrote Barras in his memoirs. 'And Madame Beauharnais was generally recognised as one of my early liaisons. With Bonaparte a frequent visitor to my apartments, he could not have remained ignorant of such a state of affairs, nor could he have believed that everything was over between her and me.'[10]

Barras, who came to loathe both Napoleon and Josephine, is not to be trusted as a chronicler. But even without his testimony, there can be very little doubt that Napoleon would have heard that Josephine was, or had recently been, Barras's mistress.

He seems also to have known something about her association with her fellow prisoner in the Carmes, General Hoche. One evening, at a party given by Thérèse Tallien, Napoleon started reading palms. For Madame Tallien he predicted all sorts of 'improbabilities' (for the outrageous Thérèse, almost nothing would have been improbable) but when the time came to read General Hoche's palm, Napoleon became suddenly less playful. With an air of solemnity, and more than a touch of malice, he said, 'Why, General, you will die in your bed.'

At this studied insult to a dashing and dedicated soldier, Hoche's colour rose, but Josephine, with one of her sweet smiles and soothing observations, stepped in and averted a row. Yet the fact that she had felt the need to do so would not have been lost on the sensitive Napoleon.

Combined, these various factors might have been the reason why, a couple of weeks after Napoleon had first called on Josephine, he stopped visiting her. It could not have been an easy decision for already he was strongly attracted. It was Josephine, interestingly enough, who made the next approach. 'You no longer come to see a friend who is fond of you,' reads her very first letter to Napoleon. 'You have completely deserted her, which is a great mistake, for she is tenderly devoted to you. Come tomorrow to lunch with me. I must see you and talk to you on matters important to your interests. Good night, my friend. A fond embrace.'[11]

He replied that very night. 'I cannot imagine the reason for the tone of your letter,' he protested. 'I beg you to believe me when I say that no one so yearns for your friendship as do I, that no one can be more eager than I for the occasion to prove it. Had my duties permitted, I would have come in person to deliver this message.'[12] He signed it 'Buonaparte'.

From then on, he could not help himself. He began to fall in love with her. And Josephine, as a natural flirt, as a natural charmer, as a natural cultivator of influential men, led him on. 'One day,' he long afterwards recalled, 'when I was sitting next to her at table, she began to pay me all manner of compliments on my military qualities. Her praise intoxicated me. From that moment I confined my conversation to her and never left her side.'[13]

On another occasion – or it may have been the same occasion – Josephine's thirteen-year-old daughter Hortense, home from school, accompanied her mother to a dinner party given by Barras at the Luxembourg Palace. 'I found myself placed between my mother and a general who, in order to talk to her, kept leaning forward so often and with so much vivacity that he wearied me and obliged me to lean back. Thus, in spite of myself, I looked attentively at his face, which was handsome and very expressive, but remarkably pale. He spoke ardently and seemed to devote all his attention to my mother.'[14]

Inevitably, they became lovers. If, for Josephine, the first occasion on which they made love was simply a diversion, a way of rounding off a pleasant evening, for Napoleon it was a momentous experience. Yet, regrettably, there is no definite date for this first love making. Napoleon, in his letter to her the following day, simply scrawled, 'Seven in the morning' at the head of the writing paper. But there is no doubt about the intensity of his feelings.

She had, apparently, given him a portrait of herself that evening; possibly a coloured sketch by her friend Isabey and one which, in its pale prettiness, captured none of the abandoned passion which Napoleon experienced that night.

'I awaken full of you,' run his breathless phrases. 'Between your portrait and the memory of our intoxicating night, my senses have no respite. Sweet and incomparable Josephine, what is this strange effect you have upon my heart? What if you were to be angry? What if I were to see you sad or troubled? Then my soul would be shattered by distress. Then your lover would find no peace, no rest. But I find none, either, when I succumb to the profound emotion that overwhelms me, when I draw from your lips, from your heart, a flame that consumes me. Ah, it was last night that I realised that your portrait is not you and that ...

'You will be leaving the city at noon. But I shall see you in three hours. Until then, *mio dolce amor*, I send you a thousand kisses – but send me none in return, for they set my blood on fire.'[15]

6

Marriage

JOSEPHINE had indeed set Napoleon's blood – and heart, and brain – 'on fire'. Never before had he experienced anything like the overwhelming passion he felt for Josephine, and he was never to experience it again. To date, his sexual activities had been limited to prostitutes; to women like the one he had met on that raw evening beneath the arcades of the Palais Royal. His only love affair, with Désirée Clary, had been more in the nature of an adolescent romance, chiefly conducted on paper. His recent proposal of marriage to Madame Permon had been the dispassionate gesture of a lonely young man in search of a mother-substitute. When set against the emotions he felt for Josephine, these experiences were as nothing.

She possessed, it has been said, 'some elusive quality that was to him of the most exquisite value.'[1] Her voluptuousness set his blood racing; her sweetness melted his heart; her decorativeness brought out all the latent romanticism of his nature. 'His whole being,' writes one of his biographers, 'was quickened: the poet and the mystic that lay in embryo within him stirred.'[2]

His aide-de-camp, Auguste Marmont, who went on to become a marshal of France, was a witness to General Buonaparte's burgeoning romance. 'He was madly in love, in the full sense of the phrase, in its widest meaning. It was, apparently, his first passion, a primordial passion, and he responded to it with all the vigour of his nature. Love so pure, so true, so exclusive had never possessed a man.... Although she no longer had the freshness of youth, she knew how to please him, and we know that to lovers the question of "why" is superfluous. One loves because one loves and nothing is less susceptible to explanation and analysis than this emotion.'[3]

Napoleon himself, whom the years made coarse and cynical, admitted, on Saint Helena, that 'I was passionately in love with her, and our friends were aware of this long before I ever dared to say a word about it.'[4]

And Josephine: what did she feel for him? Not much. Napoleon's theory that 'you could not have inspired in me so infinite a love unless you felt it too,'[5] was simply not valid. Josephine would have been flattered by the vehement attentions of this young man in his twenties. She would have been attracted by the fact that he was a man of some consequence. And she, the most feminine of women, would have responded to his aggressiveness and his masculinity. But she did not love him; not yet, at any rate. In fact, she found him rather amusing. She would refer to him as her 'funny little Corsican'; she would describe him, to her sophisticated friends, as *drôle*.

And when she was not finding him amusing, she found him rather uncomfortable. He could be so intense, so earnest, so mentally exhausting. But, passive as ever, Josephine did nothing to check his mounting passion. One could never, she reckoned, have too many admirers.

To be in love with a woman like Josephine was one thing; to want to marry her, quite another. She was the type who makes a perfect mistress but a far from perfect wife. And Napoleon's character, at this stage of his life, was still impregnated with the values of his native Corsica. The ideal Corsican wife was hardworking, thrifty, subservient, domesticated. There could hardly have been a greater contrast than between his own frugal and iron-willed mother and the extravagant and feather-light Josephine. Yet marriage is what, early in the year 1796, Napoleon proposed.

Historians have given countless reasons for Napoleon's choice of Josephine as a bride. He, in exile, added a few more. He is said to have married her because he was a snob, because he thought she had money, because he imagined she would help further his career. Napoleon, talking to General Bertrand on Saint Helena, claimed that he had checked with the banker Emmery on Josephine's prospects but that what he had heard was not reassuring: she stood to inherit almost nothing. The Beauharnais, he told Bertrand, were a 'good French family' (by 'good' Napoleon had come to mean aristocratic) and, as a member of that family, she had suited the socially ambitious general very well. To another of those dedicated Saint Helena chroniclers, he said that Barras had advised him to marry her, 'pointing out that she would constitute a link between the old regime and the new and that this would give me substance; that her old French name would offset my Corsican one; that, in sum, my standing would be improved.'⁶

There might well have been something in Barras's reasoning. Certainly, one of Josephine's attractions in Napoleon's eyes was that she was part – if only just part – of that gilded world from which he, the socially insecure Corsican, had always felt so humiliatingly excluded. But that is not the reason why he married her; it was merely one of the many qualities that combined to make her so desirable. Napoleon married Josephine because he was hopelessly, overwhelmingly, in love with her. He could never have been satisfied with her as his mistress only. He needed, as lovers have always needed, to feel that he possessed her in every way: not only sexually, but physically, mentally, emotionally and legally.

'For you even to think that I do not love you for yourself alone!!!', he once wrote after she had, apparently, accused him of wanting to marry her for some other reason, 'for whom, then? For what?... I am astonished at you, but still more astonished at myself – back at your feet, this morning, without the willpower to resent or resist. The height of weakness and abjection! What then is this strange power over me, my incomparable Josephine, that a mere thought of yours has the power to poison my life and rend my heart, when at the same time another emotion stronger still and another less sombre mood lead me back to grovel before you?'⁷

It was this sort of outpouring, or what Josephine called 'the force of his passion', that caused her to hesitate about accepting his proposal. She felt unable to cope with his ardour. She could certainly not pretend to match it. To a friend she admitted to 'a state of indifference, of tepidness'. As to whether or not she loved him, the answer, she said, was 'Well, no'.⁸

But, in the end, she accepted. Lacking the driving force of love, her reasons for marriage were more complicated than his. She was a woman who needed male admiration, protection and support. Even if Napoleon had no money other than his pay, he would be making himself responsible for her upkeep. At thirty-two, in a period when fifteen was considered a marriageable age, she was no longer in the first flush of youth; how much longer would her allure last? Perhaps, in her intuitive way, Josephine recognised that Napoleon's qualities – his enthusiasm, his energy, his efficiency – would make an excellent foil for her own nonchalance. She might even have sensed that, in marrying him, she might be hitching her wagon to a star.

'I don't know why,' she admitted to a friend, 'but sometimes this absurd self-confidence of his impresses me to the point of believing anything possible to this singular man – anything at all that might come into his mind to undertake! And with his imagination, who can guess what he might undertake?'[9]

It was a gamble worth taking.

To his own family, Napoleon said nothing. That the stiff-backed Letizia, in her patched clothes, would have approved of the frivolous Josephine in her flesh-coloured body-stockings, was beyond the realms of possibility. Even Napoleon's older brother, the more tolerant Joseph, would have disapproved of his marrying an older woman without money.

But Josephine's own two children, to whom she was devoted, had to be told. The thirteen-year-old Hortense, who was one day to play so significant a part in their story, was appalled at the prospect. 'Maman won't love us as much,' she told her equally worried brother Eugène, when the two of them first became aware of their mother's involvement with General Buonaparte. Nothing that Napoleon could do was able to soften the children's attitude towards him. He was not, in any case, especially good with youngsters of their age: his tone tended to be too teasing, his humour too barbed, his pinches too painful. When Hortense asked her mother if she intended marrying General Buonaparte, Josephine gave an evasive reply. When the girl, who shed tears with almost the same abandon as her mother, begged her not to do so, Josephine merely joined in the crying. But it was no use. 'The General,' noted Hortense ruefully, 'had already more influence than I.'[10]

Characteristically, Josephine commandeered someone else to break the news to Hortense. It was the girl's headmistress,

Madame Campan, who told her that her mother had finally accepted General Buonaparte's offer. It was, Madame Campan argued, a highly suitable match. General Buonaparte had not been implicated in 'the horrors of the Revolution' – those horrors which had led to the execution of Hortense's father, Alexandre de Beauharnais – and, in his present position, the general would be able to do a great deal for Hortense's brother, Eugène. In the end, Hortense was reconciled to the idea.

In February 1796, four months after they first met, Napoleon and Josephine called on her *homme d'affaires*, the notary Raguideau, to draw up a marriage contract. By its terms, each was to retain control of his or her own estate. With Napoleon having nothing but his pay and Josephine very little more (and most of that not paid for) the clause was, at that stage, irrelevant. Yet, with Napoleon out of the room, Raguideau advised his client against the match. Why saddle herself with a penniless young soldier, younger than herself, who might well be killed in battle, leaving her destitute? The man had nothing, argued the notary, but 'his cloak and his sword.'

Unbeknown to Raguideau, Napoleon had heard this remark through the half-open door. He never forgot it. Eight years later, reports Napoleon's first secretary, Bourrienne, when Napoleon stood dressed in all his imperial finery on the day of his coronation, he sent for the notary. 'Well, now, Raguideau,' smiled the Emperor, 'have I at last something more to recommend me than my cloak and my sword?'[11]

The couple were married on 9 March 1796. The ceremony – if the makeshift affair could be called that – took place at night in the dingiest of settings: a roughly furnished, second-storey room in what was once the Hôtel Mondragon and was now the mayor's office of the second *arrondissement*. The scene was lit by a single candle. Josephine, accompanied by her ex-lover Barras, her friend Jean Tallien and her financial adviser Jerome Calmelet, arrived promptly at eight. For two hours she waited for her bridegroom. Not until the clocks were striking ten did Napoleon come hurrying in.

The ceremony, which lasted for no more than a few minutes, was fraught with uncertainties. As a civil wedding, it was not recognised by the Church. With the mayor having tired of waiting for the groom, the ceremony was performed by a minor official lacking proper legal authority. One of the witnesses, Napoleon's aide-de-camp Lemarois, had not yet reached the required legal age and no relations were present. Because of the difficulties in obtaining baptismal certificates from Corsica and Martinique, the official had been obliged to accept sworn statements; Napoleon might even have used his brother Joseph's birth certificate. This allowed the couple to falsify their ages. With Napoleon gallantly adding two years to his, and Josephine blithely lopping four years off hers, bride and groom both passed themselves off as a compatible twenty-eight.

The form of the ceremony was hardly inspiring.

'General Buonaparte, citizen,' gabbled the acting registrar, 'do you consent to take as your lawful wife Madame Beauharnais, here present, to keep faith with her, and to observe conjugal fidelity?'

'Citizen, I do,' answered Napoleon.

'Madame Beauharnais, citizen, do you consent to take as your lawful husband General Buonaparte, here present, to keep faith with him and to observe conjugal fidelity?'

'Citizen, I do,' answered Josephine.

'General Buonaparte and Madame Beauharnais, the law unites you.'

The wedding night was spent in Josephine's house in the Rue Chantereine. There, under the swans and roses decorating her bedroom ceiling, Napoleon faced a rival for her affections; her pug dog Fortuné. When Napoleon objected to having to share the marriage bed with the dog, Josephine assured him that it was a matter of 'take it or leave it'; if he did not want Fortuné on the bed, he had better sleep elsewhere. 'So,' he afterwards reported, 'I resigned myself.'[12]

But Fortuné did not. As soon as the ardent young husband set about enjoying his conjugal rights, the dog bit him in the leg.

The honeymoon lasted for thirty-six hours. Exactly a week before, on 2 March 1796, Napoleon had been given command of the Army of Italy. He had since heard that he had to leave Paris on the evening of 11 March.

It has been claimed, chiefly by Barras, that the command had been given to Buonaparte, by Barras, as a sort of wedding present; that, for taking Josephine off his hands, Barras had rewarded

Napoleon with the Army of Italy. But not even during the gerry-mandering days of the Directory did things work quite like that. Although Barras might well have advised Napoleon to marry Josephine and although he might have hoped to benefit from any of his protégé's future successes, Barras would not have been solely responsible for Napoleon's appointment. That depended on a majority vote of all five Directors.

The truth is that Napoleon would never have married Josephine solely to be given command of the Army of Italy, and that he would never have been given the command solely because of his marriage to Josephine. Napoleon married Josephine because he was in love with her, and he was given command of the Army of Italy because of his proven military abilities. Influence no doubt played some part, but not to the extent that Barras, and others, afterwards claimed.

With his remarkable ability to concentrate his entire attention on whatever he was doing at the moment, Napoleon – in the course of that short honeymoon – devoted himself equally to his new bride and his new command. He accompanied Josephine to Saint-Germain-en-Laye to visit her two children. He was, it seems, at his most charming. Before long he had won over, not only Josephine's son Eugène, who enjoyed basking in his stepfather's reflected military glory, but Madame Campan. Hortense proved less amenable. Not even later, when all France was resounding with the glories of her stepfather's Italian campaign, was Hortense prepared to accept him.

'Do you realise that your mother has united her fate to that of a most remarkable man?' an excited Madame Campan once exclaimed. 'What gifts! What valour! Fresh conquests at every moment!'

'Madame,' replied Hortense solemnly, 'I will give him credit for all his other conquests, but I will never forgive him for having conquered my mother.'[13]

Before long, 'all Paris' was repeating Hortense's adroit remark.

Back at the Rue Chantereine, Napoleon tackled a pile of books relating to his coming campaign against the Austrians and the Piedmontese in the north of Italy. He studied them all – military memoirs, campaign histories, folio volumes of battles, books on topography – with single-minded attention. When Josephine tried to entice him away, he refused to budge. Patience, he would advise;

there would be plenty of time to make love when the war was over.

It was at this stage that Napoleon seems to have decided to change the spelling of his name from the Italian–Corsican Buonaparte to the more French-looking Bonaparte. Certainly, by the time he reached the south of France, the surname of the new commander-in-chief of a French army had been suitably Gallicised.

On the evening of 11 March Napoleon kissed Josephine goodbye and drove south. The Directory, deciding that the general's new wife would be too much of a distraction on campaign, had refused Josephine permission to travel. Perhaps they were right: Napoleon's spectacular campaign, in the course of which the names of hitherto unknown Italian villages became emblazoned in the annals of French military history, clearly suffered from no distractions. But this did not mean that he was not thinking of Josephine. Far from it. She was almost continuously on his mind. Somehow, in the midst of that tumultuous campaign, Napoleon found the time, not only to think of her but to write her the most passionate love letters.

'You are the one thought of my life,' he scrawled on 3 April. 'When I am worried by the pressure of affairs, when I am anxious as to the outcome, when men disgust me, when I am ready to curse life, then I put my hand on my heart, for it beats against your portrait ...

'By what magic have you captivated all my faculties, concentrated in yourself all my conscious existence? It constitutes a kind of death, my sweet, since there is no survival for me except in you.

'To live through Josephine – that is the story of my life.'[14]

Part Two

GENERAL AND MADAME
BONAPARTE

7

Notre Dame des Victoires

IN appointing Napoleon to the command of the Army of Italy,
the Directory was entrusting him with the task of defeating
France's most persistent enemy – Austria. Ever since 1792
France, in an effort to defend and then spread the fruits of the
Revolution, had fought alone against the monarchical powers of
Europe. In those shifting alliances of the various monarchies,
Austria had remained constant. By 1795 France had made peace
with the other allies, leaving Austria as the only major power still
actively engaged. So it was to face the Austrian armies – at
that stage allied to Piedmont and Sardinia – in largely Austrian-
controlled northern Italy, that General Bonaparte arrived in the
spring of 1796.

He succeeded brilliantly. By a combination of skill, daring
and luck, Napoleon routed the enemy and 'liberated' northern
Italy. In a matter of weeks, the eyes of all Europe were opened to
the potential of this young French general. His own eyes were
opened to something more. On the night after the famous storming
of the bridge at Lodi, Napoleon apparently felt conscious, for the
first time, of being someone exceptional; a man, as he is reported
to have put it, 'of destiny'. A mighty ambition stirred within him;
he felt, it was afterwards claimed, 'the earth move off beneath him
as though in flight.'[1]

Five days later, on 15 May 1796, he entered Milan in triumph.
As the bells rang out from every tower and campanile and the
thronging crowds hailed him as 'the Liberator', he once again

experienced that heady surge of exultation. 'They haven't seen anything yet, and the future holds successes for us far beyond what we have so far accomplished,' he confided to a subordinate. 'Fortune is a woman, and the more she does for me, the more I will demand from her . . . In our day no one has conceived anything great; it is for me to give an example.'[2]

If, from Fortune, Napoleon felt that he could demand anything he liked, he stood powerless before that other, even more capricious, woman – his wife Josephine. Militarily he might be going from victory to victory; on the domestic front he was making no advances whatsoever. None of his men, seeing their arrogant, energetic, eagle-eyed young general, would have dreamed that he was so abjectly in love. Napoleon's brusque manner and steely incisiveness masked a violently emotional, highly romantic nature. Never again were these two sides of his character to be so startlingly juxtaposed as during this period, when the triumphs of his Italian campaign were offset by the anguish of his love for Josephine. In his letters to her, Napoleon laid bare his soul to an extent that he would never do again.

'Not a day has passed that I have not loved you, not one night that I have not clasped you in my arms,' he wrote three weeks after leaving her. 'I have not drunk so much as a cup of tea without cursing the call of glory and ambition which has wrenched me from you who are my life, my soul. In the midst of military affairs, at the head of my troops, in my inspections of the camps, my adorable Josephine holds undisputed sway over my heart, possesses my mind, engrosses my thoughts . . .'[3]

Twice a day he wrote; sometimes in the stillness of dawn before the camp was astir, sometimes in a snatched moment during a lull in a battle, sometimes late at night by candlelight in his tent. Day after day his couriers went galloping along the white roads to Paris with yet another parcel of passionate love letters for their general's wife; sometimes they were instructed to remain in the capital for a few hours only before careering back with the answer.

'Love me as you love your eyes,' he begged. 'But that is not enough. As you love your very self. More than yourself, your mind, your spirit, your life, your all . . . Sweetheart, forgive me, I am raving. Human nature is weak for him who feels as keenly as he whose soul you animate.'[4]

Sometimes these letters – so vivid, so rapturous, so rich in imagery – were positively erotic. 'A kiss upon your heart,' he once

70

scrawled, 'another a little lower, another lower still, far lower!'[5]

The object of all this ardour, the recipient of all these delirious outpourings – the insouciant Josephine – simply could not respond in kind. Often she did not respond at all. Love letters, when the love is not reciprocated, are notoriously difficult to answer. She would put one of the almost indecipherable letters aside to read at a later date. She would start a letter on Monday and not finish it until Thursday. Without thinking, she would address him formally, as 'vous' instead of the more intimate 'tu'. She would break off in the middle of a letter to entertain her friends, to go to a dress fitting, or spend a few days in the country.

The bland tone of her answers would fling Napoleon into the depths of despair. 'You love me less,' he would cry out, 'you will find consolation elsewhere; someday you will cease loving me.'[6] Her last letter, he wrote on one occasion, 'was as cold as friendship. I can find there no trace of that fire which can light up your eyes, and which I have thought sometimes to see shining there.'[7]

So little affected was Josephine by these letters that she would hand them round indiscriminately to the members of her circle. 'The letter she showed me, like all the rest the general had addressed to her since his departure,' wrote her friend, the play-wright Antoine Arnault, 'was characterised by the utmost violence of passion. Josephine was amused at this emotion, which was not exempt from jealousy. I can still hear her reading a passage in which her husband, trying to suppress the anxieties [of her infidelity] which obviously tormented him, had written: "If this should be true, however, then tremble before the dagger of Othello." I can see her smile, still hear her saying in that Creole drawl of hers, "He's funny . . . Bonaparte."'[8]

This is not to say that Josephine was mocking Napoleon; she was incapable of mockery. Quite clearly, she was proud and flattered to be the object of so much devotion from so celebrated a figure, but to her sophisticated friends, she felt that she must excuse the excesses of her Corsican husband. In her worldly *milieu* such ardently expressed sentiments would have been regarded as naïve, embarrassing or, in her expression, *drôle*.

Another confidante to whom, at a later stage, Josephine showed the letters was her future lady-in-waiting, the astute Claire de Rémusat. 'They were extraordinary letters;' she notes, 'the handwriting almost indecipherable, the orthography faulty, the style bizarre and confused, but marked by a tone so impassioned, by emotions so turbulent, by expressions so vibrant and at the same time so poetic, by a love so apart from all other loves, that no woman in the world could fail to take pride in having been their inspiration. And besides, what a circumstance for a woman in which to find herself – as one of the motivating influences for the triumphal march of an entire army!'⁹

Whether or not Josephine was, as Madame de Rémusat claims, one of the motivating influences of Napoleon's triumphs in northern Italy, is debatable. Was the passion in which he was engulfed so overwhelming that it affected every aspect of his life, including his conduct of the campaign? Were his violent feelings for Josephine, denied their natural outlet, diverted into winning battles? Was the extraordinary speed with which he won his victories due to the urgency of his desire to be reunited with her? The claim seems exaggerated. Yet Napoleon did once write, 'My every action is designed with the sole purpose of reunion with you. I am driving myself to death to reach you again.'¹⁰

Madame de Rémusat goes on to make another, equally debatable, claim. The letters, she says (and she read them all) are notable for the strong vein of melancholy, of gradual disillusion, that runs through them. 'Perhaps these were the disillusionments which bruised Bonaparte's heart in its original ardour; these, perhaps, the disappointments which took their toll, made their mark, and blighted, one by one, his capacity for love. Perhaps he would have been a better man had he been more and, above all, better loved.'¹¹

But love cannot be ordered. Josephine, who had the kindest heart and the sweetest nature in the world, could none the less not feign a love that she did not feel. It would be unfair to criticise her for her 'tepidness' towards Napoleon at this stage, to blame her for the gradual hardening of his character. Her sins were all sins of omission: she was thoughtless, idle, scatterbrained, but she was never intentionally cruel.

Yet her lack of response did have a profound effect on him: always sensitive to any humiliation, he felt her indifference keenly. During these months of the Italian campaign, his finer feelings very gradually deteriorated; the combination of public triumphs and personal disappointments hardened his heart. Although he never really ceased to love Josephine, and although she would hold her fascination for him until the day she died, he was never again to love her in quite the same selfless, tender and all-consuming fashion.

But all that lay in the future. At the moment, during this triumphant spring of 1796, Napoleon's most burning desire was for Josephine to join him in Italy.

It took four months of begging by Napoleon to get Josephine to leave Paris. For one thing, she had no wish to join him; for another she was having too good a time.

Her husband's victorious Italian campaign was enabling her to bask, most gratifyingly, in reflected glory. Overnight, almost, she became a celebrity. The street outside her house was thronged with friends – and opportunists – who came to share her good fortune. Indeed, the very name of the street was to be changed from Rue Chantereine to Rue de la Victoire in honour of her husband's triumphs; while she herself came to be hailed as 'Notre Dame des Victoires'. It did not go unnoticed that those sweating and exhausted couriers who came galloping up from Italy called first at her home to deliver her husband's love letters and only then rode on to report his latest victories to the Directors at the Luxembourg.

Josephine carried off her new star status with admirable aplomb. Those qualities, which were to make her such a successful and popular Empress, were now given their first public airing. In the course of the fêtes, presentations and ceremonies which celebrated the triumphs of the French armies in Italy, Josephine impressed all who saw her by her elegance, her ease and her charm. Dressed in one of her high-waisted, neo-Grecian dresses and with garlands of flowers in her hair, she managed to look both decorative and dignified.

And all the time came Napoleon's demands that she join him. 'Come quickly, come soon to join me,' he wrote as early as 24 April. 'I warn you, if you delay longer you will find me ill....' He was sending his aide-de-camp, Colonel Junot, to Paris with captured enemy colours; 'you are to come back with him, do you understand?'[12]

Four days later he despatched yet another of those figures destined to play a leading role in his Empire – General Joachim Murat – to bring her to him. 'My happiness lies in seeing you happy, my joy in your joy, my pleasure in your pleasure,' ran his fervent sentences. 'Never was a woman loved with more devotion, more fire or more tenderness. Never has a woman been in such

73

complete mastery of another's heart, so as to dictate all its tastes and penchants, so to influence all its desires ... Adieu, Josephine, you are a monster whom I cannot explain to myself – yet every day I love you more....'[13]

Appalled by the prospect of a long and uncomfortable carriage journey over jolting roads, to be met by an ardent young soldier whom she did not particularly want to see, Josephine played for time. She no longer had the excuse that the Directory would not allow her to travel to the theatre of war; on the contrary, once Milan had been taken, the Directors gave in to Napoleon's importuning and encouraged Josephine to join him.

'We hope that the myrtle of Venus with which she will crown you will not detract from the laurels with which Victory has adorned you,'[14] is how they put it to him.

So she was obliged to find another excuse. She instructed Murat to tell Napoleon that she was pregnant and that, as such, she could not possibly undertake the arduous journey. Her news brought an ecstatic reaction from her husband. But, as an excuse for not joining him, it cut no ice whatsoever. No son of a Corsican mother would consider mere pregnancy a good enough reason for not travelling. Had Napoleon himself not been conceived and carried in embryo while his mother was accompanying his father during a guerrilla campaign?

'Ah, my beautiful one,' wrote Napoleon to Josephine at the end of May, 'take good care of yourself, be gay, take exercise, let nothing dismay you, worry about nothing, have no fear about your journey. Travel by easy stages. All I can think about is seeing you, with your little swollen belly. You must look charming.'[15]

With pregnancy not proving excuse enough, Josephine now claimed that she was ill. The news, and her dilatory replies to his letters, drove her husband almost frantic. 'My life,' he wrote, 'is a perpetual nightmare.'[16] Sometimes he imagined that she was dangerously ill; sometimes that she had recovered and was already on her way to him; sometimes that she was being unfaithful. One day he convinced himself that she had arrived; he came dashing back to Milan from the battlefield at Borghetto to find that she was not there after all. 'Sorrow crushed my soul,'[17] he told her.

'When you write, dearest,' he begged in yet another of those long, anguished letters, 'assure me you realise that I love you with a love beyond the limits of imagination, that every minute of my life is consecrated to you, that never an hour passes without my thinking of you, that I have never thought of another woman, that they are all, in my eyes, lacking grace, wit and beauty. That you, you alone, and all of you, as I see you, as you are – only you can please me, absorb the faculties of my soul; that you pervade my soul to its farthest reaches; that there is no corner of my heart into which you do not see, no thought of mine which is not subordinate to you. That my arms, my strength, my mind are all yours. That my soul lives in your body, and that the day upon which you should change or cease to live would be the day of my death. That the world is beautiful only because you inhabit it. If you do not realise and believe all this, you do not love me. A magnetic fluid flows between persons who love each other.'[18]

If any such magnetic fluid was flowing out of Josephine, it was not flowing towards him. For by now Josephine had a much stronger reason for not joining Napoleon than mere disinclination. She had fallen in love with someone else.

Late in April 1796, two months after her marriage to Napoleon, Josephine had been introduced to a Lieutenant Hippolyte Charles. Eight years younger than her, the twenty-four-year-old Hippolyte Charles was, in every way other than a shared smallness of stature, Napoleon's opposite: dashingly handsome, flamboyantly uniformed, gallantly mannered, socially accomplished, a positive fountain of quips and puns and small talk. With his talent for conversation and his knowledge of fashion, Hippolyte Charles was able to interest Josephine to a degree never achieved by her more serious-minded husband.

At the time, and for the next century and a half, the precise nature of the relationship between Josephine and the dapper Lieutenant Charles was uncertain. Some imagined that the *soignée* Madame Bonaparte was merely diverted by the company of the amusing young man; others assumed that she was simply enjoying a light-hearted and purely sexual affair with him.

But in the 1950s, among an accumulation of documents in Charles's ancestral home, the historian Louis Hastier uncovered a series of letters from Josephine. They established, beyond a shadow of doubt, that Josephine was madly in love with the young man. Their passionate phrases, their note of delirium, their vehement protestations equal anything that Napoleon was writing to her at the time. In spite of two marriages and at least two extra-marital liaisons, Josephine appears to have been experiencing the ecstasy and the anguish of first love. No amount of wooing then, on Napoleon's part, would have won her heart; she had lost it to another.

And eventually, when not even Josephine could withstand her husband's frenzied entreaties any longer (the Directors, afraid that General Bonaparte might desert the battlefront and return to his wife, added some entreaties of their own), she arranged for Hippolyte Charles to accompany her. As an adjutant to General Leclerc, who had recently joined the Army of Italy, Lieutenant Charles would be travelling as a 'special cavalier' to General Bonaparte's wife.

Finally, on 26 June 1796, Josephine set out. Her lumbering, three-carriage caravan (for Josephine was bringing, besides Hippolyte Charles, several servants and a trousseau of new clothes) was escorted by a mounted guard. In her carriage drove her brother-in-law Joseph Bonaparte, her husband's aide-de-camp Colonel Junot and, of course, Lieutenant Charles. Also in the carriage was another of Napoleon's rivals for her affections – her dog, Fortuné.

8

General Bonaparte's Court

JOSEPHINE'S arrival in Milan, in July 1796, coincided with the start of the most spectacular stage of her husband's Italian campaign. Three successive efforts by the Austrian armies to break the French siege of Mantua resulted in some of Napoleon's most celebrated victories – Castiglione, Arcola, Rivoli. Finally, with Mantua captured, the French drove the Austrians back on to their own soil, so that by March 1797, General Bonaparte stood within a hundred miles of Vienna.

Beaten, the Austrians requested an armistice. By October that year, the Treaty of Campo Formio had been signed. Skilfully presented by Napoleon – who was fast becoming an accomplished self-publicist – the Treaty of Campo Formio was generally regarded as the finale to a brilliant campaign waged by a brilliant young general. This success was accompanied by his equally thorough political re-organisation of most of northern Italy into the new Cisalpine Republic.

With Josephine, though, his campaign was progressing anything but brilliantly. The sight of her, standing in the great loggia of the rose-coloured Palazzo Serbelloni in Milan, had almost overwhelmed him. 'A few days ago I thought I loved you,' he wrote from the battlefront (for he was always having to leave her to take command of operations), 'but now since I have seen you again I love you a thousand times more. Every day since I met you I have loved you more... Thousands of kisses – one even for Fortuné, wicked beast that he is!'[1]

To the embarrassment of others in the room, Napoleon would play with her like a child, tease her until she cried, or fondle what he called her 'beautiful body' boldly and unashamedly. On paper – in his letters from the front – he was no less ardent. 'Good God,' he wrote in one of his erotic outpourings, 'how I wish I could drop in on you tonight and watch you at your dressing table, with one little shoulder bare and one little white breast showing, firm and elastic... you well know that I never forget the little visits to the little black forest. I give it a thousand kisses and impatiently await the moment of my return, to be yours, utterly yours... To live in Josephine, that is to live in Elysium. A kiss upon your lips, your eyes, your shoulder, your breast, everywhere, everywhere, every-where!'[2]

It is no wonder that, over half a century later, a worried Prosper Mérimée, in preparing Napoleon's correspondence for publication, should report that these Italian love letters were 'a question of hardly anything but kisses, in places the names of which are not found in the Dictionary of the French Academy.'[3]

Yet, to Napoleon's disappointment, the great surge of his passion still seemed to raise no corresponding passion in her. She submitted, kindly enough, to his love making but she was incapable of making any positive contribution towards their relationship. She answered his long, frequent and burning love letters from the battlefield with a few scrawled lines or not at all. She was often out, shopping or gossiping, when he came dashing back to Milan especially to see her.

Much of her time, during Napoleon's absences, was spent with Hippolyte Charles. 'Lieutenant Charles appeared as a lunch-eon guest at the Serbelloni Palace as soon as the general left the city,' reported one member of his staff. 'Josephine's interest in the young officer was no secret; if only a tender friendship, it occupied much of her time.'[4]

Napoleon certainly did not suspect that there was anything more to Josephine's association with Charles than friendship. He assumed that his wife regarded this pretty, vivacious young man with his 'hairdresser's elegance' as a diversion; as a valuable lunchtime guest or companion with whom she could discuss her clothes. With his riotously curled black hair, his tasselled red leather boots and his silver-embroidered, fur-lined jacket slung over one shoulder, Lieutenant Charles could hardly be thought of as a rival for his wife's affections. That Hippolyte spent his nights as well as his days with Josephine (and the couple were, apparently, very discreet), did not occur to Napoleon. He would have seen the young man as a link between Josephine and the life she had left behind in Paris.

To her friends and relations in Paris Josephine found the time to write the letters she should have been writing to Napoleon. In them, she complained that she was 'terribly bored' in Italy. She would gladly exchange all her present advantages – the *palazzi* in which she lived, the crowds who cheered her, the princes who fêted her, the husband who adored her – for the joy of being back in her house in the Rue Chantereine.

Yet everyone, or almost everyone, who met Josephine during the eighteen months she spent in Italy, was impressed by her many good qualities. One of these admirers was the then unknown young artist, Antoine Gros. Appreciating his talent, Josephine asked him to paint a portrait of Napoleon. Although Napoleon agreed to pose for Gros, he had neither the time nor the temperament for prolonged sittings. Josephine solved the problem by enticing her husband, during after lunch coffee one day, to sit on her lap. This allowed Gros to begin his sketches. Each day, after that, the scene would be re-enacted. Few, seeing the finished painting – that heroic portrait of the steely-eyed General Bonaparte, flag in hand, leading his men across the bridge at Arcola – knew that the subject had been lamely perched on his wife's knees during the sittings.

To Gros, Josephine was 'the very angel of goodness'. Another witness, Miot de Mélito, claimed that 'never has a woman combined greater kindness with so many natural graces; never has a woman done so many good deeds as she – with greater pleasure in the doing.'[5]

And, of course, to her besotted husband, she remained, in spite of everything, 'my beautiful and good, my utterly incomparable, utterly divine Josephine!'[6]

'All day long he adores me,' reported the bemused Josephine to her Aunt Edmée, 'as if I were a goddess.'[7]

In the summer of 1797 Josephine came up against a group of people who remained resolutely unimpressed by her seductive charms: her husband's family.

To escape the heat of Milan, Napoleon had moved into the

summer palace of Mombello. Set in an elaborately landscaped garden, this great marble *palazzo* took on, during General Bonaparte's stay, an almost regal atmosphere. 'Never,' wrote one observer, 'did military headquarters so closely resemble a royal court; the *ambiance* was exactly that of the Tuileries Palace a few years later.'[8] Protected by guards, attended by aides, surrounded by admirers, granting audiences to a variety of people, Napoleon behaved with all the ease and authority of a man born to the purple.

He was even beginning to take on the appearance of a person of consequence. The edgy, half-starved looking young lieutenant of Laure Permon's pen-picture was giving way to the more classical features of the young conqueror: firm-jawed, eagle-eyed, with a profile like 'an antique Greek or Roman coin.'[9] He might still have been slight and long-haired but he had an undeniable presence. 'Nothing could be so remarkable,' wrote one visitor to Milan, 'as the sight of that small man in the midst of giants, all so dominated by his personality that none with whom he spoke appeared taller than he.'[10]

And, as a perfect contrast to the abrupt, imperious commander-in-chief was his wife. With her dulcet manners and her floating garments, Josephine could always be relied upon to create a harmonious atmosphere. Nor, at the same time, could anyone queen it better than she.

By no one, during a fortnight of that summer at Mombello, was Josephine watched more closely than by the assorted Bonaparte clan. Napoleon had assembled almost his entire family at Mombello in June; of them all, his brothers Joseph and Louis were the only ones whom Josephine had met before. As she moved amongst them, with her carefully made-up face, her expensive clothes and with her dog trotting at her heels, she confirmed everything that they had heard about her: that she was extravagant, fickle and well past the first flush of youth.

Napoleon's mother, Letizia Bonaparte, was the most censorious of them all. The first she had heard of her son's marriage was when, on his way to take command of the Army in Italy, he had called on her in the south of France. He had brought her a letter from Josephine. Or rather, he had brought her a letter which Josephine, too lazy to write herself, had copied from a draft written by Napoleon. Its dutiful phrases did not impress Madame Letizia. To her, Josephine remained the most unsuitable choice for her son. A penniless widow, a mere fourteen years younger than Letizia herself, with two almost grown-up children could hardly be considered much of a catch.

Since the ill-educated Letizia was incapable of composing an answer to her daughter-in-law's letter, Napoleon had been obliged to write a second draft: this time an acknowledgement of his own letter.

On finally meeting Josephine at Mombello, all Letizia's worst suspicions were confirmed. Although, according to Napoleon, his wife 'showered her mother-in-law with courtesies and attentions',[11] Letizia remained unimpressed. Ashamed of her own faulty French and of her lack of social polish, she failed to respond to Josephine's advances. In any case, to the ramrod-backed and parsimonious Letizia, her son's wife represented almost everything she disliked in a woman. And as far as Letizia's sharp eye could make out, Josephine did not even fulfil the most basic wifely qualification: she showed no signs of bearing Napoleon a child. This, by Letizia's reasoning, would be the unforgiveable failing.

Napoleon's older brother, Joseph, did not allow himself to look nearly so disapproving. Knowing how passionately his brother loved Josephine, he saw no advantage in siding openly with the rest of his family against her. It would be better if he and his submissive wife Julie minded their own business and accepted whatever Napoleon felt inclined to offer. The luxury-loving Joseph would always be one for accepting whatever was going. His reticence was richly rewarded: Napoleon arranged for Joseph to be appointed French ambassador to Rome.

Napoleon's oldest sister, the twenty-year-old Elisa, could not bring herself to be more than polite to Josephine. A serious-minded, self-opinionated and singularly graceless young woman, Elisa resented her sister-in-law's frivolous tastes and sophisticated aura. Yet, no more than Joseph, could Elisa allow herself to appear too disapproving. Contrary to Napoleon's express wishes, Elisa had recently married a thirty-five-year-old nonenity by the name of Felix Bacciochi. Now, on meeting her all-powerful brother at Mombello, she needed to do everything she could – which included being civil to Josephine – to reconcile him to the match.

To her great relief, Napoleon accepted the fact of Elisa's marriage to Bacciochi quite calmly. Although acquaintance did not improve his opinion of Bacciochi, Napoleon gave his sister a dowry and arranged a military command for her husband in his native Corsica. On one thing, though, he did insist: that the Bacciochis' previous civil marriage be followed by a religious ceremony – a benediction in the oratory at Mombello. For as Napoleon rose to a position of power in the world, so did he begin to pay lip service to the world's other established powers.

Louis, the fifth Bonaparte child and, at this stage, Napoleon's favourite brother, seemed to resent Josephine less than did the others. It might have been that he was better mannered or simply that he was too self-obsessed to be bothered with these family squabbles. At nineteen, Louis's character was undergoing a change. Hitherto, he had been Napoleon's devoted pupil and, as his aide-de-camp during this Italian campaign, he had acquitted himself very well. But at about this time, Louis began to lose his taste for soldiering, and with it he lost the cheerfulness and the willingness to please which had so endeared him to Napoleon. He became quieter, graver, gloomier. His health became his chief preoccupation and from now on he was seldom happier than when consulting his doctors about the vague pains which plagued but never actually incapacitated him. His character, which had once seemed so open and uncomplicated, now became shuttered and enigmatic. But at Mombello, Josephine was grateful for his presence, for if he was not actually friendly towards her, he was at least polite.

One could not say as much for Pauline, the sixth Bonaparte. She, of them all, caused Josephine the most distress. At seventeen Pauline had more than the usual Bonaparte good looks: she was radiantly beautiful. Grey-eyed, chestnut-haired, with a flawlessly white skin and a soft, seductive body, Pauline was already setting the hearts of Napoleon's young officers aflutter. But for all her dewy freshness, when set against the soignée Josephine, Pauline seemed countrified, almost gauche. To mask her jealousy of her polished sister-in-law, Pauline behaved outrageously; she giggled incessantly, she flirted with the officers, she repeated their smutty gossip (a great deal of which concerned her brother's wife) and, when Josephine's back was turned, stuck her tongue out at her.

Napoleon very wisely decided that the best thing to do with this badly behaved, hot-blooded young girl was to marry her off as quickly as possible. He decided to do it there and then. There was a husband to hand in the person of General Charles-Victor Leclerc, the twenty-five-year-old friend of Napoleon's to whose staff Lieutenant Hippolyte Charles happened to be attached.

Leclerc was both handsome and rich. Pauline seemed willing enough (the rumour that it was a 'musket wedding', that Pauline and Leclerc had been discovered by Napoleon in a compromising position, is impossible to prove), and she and Leclerc were married with a nuptial mass in the palace oratory.

At fifteen, Caroline Bonaparte was too young to cause any serious trouble. But she shared her sister Pauline's envy of Josephine's accomplishments and joined in her laughter at Josephine's expense.

Also at Mombello was the man whom Caroline would one day marry. In a milieu of exceptionally handsome men, Joachim Murat was the most handsome of them all. Magnificently built, superbly uniformed, swaggeringly mannered, Murat was nick-named 'Franconi', after the renowned circus master. His passion for soldiering was matched only by his passion for love-making; for fearlessness on the battlefield and prowess in bed, Joachim Murat had no rival. At thirty years of age, despite his crowded career, he still retained an almost boyish enthusiasm for life. And at Mombello even he, although not yet a member of the family, slandered Josephine by hinting to his fellow officers that he had seduced her in Paris the year before.

Murat's innuendos were repeated to Napoleon, apparently by his sister Pauline. He may or may not have believed them but, three years later, when Josephine begged Napoleon to allow his sister Caroline to marry Murat, he seemed distinctly relieved. Napoleon's secretary Bourrienne, who had been with him in Italy, concluded that 'Napoleon interpreted his wife's eagerness to promote the match as a proof that the rumours of her intimacy with Murat had been slanderous and unfounded.'[12]

Jerome, the youngest Bonaparte child, who had recently been sent by Napoleon to school in Paris, now joined the family at Mombello during the holidays. At thirteen years of age he was already showing signs of becoming the best looking and most frivolous of the Bonaparte boys. Jaunty, insouciant and quick witted, Jerome was known by his friends as 'Fifi'.

Only Lucien, the intelligent, ill-tempered, incorrigible black sheep of the family was absent. He was still smarting under Napoleon's outspoken disapproval of his marriage to the simple Christine Boyer three years before. Not content with the appointment Napoleon gave him as a commissioner with the Army of the North, Lucien had begged to be allowed to return to Marseilles.

But Napoleon, considering Marseilles to be too explosive a city for someone of Lucien's temperament, had him posted to Corsica instead. By some tortuous process, Lucien saw Josephine's hand in this thwarting of his wishes.

Josephine had at least one ally at Mombello in the person of her son Eugène. Napoleon had recently sent for him and made him one of his aides-de-camp. Now sixteen years of age, Eugène, like his mother, was noted less for physical beauty than for an attractiveness of manner. And like her, he had a certain suppleness of temperament which was to stand him in very good stead in the years ahead.

Although Josephine's daughter Hortense could not be present, Napoleon did not forget her. The 'hundred pretty things' which he had once promised her in a postscript to a letter, began arriving in a steady stream at Madame Campan's school. And with the arrival of dozens of these jewelled and enamelled trinkets from Italy, Hortense's very feminine heart began to warm towards her stepfather.

The Bonaparte family left Mombello after a stay of two weeks. It must have been the longest fortnight of Josephine's life. If it had done nothing else, their stay had confirmed their resentment against Napoleon's wife; from now on there would not even be a show of friendliness towards her. To them, Josephine remained always 'the Creole', an outsider and an interloper. She, in turn, would always refer to them as 'those monsters'. The vendetta between the Bonapartes and the Beauharnais, which was to affect Josephine's whole life, was now underway.

9

The Crisis

B Y early January 1798 Napoleon and Josephine were back in their home in the re-named Rue de la Victoire. They had returned from Italy by different routes: he by the shortest, she by a way which, even by her dilatory standards, took a suspiciously long time. She missed several of the celebrations held in his honour, and three times Talleyrand, the urbane Minister of Foreign Affairs, was obliged to postpone a reception for General and Madame Bonaparte, and to replace the especially ordered and cripplingly expensive floral decorations.

Josephine's tardiness is explained by the fact that she had been secretly joined on her journey home by Hippolyte Charles. The lovers had behaved with such circumspection that Napoleon had been quite unaware that they had travelled together. Not until within 'three posting stations of Paris'[1] had Hippolyte Charles parted from her.

As always, Napoleon's irritation with his wife evaporated the minute he set eyes on her. When the celebrated couple were finally able to attend Talleyrand's frequently postponed gala, it was noticed that Napoleon could not bear to leave her side. He resented any time that he was obliged to spend in conversation with anyone else.

He certainly resented the conversation of the famous Madame de Staël. The formidable bluestocking, Germaine de Staël, a fellow guest at Talleyrand's glittering reception, imagined that this would be an excellent opportunity to engage the 'idol of the nation' in a worthy verbal exchange. Already, in a torrent of letters, Madame de Staël had declared her admiration for the victorious general. She had tried to convince Napoleon that the two of them – she the great intellectual and he the man of destiny – were made for each other. Nature, she trumpeted, had destined 'a soul of fire' such as hers, to the 'adoration of a hero', such as he. How could he possibly be satisfied with the milk-and-water Josephine?

'What effrontery!' Napoleon had exclaimed. 'To dare to compare herself with Josephine!'[2]

On her hero's return to Paris, the determined Madame de Staël had even managed to force her way into his home in the Rue de la Victoire. Brushing past a footman, who protested that the general was naked in his bathtub, she cried out, 'No matter. Genius has no sex!'[3]

Now, at the Talleyrand reception, Madame de Staël again tried to draw Napoleon's attention to herself.

'Who is the woman, General, whom you love the most?'

'My wife, Madame,' answered Napoleon.

'Yes, yes, of course,' she insisted, 'but which is the one whom you could most admire?'

'The one who best manages her household.'

'Very well, then, granted. But who is the woman whom you would consider pre-eminent among her sex?'

'The one who gave birth to the greatest number of children.'[4]

Not only did this exchange put Germaine de Staël in her place, it accurately reflected Napoleon's views. Women, Napoleon once said, were at the bottom of all intrigues and should be kept at home, away from politics. And although Josephine might well have agreed with this, she would hardly have welcomed his reference, in this exchange with Madame de Staël, to fecundity. She, after almost two years of marriage, still showed no signs of bearing a child.

Nor, of course, would Josephine have met her husband's requirements in the matter of household management. He had been greeted, on his return to Paris, with a bill of outrageous proportions for Josephine's refurbishing of the house in the Rue de la Victoire. From Italy she had sent instructions for the remodelling, refurnishing and redecorating of the house. Everything was to be in 'the latest elegance'; no expense, she implied, was to be spared. Nor was it. For the creation of a more military decor – rooms that resembled tents, stools that looked like drums, bedposts made out of cannon – Napoleon was obliged to foot a bill over seven times larger than the value of the house itself. It was no wonder that he decided to buy the house instead of leasing it; it was the only way he could safeguard the vast sum he had been forced to pay out.

To cover the cost of her various other extravagances, about which Napoleon knew very little, Josephine began dabbling in that most lucrative of enterprises – the granting of army contracts. A great believer in cultivating men in high places, she had kept her relationship with Director Barras in repair. Now, through him and others and by making use of her unique position as Bonaparte's wife (but without Bonaparte's knowledge), Josephine was able to reap substantial financial rewards from various questionable operations.

But Josephine's interest in army contracting was not purely financial. It allowed her to do something for her lover, Hippolyte Charles: through her influence he, too, was able to enjoy some of the handsome profits that were being made by suppliers to the military. The couple's chief contact was with the Bodin company of Lyons.

Inevitably, Napoleon got to hear about it. He was told – and with what relish one may imagine – by his brother Joseph. Joseph's accusations against Josephine were backed up by yet another Bonaparte: the beautiful Pauline, recently married to General Leclerc. Napoleon, thus primed by his brother and sister, lost no time in tackling Josephine. Was she responsible for the procuring of a purveyor's contract with the Army of Italy for a certain Citizen Bodin? And was it true that Hippolyte Charles was living in Citizen Bodin's house and that she visited him there every day?

Dissolving, as always, into tears, Josephine denied all knowledge of the matter. If Napoleon wanted a divorce, she sobbed, he had only to say so.

He, of course, wanted nothing of the sort. Only too anxious to believe in his wife's innocence, he accepted her tearful refutations. He even believed her when she promised to break off all communications with Hippolyte Charles.

Yet, on the very day after this violent domestic scene, Josephine wrote a distraught letter to Charles. In it she explained what had happened, instructed him to tell Bodin to deny that he knew her, and promised to meet her lover again as soon as possible. 'No matter how they torment me,' she wrote, 'they shall never separate me from my Hippolyte! My last sigh shall be for him ... Goodbye, my Hippolyte, a thousand kisses as fiery as my heart, and as loving.'[5]

A few days later she wrote to assure him that she would be coming to see him, at Bodin's as usual, that evening. 'Only you can restore me to happiness,' she gushed. 'Tell me that you love me, that you love me alone! That will make me the happiest of women ... Adieu, I send you a thousand tender kisses – and I am yours, all yours.'[6]

Napoleon's overwhelming love for Josephine was not the only reason for his readiness to believe in her innocence: he was, frankly, far too busy to give much time to his marital troubles. Soon after arriving home from Italy, he had spent twelve days on an inspection of the naval and military installations along the Channel coast. The Directory had offered him the command of an expeditionary force against yet another of Republican France's enemies, Britain. But, having decided that the chances of a successful invasion were slight, Napoleon gave his support to a counter-suggestion: an expedition against Egypt, to cut Britain's lifeline to the East. Here, the chances of success would be higher and the chances of personal glory – in which Napoleon was becoming increasingly interested – infinitely greater. Indeed, the spell of the East was being cast over his mind no less powerfully than it had been over the minds of Caesar and Alexander.

With characteristic zest, Napoleon set about planning his Egyptian campaign; a campaign apparently intended as a prelude to a French invasion of India. It was intended as something else as well: a civilising mission, in the course of which an ambitious scientific and cultural investigation would be undertaken. And so, along with the army, would go a second army: a civilian army, or 'living encyclopaedia' of scientists, zoologists, orientalists, artists and writers.

The commander's wife was not one of their number. Although Josephine accompanied Napoleon to Toulon, from where the mighty French armada was to set sail, it was decided that it would be too risky for her to go with him. The French fleet might well be attacked by the British. So it was agreed that, all going well, she would join him at some later stage.

The parting of Napoleon and Josephine on 19 May 1798

was, says Bourrienne, 'affecting in the extreme. Those who knew Madame Bonaparte are aware that few women were ever more delightful or more fascinating; and Napoleon, passionately in love with her, had brought her with him to Toulon to enjoy her company, to put off the cruel parting until the last possible moment.'[7]

Napoleon's last sight of Josephine would have been of her standing on a balcony overlooking Toulon harbour, waving her scarf at her husband's ship *L'Orient* as it 'pulled majestically into the open sea, to the accompaniment of wild shouts of acclamation from the shore, the fanfare of regimental bands on deck and the boom of the cannon from the city forts and from the battleships.'[8]

Just before leaving Toulon, Napoleon, who was never prudish, received one of his officers, General Dumas, while still in bed. Beside him lay Josephine. Both, apparently, were naked under the sheets. Once they had conquered Egypt, Napoleon assured Dumas, the two of them would send for their wives and do their utmost to produce sons. Dumas would stand godfather to Napoleon's son, and Napoleon to his. With this, Napoleon gave Josephine a resounding smack on her bottom: a bottom which, he once claimed, was the sweetest in the world.

In the hope of fulfilling her husband's desire for a son, Josephine, on leaving Toulon, made for the spa of Plombières. Set among the pine forests of the Vosges mountains, Plombières had been famous, since Roman times, for its 'waters of fertility'. Now thirty-five, Josephine was beginning to worry about the fact that she had still not borne her husband a child; a worry augmented by the attitude of Napoleon's family who made no secret of their suspicions that she might have become sterile. In a letter to Barras written from Plombières, Josephine claimed that Joseph Bonaparte (a 'vile, abominable creature') would 'not rest until he has succeeded in bringing about a rift between my husband and me.'[9]

Whatever good the waters might have done were apparently nullified by an accident, on 20 June. Josephine had been sitting sewing in an upstairs room when one of her company, knowing how devoted Josephine was to dogs, called her out on to the balcony to see a particularly handsome little dog trotting by. The entire company rushed out, the balcony collapsed under their weight and Josephine fell twenty feet. She was not seriously injured but the local doctor, conscious of his tremendous responsibility, subjected her to a variety of bizarre treatments which included leeches, compresses of hot boiled potatoes and the wrapping of the patient in the skin of a freshly slaughtered sheep. That she survived the cure was more miraculous than her having survived the fall.

For two months longer Josephine remained at Plombières. The plan seems to have been that, once fully recovered, she would follow Napoleon to Egypt. 'He tells me to come as quickly as possible to join him, that he cannot bear to be separated from me,'[10] she reported to Barras. And this time she was making no excuses, in spite of the fact that a journey to Egypt would be far more hazardous than one to Italy. It appears that, by now, Josephine had come to a better appreciation of the man she had married. Even she must have realised that he was someone exceptional; that all the deference with which she was treated, the acclamation with which she was received, the expensive gifts with which she was presented, was due to the fact that she was the wife of a national hero.

Beside this conqueror, Hippolyte Charles – for all his attractions – must have appeared very lightweight indeed. Josephine might even, by now, have begun to tire of her young lover; or he of her. Or perhaps, as Bonaparte grew in stature and importance, so did the astute Charles begin to appreciate the extent to which he was playing with fire. It might be advisable to draw back. If Napoleon were to be convinced that Charles was Josephine's lover, he might get very badly burnt indeed.

But whatever the reason, Josephine left Plombières for Paris early in September with the firm intention of setting out from there to join her husband in Egypt. Two momentous events, one military and the other domestic, prevented her from carrying out her plan. Nelson destroyed the French fleet at Aboukir Bay, and Napoleon heard the full story of Josephine's infidelity.

The glory which Napoleon had sought in the East turned out to be of a somewhat uncertain variety. By good fortune, as much as anything, the French captured Malta and disembarked safely on the Egyptian coast. The famous Battle of the Pyramids, in which Napoleon's troops routed the gorgeously costumed and archaically armed Mameluke army could hardly have been regarded as a fair fight: it was more a case of a modern fighting force mowing down a medieval one. But it did allow Napoleon to enter Cairo in triumph on 23 July 1798. The sweetness of this triumph was soured a few days later by the equally famous, if inaccurately named, Battle of the Nile, in which Nelson destroyed the French fleet in Aboukir Bay.

In fact, Napoleon's Near Eastern glories tended to be civilian rather than military. Displaying his great qualities of resourcefulness, intelligence and leadership, he set about colonising Egypt; he organised the administration, he improved the economy, he supervised a variety of scientific, geographic and archeological projects. One of the most important French discoveries was the Rosetta Stone, which supplied the key for the deciphering of hieroglyphics. By a combination of skill and brutality, Napoleon established himself as the undoubted master of Egypt – the Sultan El Kebir or Great Sultan.

But there was no sign of a sultana. And it was not only the fact that Nelson, by destroying the French fleet, had destroyed Josephine's chances of travelling to Egypt that prevented her from joining Napoleon: by now Napoleon did not want her to join him.

Not long after arriving in Egypt, while the invading French army was still marching towards Cairo, Napoleon was shown a letter which General Junot had just received from France. In it was a full account of Josephine's affair with Hippolyte Charles. This was not, of course, the first that Napoleon had heard of his wife's association with Charles but this time he was more ready to believe it. He was told, among other things, that the couple had travelled back in the same carriage from Italy to 'within three posting stations' of Paris; that they frequently shared a private box at the theatre; that Charles had given her a little dog to replace Fortuné, who had been killed in a dog fight; and that she was still seeing her lover almost daily.

As Napoleon read these accusations (and had them confirmed by two more of his officers) his 'pale face turned paler than ever', reports his secretary Bourrienne, who claims to have been standing nearby. 'His features were suddenly convulsed, a wild look came into his eyes, and several times he struck his head with his fists.'

Leaving Junot, Napoleon hurried across to Bourrienne. The secretary had never seen his employer so distraught. 'Unless one is familiar with the violence of the wrath of which Napoleon was capable when aroused, it is impossible to imagine what he was like during this terrible scene,' he writes. Napoleon roundly attacked Bourrienne for not having told him about Josephine's unfaithfulness. 'There's a true friend for you,' he sneered. 'Josephine! And I six hundred leagues away! You should have told me! Josephine – to have deceived me like this! Damn them, I shall exterminate that whole breed of fops and coxcombs! As for her, divorce! Yes, divorce – a public divorce, open scandal! I must write immediately. I know everything. It's your fault, you should have told me.'

Bourrienne tried to calm him. He denied any knowledge of Josephine's unfaithfulness. He suggested that the stories might be nothing more than malicious gossip. He blamed Junot for accusing a woman who was not there to defend herself. He contrasted the unimportance of these rumours with the glory of Napoleon's achievements.

'My glory!' scoffed Napoleon.'Oh, what I wouldn't give for Junot's news to be untrue! I love that woman so deeply! But if she is guilty, then divorce must separate us forever. I will not be the laughing-stock of Paris! I will write to Joseph and tell him to have the divorce announced.'

Bourrienne begged him not to write to his brother: the rumours might be false, the letter might be intercepted. 'As to a divorce,' advised the secretary, 'there is plenty of time to think of that later, after due consideration.'[11]

Quite possibly Bourrienne, in recalling the scene, exaggerated his own role. Nevertheless, Napoleon decided against an immediate divorce. His wrath eventually subsided but it left him feeling deeply depressed and disillusioned. Already Josephine's lack of response during the early days of their marriage had begun to harden his heart; now her reputed unfaithfulness hardened it irrevocably. For until this moment, and in spite of her vagueness and want of ardour, Josephine had provided Napoleon's life with a sweet centre. In contrast to the clamour and brutality of his days, she had represented – or had appeared to represent – something that was fine and good and unselfish. But her unfaithfulness delivered his nature a blow from which he never recovered. 'My emotions are spent, withered...,' he admitted to his brother Joseph. Nothing remains for me but to become a complete egoist.'

In the same pouch as Napoleon's letter to Joseph went one for Josephine written by her son, the sixteen-year-old Eugène. The boy was in Egypt with his stepfather, as an aide-de-camp.

'I have so many things to tell you, I don't know where to

begin,' he wrote on 25 July. 'For the last five days Bonaparte has appeared exceedingly sad, and this came about as a result of a talk he had with Junot and Jullien – even Berthier joining in. He was more seriously affected by this conversation than I had realised....'

Eugène then went on to repeat to his mother what Napoleon had been told by Junot about her affair with Hippolyte Charles. 'As you can well imagine, Mama, I do not believe a word of this, but what is certain is that the general is deeply affected by it. Still, he redoubles his kindness to me; he seems to be saying, by his actions, that children cannot be held responsible for their mother's frailties. But your son tells himself that all this gossip has been fabricated by your enemies, and he loves you no less, no less yearns to embrace you....'[12]

Written by a boy of sixteen, the letter could hardly have been more tactful or tender. But then Josephine was extraordinarily lucky in her children. Both Eugène and Hortense were exceptionally loyal, kindhearted and devoted young people. Their attitude towards their mother was always solicitous and protective; she seemed more like a sister than a mother to them, and a younger sister at that.

But neither Eugène's chivalrous letter to his mother, nor Napoleon's disillusioned letter to his brother, ever reached Paris. The ship carrying them was seized by the British and the highly confidential documents sent to London.

Sensitive, unforgiving, determined not to be labelled as a 'cuckold' and so become 'the laughing-stock of Paris', Napoleon set about getting his own back on Josephine. Deliberately he embarked on a liaison which would offset – and would be seen to offset – his wife's infidelity. It was the first of those short-lived extra-marital adventures that were to punctuate his years of marriage to Josephine. He had certainly not been unfaithful to her before.

His secretary Bourrienne was commissioned to round up several Egyptian beauties for his master's inspection. None passed the test. In Napoleon's eyes, they were all too fat and cumbersome. His taste was for small, slender, graceful, very feminine women dressed, for preference, in white. There was certainly nothing about these obese houris with their hennaed hair and jangling bracelets to tempt him. So he chose one of the few European women available. This was Pauline Fourès, the nineteen-year-old wife of a lieutenant in the Chasseurs, who had managed to get to Egypt by putting on one of her husband's uniforms and stowing away on his ship.

With her 'rose-petal complexion, beautiful teeth and a good geometrical figure',[13] Pauline suited Napoleon's purposes very well. Having sent Lieutenant Fourès upriver, he staged a very public seduction scene (he spilt some wine on her dress at a dinner party and ushered her upstairs to sponge it off), thus ensuring that the affair would be widely talked about. On his return to Cairo, the cuckolded Lieutenant Fourès was shipped off for a second time – on this occasion to carry 'urgent' despatches to France. With the husband out of the way, the wife – rose-petal complexion, beautiful teeth, good geometrical figure and all – was installed in a villa close to Napoleon's headquarters.

One day out of port, the ship carrying Fourès was captured by the British. With considerably more malice than chivalry, the British captain – knowing all about Bonaparte's *amour* – returned the captive husband to Egyptian soil. Poor Fourès was obliged to obtain a civil divorce and Pauline was able to bask, unencumbered, in her position as Napoleon's acknowledged mistress. Bask she certainly did. When not sitting beside her lover in his open carriage, she would be riding beside him, sporting a 'general's' uniform of tight white trousers, gold-braided blue coat and riotously plumed hat. The soldiers called her 'Madame Generale'.

The only person seriously upset by Napoleon's studied display of infidelity was his stepson Eugène. As one of General Bonaparte's aides-de-camp, Eugène was often obliged to ride escort behind his carriage. When the youth could bear the humiliation no longer, he applied for a transfer to another regiment. Napoleon was furious and treated Eugène to one of his celebrated diatribes. But, significantly, the public drives with Pauline ceased from that moment on.

If one can believe Bourrienne, Napoleon promised to marry Pauline Fourès if she produced a child. When she showed no signs of doing so, he complained that 'the little idiot' did not know how to have one. To this Pauline replied, most emphatically, that the fault was not hers. This seems to have been one of the first occasions on which doubt was cast on Napoleon's ability to father a child. The fact that Josephine had already borne two children further encouraged the doubts; it certainly strengthened Josephine's contention that the fault lay with him, and not her. But she was fortunate in that Pauline did not bear Napoleon a son: in his present mood, he might well have divorced his childless and unfaithful wife to marry a younger woman capable of giving him children.

But once Napoleon had left Egypt, he never saw Pauline again; although, under the Empire, he did buy her a house and grant her a liberal allowance. Having outlived the fall of the First Empire, Pauline Fourès very nearly outlived the fall of the Second; she died, in her ninetieth year, in 1869, in a Paris apartment surrounded by an assortment of fluttering uncaged birds and wildly chattering monkeys.

With news sometimes taking months to reach Paris from Cairo, Josephine was still blissfully unaware of Napoleon's changed feelings towards her. Not until November 1798 – four months after Junot had first told Napoleon about her infidelity – did she come to hear about it. When she did, it was in the most embarrassing fashion possible. Those highly confidential letters – from Napoleon to Joseph, and from Eugène to Josephine – which had been captured by the British, were published in London. Copies were immediately rushed to France. In no time, all Paris was talking about the crisis in the Bonaparte marriage. That Napoleon was intending to divorce her, Josephine had very little doubt. Her apprehensions were confirmed when she came to hear about his affair with Pauline Fourès.

Yet, by the time the news reached her, the initial wave of Napoleon's wrath had subsided. Writing to Joseph that October and entrusting the letter to their brother Louis who was deserting the discomforts of Egypt for the luxuries of home, Napoleon urged Joseph to 'show some courtesy to my wife, go and see her occasionally. I am likewise asking Louis to give her some good counsel.'[14] One may be sure that Joseph discouraged Louis from passing on any such good counsel.

Josephine was certainly in need of it. Not only had she resumed her former intimacy with Hippolyte Charles but she was up to her neck in yet another unsavoury scandal – this one concerning the affairs of those notorious army contractors, the Bodin company. The collapse of the company, in which she and Charles were deeply involved, put a strain on their relationship;

by February 1799 she was writing him what reads like a bitter letter of renunciation. 'You can be assured . . . ,' she says, 'that you will no longer be tormented by my letters or by my presence. The self-respecting woman who has been the victim of deceit retires and says nothing.'[15]

But even this did not result in a final break with Charles. Certain that, even if Napoleon were to arrive back safely from Egypt, he would divorce her, Josephine did not want to sever all connections with Hippolyte Charles. She might yet have need of him. For her, the support of a man was essential; security was what she prized above all else. Already, her long-standing relationship with Barras was beginning to cool; to replace it, she began to cultivate the friendship of yet another member of the Directory, the fifty-two-year-old Louis-Jerome Gohier. The friendship remained platonic and Gohier did his best to give Josephine some sound advice: this was that she should break with Charles. With the irresolute Josephine feeling unable to take such a step, Gohier then advised her to take another: she should divorce Napoleon and marry Charles. This advice, too, she considered too drastic.

Never one for facing up to her responsibilities – except where her children were concerned – Josephine simply floundered from day to day, hoping that someone would make up her mind for her, and expecting the worst.

Adding considerably to Josephine's discomfort was the fact that, by now, all her dreaded in-laws, the Bonaparte family, were living in Paris. For as much as they delighted in the bounty which was now flowing their way, so they resented the fact that Josephine stood to benefit most from it.

With the urbane Joseph's spell as ambassador to Rome having been cut short by a riot, he and his wife Julie had settled into, not one, but two luxurious French homes: a town house in the Rue de Rocher and a country place at Mortefontaine, near Chantilly. Here they were joined by Madame Letizia. The dramatic change in the family's fortunes brought no diminution of Letizia's deep-rooted parsimony. While the rest of them spent money like water, she watched every franc. She had to save, she claimed, for her sons; they were not all in what she called 'settled positions' yet. Of her profligate daughter-in-law Josephine, she disapproved strongly. Against the rock-like taciturnity of Madame Letizia, all

Josephine's charm and spontaneity dissolved like so much froth.

Every bit as antagonistic towards Josephine was the third Bonaparte son, the fiery Lucien. Unable to keep out of politics, Lucien had managed to get himself elected as Corsican deputy to the Council of Five Hundred. The fact that he was far too young to stand for election (he was twenty-three at the time and a candidate had to be at least twenty-five) was conveniently glossed over and he took his seat in April 1798. Never one to hang back, Lucien was soon one of the most voluble members of the assembly. Nor were his speeches mere verbiage; buried under the florid phraseology and the classical allusions was a great deal of common sense. Lucien could be foolish but he was no fool. His listeners began to take the ardent young man more seriously and before the year was out he had become a real force in the Council. His position was to stand his brother Napoleon in very good stead. Like Joseph, Lucien bought himself both a town and a country house, and, although he could not match his brother's qualities as a host, his estate at Plessy was equal to Joseph's in magnificence.

The three Bonaparte sisters – Elisa, Pauline and Caroline – were also in Paris. Elisa, with her intellectual pretensions, was finding both her stolid husband, Felix Bacciochi, and life on Corsica (where Napoleon had organised a military command for Bacciochi) far too dull for her taste. As a result, she was spending more and more time in Paris.

The lovely Pauline was finding her husband, Victor Leclerc, equally dull. But, unlike the plain Elisa, Pauline had no difficulty whatsoever in attracting other, more vivacious, men. Already, with her seductive looks, suggestive clothes and numerous admirers, Pauline was the talk of Directoire society.

The youngest Bonaparte girl, the headstrong Caroline, Napoleon had sent to join Josephine's daughter Hortense at Madame Campan's school. 'I counted on finding a real friend in Caroline Bonaparte,'[16] wrote Hortense. She blamed her subsequent disillusion on Napoleon. Her stepfather, she claimed, made the mistake of always holding her up as an example to Caroline. In vain did the sweet-natured but possibly patronising Hortense try to help the disgruntled girl. The spiteful Caroline repaid her kindness by complaining that Hortense was showing off at her expense. In true Corsican fashion, the Bonaparte vendetta was being extended to the second generation.

Both before and after his spell as aide-de-camp to his brother

Napoleon in Egypt, Louis Bonaparte would sometimes visit the two girls at Madame Campan's. 'He seemed particularly interested in me,' noted Hortense in some alarm, adding that there was something about his bearing that she mistrusted. Of a generous, sunny disposition herself, Hortense disliked Louis's withdrawn, melancholy temperament. If he was showing some interest in Hortense at this time, she was certainly not returning it.

Neither of these two ill-matched young people could ever have foreseen the roles in which they were one day to be cast in the Bonaparte–Beauharnais drama.

As an escape from the prying Bonaparte eyes and from the relentless pressures of her life, Josephine set about acquiring what was to be her most lasting memorial: the Château of Malmaison.

Lying about ten miles down the Seine from Paris, on the outskirts of the village of Rueil, Malmaison was more of a manor house than a château. Its ill-omened name – 'Evil House' – reflected the fact that a leper hospital had stood on the site in medieval times. But any such unfortunate associations had long since been dispelled. Malmaison was a large, handsome, unpretentious home set in three hundred acres of lawns, woods, vineyards and farmland. Since the Revolution, the property had been badly neglected.

Appreciating its potential, and blithely ignoring that she could not possibly afford the three hundred thousand francs that was being asked for it, Josephine started negotiations. But even after the asking price had been reduced and lenient terms of credit extended, she was still unable to find the money for the deposit. Joseph Bonaparte – expecting his brother to divorce her when he returned – had discontinued her allowance, and the collapse of the Bodin company had cut off her only other source of revenue. But never one to allow a lack of funds to prevent her from buying whatever she wanted, Josephine simply borrowed the deposit: some say from Barras, others from the estate steward. The contract was signed on 21 April 1799 and within days Josephine had moved in.

Whatever Josephine lacked in hard cash she made up for in exquisite taste. Before long Malmaison was being transformed. Napoleon's Italian campaign had yielded a rich booty: as the French armies had advanced into Italy, so, in the opposite direction, had travelled the spoils of that victorious campaign. At Malmaison, Josephine was able to display those paintings, statues, mosaics and *objets* which Napoleon had sent home. There were more personal treasures too. 'It was at Malmaison,' writes one visitor that summer, 'that Madame Bonaparte showed us the prodigious quantity of pearls, diamonds and cameos which at that time comprised her jewel collection, already as fabulous a treasure as any in the *Arabian Nights*, and later to be augmented further still...

'Surrounded by all these treasures, Madame Bonaparte often lacked the cash to pay her day-to-day expenses and, to extricate herself from this predicament, she resorted to selling her influence in high places, compromising herself by imprudent associates.'

In her indiscreet way, Josephine regaled this particular visitor – her future lady-in-waiting, the young Claire de Rémusat – with all sorts of confidential information about Napoleon and his 'detestable' brothers. She seemed, says Madame de Rémusat, 'forlorn and isolated...prey to anxiety, despairing of her husband's return, on worse terms than ever with her brothers-in-law and furnishing them steadily with all too much concrete evidence to support their accusations against her.'[17]

Confused and apprehensive, Josephine finally turned to her old associate, Barras, for advice. Their friendship might have cooled of late but she still felt able to write to him, beseeching him to see her, if only for a quarter of an hour. 'I must talk to you! I need your counsel,' she begged. 'You owe it to the wife of Bonaparte as well as to our own friendship, yours and mine....'[18]

Barras saw her and the advice he gave her was excellent. She must work towards a reconciliation with her husband; it was her only hope. Acting on this, Josephine wrote to Napoleon. It was not apparently (for it has been lost) a letter of contrition but one of injured innocence. In an accompanying letter to Eugène, Josephine struck the same note. She was living for the moment, she declared, when she would be reunited with all she held dear in this world; 'especially if I find Bonaparte as he was when he left me – as he should never have ceased to be!'[19]

10

Reconciliation

NEVER one for sitting idle, and still in search of the elusive Near Eastern glory, Napoleon marched his army out of Cairo in the early days of February 1799. He was headed for the Holy Land, ostensibly to defeat a Turkish army but quite possibly to strike a yet more spectacular blow in the form of the capture of Constantinople or even the conquest of India.

Napoleon smashed the Turks easily enough at the Battle of Mount Tabor but by then he was bogged down in a siege of the Turkish-held fortress of Acre. For over two months, with increasing frustration, he laid siege to Acre. Finally, while admitting defeat in private but claiming victory to the Directory back in Paris, he abandoned the siege and marched his depleted troops back to Egypt.

Here, he redeemed himself, on 25 July 1799, by routing yet another invading Turkish army. Nothing, though, could disguise the fact that – strategically and personally – Egypt had become a *cul de sac* for Napoleon.

This conviction was strengthened when a packet of newspapers fell into his hands. In them he read, for the first time, about the dangers facing France. A powerful new coalition of Austria, Britain and Russia had inflicted crushing defeats on the French armies while the French Republic itself was facing serious internal upheaval. This, he immediately decided, was no time to be sitting about in Cairo: he must get back to France as soon as possible. His place, he declared ringingly, was where he could be of the most use: the most use, one suspects, to himself.

On 23 August 1799, having entrusted the army to General Kléber, Napoleon and a small party – including his stepson Eugène – slipped secretly out of Egypt and set sail for home. Six weeks later, on 9 October, the little squadron arrived off Frejus, in the south of France.

Josephine was dining at the home of her new friend, Louis-Jerome Gohier, by now President of the Directory, on the evening of 10 October 1799, when a message, conveyed by the miraculous new signalling system of semaphore, announced that Napoleon had landed in France the day before.

For once, she acted with iron resolve. 'I am going to meet him,' she announced to Gohier. 'It is important for me to reach him ahead of his brothers, who have always hated me.' Not, she hastily added, turning to Madame Gohier, that she had anything to hide. 'When Bonaparte learns that it is in your company, Madame, that I have spent my time during his absence, he will be flattered as well as grateful for the cordial welcome given me in your home.'[1]

What Madame Gohier (who had once been her husband's cook) thought of this outrageous statement – part warning, part promise and all nonsense – one does not know. Like many people in authority, the Gohiers were keeping their options open: who knew what the future might hold for the returning General Bonaparte, or his wife?

At dawn the next morning, with Hortense as her only companion, the worried Josephine drove south at breakneck speed to meet her husband. But the Bonapartes had started out even earlier. Already Joseph, Lucien and Louis, with Pauline's husband, Leclerc, were thundering south, three hours ahead of her. Both coaches were careering down the Burgundy road to Lyons. In every town and village through which they passed, they saw *arcs de triomphe* being erected; whenever they stopped to change horses, people crowded round to ask if it were true that 'the Saviour' was on his way home.

Before reaching Lyons, Josephine was greeted with alarming news. Napoleon had already left Lyons, but he was making for Paris by another route; this was why she had not encountered him on the Burgundy road. His brothers, who had also discovered the error, had already turned round and were racing after him. Sick with apprehension and now two days late, Josephine turned back to Paris.

Napoleon arrived back at the Rue de la Victoire to find the house empty. 'The effect upon him of that homecoming,' writes Laure Permon, 'was profound and terrible: the house was deserted, its mistress missing. His wife's absence he interpreted as an admission of her unworthiness to come into the presence of his mother and sisters, an admission of her fear to face the man she had wronged.'[2]

That, at least, is how the Bonapartes interpreted it. For, having heard of Napoleon's arrival, Madame Letizia, accompanied by his sisters Elisa and Pauline, lost no time in hurrying over to greet him. A few hours later his brothers, exhausted but victorious, tumbled out of their coach. The assembled Bonapartes were now able to give their brother a full account of Josephine's transgressions, not least her long liaison with Hippolyte Charles. The fact that she was not there to greet him seemed to confirm everything they said. There was only one possible course of action, they urged: he must divorce her immediately.

Napoleon was given more disinterested advice as well. Several of his colleagues advised him to forgive her, to treat the matter more philosophically, to postpone any decision until later. The worldly Barras warned him of the political consequences of a divorce: even in these free-thinking days, it was a stain on the record of a man in the public eye. Sometimes Napoleon seemed to be swayed by such arguments; at others he cried out that he would never forgive her, that he was determined to rid himself of her once and for all.

It is some measure of Napoleon's obsession with Josephine that he – the most rational and decisive of men – was plunged into such a state of confusion. It was not that he did not believe that she had been unfaithful to him; it was that he could not bear the thought of parting from her. Normally so touchy, so vindictive, so unforgiving, he was none of these things when it came to Josephine. His other, more renowned characteristics – his analytical mind and his steely resolve – likewise deserted him when faced by Josephine's magic. Disillusioned he certainly was, but he was no less bewitched.

Yet by the time Josephine finally arrived home during the night of 18 October – three days after Napoleon – he seems to have made up his mind to have nothing more to do with her. Hurrying upstairs, she found their bedroom empty; Napoleon had locked himself in his study. No amount of knocking, pleading or crying would get him to open the door to her. All night long she remained outside the door, the house hushed about her, 'the deathly stillness and suspense broken only by her sobs.'[3]

At dawn, acting on the suggestion of her astute maid, Josephine fetched Eugène and Hortense and the three of them stood there in the half-light, beseeching him to let them in. Finally, because he was devoted to his stepchildren, Napoleon opened the door. They could see that his own eyes were red with weeping. Napoleon embraced Eugène, while Josephine and Hortense knelt on the floor, hugging his knees.

'What was there to say?' Napoleon afterwards somewhat shamefacedly explained. 'One cannot be human without being heir to human weaknesses.'[4]

Once the children had returned to bed and Josephine was alone with her husband, she managed, as always, to convince him – or at least half convince him – of the baselessness of his brothers' accusations. And she also managed, of course, to weave her old irresistible, seductive spell. In the face of Josephine's sweetly drawled blandishments and sexual allure, all Napoleon's resolve melted.

Later that morning Lucien Bonaparte arrived to see his brother. He was told that Napoleon was not yet up. He knocked on the bedroom door and Napoleon shouted to him to come in. There, to his chagrin and consternation, Lucien was greeted by the sight of Napoleon and Josephine in bed together, in a state of 'unmistakable, total reconciliation.'[5]

This celebrated scene – of the weeping Josephine's night-long vigil outside Napoleon's bolted door – marks a climax in their marriage. From this point on, the relationship between them changed. The experience had jolted Josephine out of her old complacency and indifference; never again would she be in a position to make light-hearted references to her husband's helpless devotion, never again would she take his love for granted. On the other hand, it had torn the last of the scales from Napoleon's eyes. Josephine no longer appeared to him as some almost mystical amalgam of everything that was sweet and lovely. Although she would never cease to fascinate him or to be inexpressibly dear to him, he now saw her for what she was.

From this point on, their roles were reversed. Josephine was to become the wooer, and Napoleon the wooed; she the faithful one and he the philanderer; she the one to suffer pangs of jealousy, he to take his pleasures wherever he found them. The marriage was henceforth to be on his terms, not hers. And perhaps this is how Josephine preferred it. Submissive herself, it had not suited her to have so submissive, so abject, so adoring a lover as the young Napoleon. Now that he had revealed himself as the more masterful partner, she found herself responding with more ardour. Until that fateful night, it had been Napoleon who had been in love with Josephine; now it was she who was in love with him.

With their reconciliation, the cause of their matrimonial upheaval – the debonair Hippolyte Charles – disappeared from the scene. Josephine had sworn never to see him again, and although she might well have contacted him once or twice more for business reasons, she clearly kept her word. And Charles, unlike those others such as Barras and Hoche, who afterwards boasted of their intimate association with the late Empress Josephine, kept his lips sealed. Although the affair between Madame Bonaparte and Lieutenant, afterwards Captain, Charles was talked about at the time, there was no written proof to back up the rumours; there was certainly nothing in black and white to indicate that it had been anything more than a little light-hearted dalliance on Josephine's part. When Charles died, almost a quarter of a century after Josephine, the full story of the affair was assumed to have died with him; for Charles had ordered all Josephine's love letters to be destroyed. But they were not all destroyed. And only with the discovery, in the 1950s, of a selection of these passionate letters to him, could the depth of her feelings be appreciated.

Yet Napoleon seems to have appreciated them. In spite of all Josephine's pretty protestations of innocence or, at least of her avowal of the unimportance of the affair, Napoleon always regarded Charles as a deadly rival. Laure Permon, by then married to one of Napoleon's old comrades-in-arms, Andoch Junot, once claimed that Napoleon never allowed Charles's name to be mentioned in his presence, and went on to give an example of his enduring obsession with his wife's ex-lover.

One day while Napoleon, by then Emperor of the French,

was out walking incognito with General Duroc through the streets of Paris, the General felt his arm being gripped so tightly that he imagined Napoleon was about to fall. He noticed that 'the Emperor's face had paled even beyond its normal pallor'. The worried Duroc was about to call for help when Napoleon silenced him. 'There's nothing wrong with me. Be quiet,' snapped the Emperor.

'A carriage had sped past and the passenger in the carriage had been Monsieur Charles, and Napoleon had caught sight of him – for the first time since the Italian campaign,' explained Laure Junot.

Duroc's story astounded her, she claims, for she had never believed that Napoleon, whom she considered heartless, was capable of such 'profound emotion.'[6]

Napoleon's domestic drama was followed, three weeks later, by a national drama of epic proportions.

With France in a state of political, military and economic confusion, it was felt – in certain government and intellectual circles and by a great many ordinary French people – that the time was ripe for the establishment of a more stable regime. The Directory was feeble and discredited; the country was on the verge of bankruptcy with inflation and unemployment dangerously high; large areas of western France were in the hands of royalist rebels. Only a strong man would be able to bring order to this chaotic situation.

This was certainly the view of one of the Directors, Emmanuel Sieyès. What he was looking for, declared Sieyès, was 'a sabre'. He did not need to look far. Napoleon, who had recently proclaimed that his sabre would never be drawn 'except for the defence of the Republic and its government',[7] was apparently ready to draw it now. He was not drawing it, though, so much in the defence of the Republic and its government, as in the furtherance of his own career.

Napoleon's exercise of power, both in northern Italy and in Egypt, had given him great confidence in his own abilities. This, allied perhaps to his romantic sense of destiny, convinced him that the time had come for him to play a more active political role. As 'the Saviour of France', his was the one name that was widely known among the people; against the blur of faces of the men who governed France, his austere Roman profile was the only instantly recognisable one. This popularity must be put to good use. So, together with Sieyès and others, Napoleon planned a *coup d'état*.

In the weeks between Napoleon's return from Egypt and the famous *coup d'état* of 18 Brumaire (9 November 1799), he spent much of his time closeted in his study in the Rue de la Victoire. At all hours of the day and night the conspirators came and went. Singly, or in groups, soldiers, ministers of state, representatives of the Council of Ancients and the Council of Five Hundred, Directors, and, of course, Napoleon's brothers Joseph and Lucien, answered Napoleon's summons. At times the house teemed with mutually antagonistic individuals and factions as they waited to be admitted into the general's study.

Throughout this tense period, Josephine played a not unimportant role. It is some indication of Napoleon's confidence in her abilities that she knew all about the conspiracy from the start. 'Josephine was in the secret,' affirms General Count Philippe de Ségur, 'nothing was concealed from her. At every conference at which she was present, her discretion, her grace, her gentle manner, her cool composure, ready ingenuity and wit were of great service. She justified Bonaparte's renewed confidence in her.'[8] She was, in short, of considerable value to Napoleon. While he plotted in the study, she held court in the salon: reconciling, reassuring, lightening the atmosphere, smoothing ruffled feathers, employing all the tact and diplomacy for which she was well known.

On occasions, Josephine played a more active part in the conspiracy than this. Napoleon, uncertain whether the President of the Directory, Josephine's old admirer, Gohier, was willing to support the proposed *coup*, used her to put him off the scent. When, for instance, talk of a conspiracy was raised in Gohier's presence, Josephine, acting the helpless little female, would imply in a 'tremulous, incredulous tone of voice,'[9] that it was the first she had ever heard of it.

And on the evening before the *coup*, Napoleon – anxious to have Gohier on his side the following day – got Josephine to write him a letter. 'Please come, my dear Gohier, both you and your wife, to breakfast with me at eight in the morning. Do not fail me. I must talk to you on matters of the utmost importance. Farewell, my dear Gohier; count always on my sincere friendship.'[10] Finally suspecting that something was afoot, Gohier declined the invitation. But Madame Gohier came. What she saw confirmed all her husband's suspicions. The courtyard of the house in the Rue de la Victoire was full of generals on horseback. But, as not even Josephine's entreaties to Madame Gohier to persuade her husband to throw in his lot with Napoleon could change the President's mind, Gohier was put under house arrest at the Luxembourg. Josephine's other long-standing friend in the Directory, Barras, was likewise deposed.

On the morning of 9 November 1799, with over sixty officers clattering behind him, Napoleon rode out of the gates of the Rue de la Victoire house towards the Tuileries, where the Council of Ancients was assembled. 'Josephine and I were left alone,' reports Bourrienne. 'She was consumed by anxiety. I assured her that every move in the plan had been so meticulously prepared that success was certain.'[11]

It was, in fact, by no means certain. The first stage went well enough. Such members of the Council of Ancients who had managed to attend the deliberately hastily summoned session were bullied, by threats of an entirely fictitious terrorist plot, into appointing Napoleon commander-in-chief of all the troops in the capital, and into agreeing to transfer the sittings of the two legislative houses to the palace of Saint-Cloud, where, away from the centre of Paris, they could be even more easily bullied. Napoleon returned to Josephine that evening, well enough pleased with the progress so far.

The trouble came the following day. When Napoleon, at Saint-Cloud, addressed first the Council of Ancients and then the Council of Five Hundred in an attempt to get them to authorise a new provisional government, he proved himself no orator. He was simply shouted down. 'Down with the tyrant!' and 'Outlaw the dictator!' yelled the deputies. White-faced and flustered, Napoleon had to be rescued from the hall. His brother Lucien who was, besides being President of the Council of Five Hundred, a far more forceful speaker, fared no better. He, too, had to be rescued by the soldiers.

With oratory having failed, the Bonapartes resorted to force. Although Napoleon was still too shaken to take command of the situation, his brother Lucien leapt on to his horse and addressed the troops. He urged them to 'march against the traitors who were in the pay of England' and swore that he himself would stab his brother Napoleon in the heart if he in any way tampered with the liberties of France.

Apparently convinced by this rhetoric and led by Generals Leclerc and Murat (one present and one future Bonaparte brother-in-law), the soldiers invaded the chamber. Their gleaming bayonets did the trick. The deputies fled, scattering their red republican togas across the gardens as they disappeared into the fast failing light.

Such deputies as could be herded up were later obliged to agree to the abolition of the Directory and the establishment of a consulate of three: two former directors, Sieyès and Ducos and, as First Consul, General Bonaparte. It was subsequently decided that the functions of the other two consuls would be advisory and consultative only. For all practical purposes, Napoleon was now master of France.

With, as Bourrienne drily puts it, 'the logic of the bayonet' having won the day, he accompanied the exhausted Napoleon back to the Rue de la Victoire. Throughout the drive, Napoleon said not a word. It was almost dawn by the time they arrived home. The worried Josephine was still awake; in her soothing company Napoleon regained, says his secretary, 'his usual confidence'. Together the three of them – Napoleon, Josephine and Bourrienne – sat discussing the day's tumultuous events.

It was already getting light on that morning of 11 November 1799 when Napoleon finally dismissed his secretary. 'By the way, Bourrienne,' he reminded him in his bantering fashion, 'tomorrow we sleep at the Luxembourg.'[12]

1 The dawn of the legend: the heroic painting, by Philippoteaux, of General Bonaparte at the Battle of Rivoli in 1797.

2 Napoleon's mother, the beautiful and iron-willed Letizia Bonaparte.

3 Napoleon's older brother, the urbane Joseph Bonaparte.

4   The eagle-eyed young General Bonaparte soon after his marriage to Josephine de Beauharnais. From a miniature by Guerin.

5   Isabey's sketch of Josephine in the year after her marriage to Napoleon;
one of the few portraits to capture her allure.

7   Lucien Bonaparte,
Napoleon's irascible and
rebellious brother.

8   Napoleon's oldest sister, the
pretentious Elisa Bonaparte
Bacciochi.

9   Josephine's daughter, the
sympathetic Hortense de
Beauharnais, afterwards Queen of
Holland.

10   Napoleon's taciturn brother
Louis, afterwards King of Holland,
whose marriage to Hortense was
engineered by Josephine.

6   (*Left*) The always elegant Josephine, as First Lady, receiving ambassadors
at the Tuileries.

11 Gérard's portrait of the redoubtable Letizia Bonaparte, soon to be transformed into Madame Mère.

12 The swashbuckling Joachim Murat, King of Naples.

13 Napoleon's attractive and ambitious sister Caroline Murat, afterwards Queen of Naples.

14 (*Right*) Napoleon in his specially designed uniform as First Consul, by Ingres.

15 Josephine, as wife of the First Consul, by Appiani.

16 Josephine's son, the good-natured Eugène de Beauharnais, as Viceroy of Italy.

Part Three

FIRST CONSUL AND FIRST LADY

11

The Partnership

NAPOLEON Bonaparte turned thirty in the year that he became First Consul. Although he had not yet developed into the plump and imperious figure of later life, he was beginning to fill out. He was five foot six inches tall, with a large head and a deep chest. His body was well made but not particularly powerful. Against those other famous soldiers of the period – Massena, Kléber and Murat – he appeared almost puny. His hands and feet were small.

Napoleon was considered handsome, with a sensuous, somewhat Italianate face. His complexion was cameo-like, smooth, clear and sallow. His eyes, which were his best feature, were blueish-grey and his gaze unflinching. Sometimes gentle, almost caressing, those eyes could suddenly become hard and forbidding; more than any other man's they seemed, says one witness, 'to depict the divers emotions which stirred him.'[1] His mouth, too, tended to express his feelings: thin-lipped in anger and twisted in irony, it could transform his face when breaking into a wide, enchanting smile. His chestnut-brown hair, which was already thinning, he was soon to cut very short in the style of the ancient Greeks and Romans; *le petit tondu* – the little crop head – they called him.

Napoleon's face, noted the Englishwoman Fanny Burney, 'is of a deeply impressive cast, pale even to sallowness, while not only in the eye but in every feature – care, thought, melancholy and meditation are strongly marked, with so much of character, nay, genius, and so penetrating a seriousness, or rather sadness, as powerfully to sink into the observer's mind.' She had been expecting to find a swashbuckling soldier: what she saw was someone with 'far more the air of a student than a warrior.'[2]

But Napoleon was a consummate actor and Fanny Burney was merely seeing him in one of his many roles. Far more typical was that other Napoleon – the restless, energetic, dynamic young man who could never sit still and who could never stop talking. When he was annoyed, his words tumbled out at breakneck speed, 'like a torrent'. He had a very quick temper. Often he lost it over trifles – at the ineptitude of a servant, perhaps – but he had also been known to strike a general across the face on the battlefield. He ate extraordinarily quickly: guests at the First Consul's table would find that he, who had been served first, had cleared his plate before they had been able to touch theirs. When, after fifteen or twenty minutes, he rose, they were obliged to leave the table with him. Those like his stepson, Eugène, who knew him well, made sure of eating a hearty meal before they sat down to dine with him.

Although he could display remarkable social assurance, and his charm, when he chose to exercise it, could be overwhelming, Napoleon did not really enjoy the dinners and receptions which became so much a part of his life once he moved into the Luxembourg Palace. He much preferred to be closeted in his study with one or two of the guests, talking official business. And although he could do without sleep when necessary, he disliked staying up late. No matter how illustrious the company, at eleven Napoleon would break up the party by saying abruptly to Josephine, 'Let's go to bed.'

The couple's new home, the Luxembourg Palace, was a far cry from Josephine's fashionably decorated little house in the Rue de la Victoire. Once a splendid royal residence, the Luxembourg had suffered during the Revolution; Louis XVI and Marie Antoinette had been confined there, and during the Terror it had become a prison. Under the Directory, each of the Directors had been allotted an apartment, and although some, like Barras, had introduced a note of luxury, the Palace remained a shabby, echoing, inhospitable place. Napoleon and Josephine were housed in the wing to the right of the main entrance, overlooking the Rue Vaugirard. In this same Rue Vaugirard, less than half a mile away, Josephine had been imprisoned in the Convent of the Carmelites.

It seemed almost unbelievable that that should have been a mere six years before. Then she had been an unknown, unimportant, lower-ranking member of the aristocracy awaiting execution; now she was the First Lady of the French Republic.

But it was her connections, tenuous though they might have been, with the *ancien régime*, that were proving so invaluable to Napoleon. For he was determined to put an end both to the egalitarian atmosphere of the early days of the Revolution and to the disreputable society of the Directory. The tone of public life was to be improved; what the First Consul was after was order, respectability and formality. He was anxious to recreate something of the mannered world on whose fringes his wife had once moved. And as Josephine was the only member of his family and close circle who had ever moved in that world, he relied on her to help set the tone.

Josephine's most recent associates – that raffish crew of speculators, profiteers and adventurers who had flourished under the Directory – were sent packing. Admission to the Luxembourg was by invitation only; manners became more formal, behaviour more polished. The titles *monsieur* and *madame* replaced the Revolutionary *citoyen* and *citoyenne*; the use of *vous* replaced the more familiar *tu*; it became increasingly common to address the First Consul as 'Your Highness'.

With his capacity for interesting himself in all aspects of the world about him, Napoleon even turned his attention to women's fashion. He decided that the gauzy, half-naked *Directoire* dresses were both indecent and unpatriotic; why should Frenchwomen dress themselves in flimsy fabrics from British India at the expense of French silks and satins? To emphasise his point, Napoleon, at one evening reception, ordered the fires to be stoked higher and higher until the rooms were like a furnace. 'I wanted to be sure to get it warm enough,' he declared loudly, 'because the weather is cold and these ladies are practically naked.'[3]

If he discovered that Josephine or her daughter Hortense were wearing English muslin as opposed to French lawn from Saint-Quentin, he would, says Hortense, 'instantly tear the guilty garment in two.'[4]

Gradually Napoleon created a less military, more regal setting for himself. With his own natural air of command and with his elegant, engagingly mannered wife on his arm, he presided over the new consular society as though born to the position. 'It was not exactly a court,' explained the visiting Princess Dolgoruki, 'but it was no longer a camp.'[5]

But much of the First Consul's time during this period at the Luxembourg was taken up with the creation of a new Constitution. The result, when stripped of all the histrionic phraseology, myriad clauses and complicated electoral system, was a dictatorship, with all effective power in the hands of the First Consul. All three consuls (Sieyès and Ducos were replaced by Cambacérès and Lebrun) were appointed for ten years. In a plebiscite on 7 February 1800, the electorate voted overwhelmingly in favour of the new Constitution.

That was all the encouragement Napoleon needed. Ten days later he left the Luxembourg and took up residence in the Tuileries, the old palace of the kings of France. In splendid procession he passed through the gates on which were written 'August 10 1792 – Royalty in France is abolished and shall never be re-established'. What Napoleon thought of the inscription one does not know but, late that night, he did reveal something of his feelings to Josephine.

'Come, little Creole,' he said, as he helped her into the sumptuously canopied bed in which successive Bourbon kings had slept, 'get into the bed of your masters.'[6]

Today almost nothing remains of the Tuileries Palace. For over three centuries this ornate building, with its great central dome, was the principal Paris residence of the rulers of France. It filled the vast empty space that now stretches between the Pavillon de Flore, overlooking the Seine, and the Pavillon de Marsan, overlooking the Rue de Rivoli. The Palace was gutted by fire during the upheavals of the Paris Commune in 1871 and was demolished a decade later. Only its name is perpetuated in the gardens that now lie between the Place de la Concorde and the Louvre.

For fifteen years of its long history – from 1800 until 1815, except for one interruption – the Tuileries was the official home of Napoleon; for the first ten of those years, he shared it with Josephine. When they took up residence in February 1800, almost all traces of royal splendour had disappeared. During the Republican years, the palace had become a rabbit warren of offices; the crudely whitewashed corridors thronged with stall holders, lemonade sellers, touts and professional beggars.

There was even a barber's shop and a draper's shop.

The First Consul, determined to restore the dignity of the building, lost no time in clearing out this rabble and in employing the architect, Felix Lecomte, to renovate the old royal apartments. Those famous Republican symbols – the red caps of liberty painted on the walls, and the trees of liberty planted in the courtyard – he ordered to be, respectively, painted out and chopped down. 'Get rid of those things,' he snapped. 'I don't want any of that non-sense.'[7]

Napoleon moved into the suite of eight rooms on the first floor which had once been occupied by Louis XVI. Josephine lived in Queen Marie Antoinette's old apartments, directly below. Their living quarters were linked by a small interior staircase leading off his study. Although the First Consul seems to have adapted, readily enough, to his new surroundings, Josephine was uneasy. 'I remember the sadness that overwhelmed my mother during our first days at the Tuileries,' writes Hortense. 'She was obsessed with the thought of Marie Antoinette, saw her tragic figure every-where. The palace was haunted for me too by the poor Queen, for Madame Campan had told me so many harrowing stories of her royal mistress's last tragic hours there.'[8]

There were more recent and no less grim associations as well. Josephine's bedroom had once accommodated the Committee of Public Safety – that ruthless gang of twelve, headed by Robespierre, who had sent so many aristocrats, Josephine's first husband included, to their deaths during the Reign of Terror. From the nearby entrance hall, Robespierre himself had eventually been dragged off to the guillotine.

'I know I shall not be happy here,' confided Josephine to Hortense. 'The darkest presentiments came over me the minute I entered.'[9]

But as the spending of money was the one certain way of cheering herself up, Josephine set about transforming her mel-ancholy surroundings. By introducing bright colours – the fur-niture in one salon was upholstered in violet-blue silk taffeta; for another she chose yellow and golden-brown satin fringed with red – she immediately lightened the atmosphere. She filled the rooms with paintings and mirrors, with urns of rose-coloured granite and vases of Sèvres porcelain. Each day the celebrated florist, Madame Bernard, arrived with baskets full of fresh flowers. Josephine's private suite – boudoir, bedroom, dressing-room and bathroom – was decorated in the height of fashion: mirrored walls, blue and white striped fabrics, gold fringes. Her mahogany bed, elaborately ornamented in bronze gilt, stood in an alcove.

To this bed, every night, came Napoleon. 'At the Luxembourg, at Malmaison and at the Tuileries during the early years,' claims Bourrienne, 'the First Consul always slept with his wife.'[10]

For, during these early years, she never lost her sexual fascination for him. She was always careful to come to bed looking as attractive as she did on public occasions: 'all charm and grace,' as Napoleon afterwards put it, 'in bed as elsewhere.'[11]

Nor was her husband the only one to be aware of Josephine's allure. Napoleon's future valet, the young Louis-Constant Wairy, known always as Constant, who joined the household at about this time, gives an almost lyrical description of Josephine. Her every movement, he says, was a delight; she almost floated as she walked. Even in these early days, wearing a simple red handkerchief tied, Creole-style, around her head, she carried herself like a queen. 'If she smiled, involuntarily one smiled too, just as one became sad if she showed signs of grief.' As Napoleon's eyes were his most compelling feature, so, in a different way, were Josephine's. Hers were amber, with large, almond-shaped lids and long sweeping lashes. 'When thus dreamily she gazed at you,' reports Constant breathlessly, 'you felt drawn towards her as by a resistless force.'[12]

Not only physically but temperamentally, Josephine was proving to be the perfect mate for Napoleon. Their marriage had by now settled down into a partnership of mutual accommodation. With the almost delirious ardour of his early married life having subsided, he displayed towards her a steady affection and a touching tenderness. She, in turn, who was coming to love him more and more, had learned to adjust to his every mood. She had made herself, in a way, indispensable to him. 'Josephine possessed an exact knowledge of all the intricacies of my character, and with it an admirable tact,'[13] Napoleon once explained. She appreciated all his likes and dislikes. If, as invariably happened, he kept her waiting, she never complained. She knew when to keep silent, when to divert him with a bit of gossip, even when to relieve him of his coffee cup as he launched forth on some theory. Josephine was the one person, claimed her daughter Hortense, who could sometimes persuade him to change his mind.

'People do not understand Napoleon,' Josephine would say,

'he is quick tempered but he has a good heart.'[14]

He delighted in her company. Leaving his study at night, he would send for Josephine to read to him. And she, no matter how interesting her circle of guests or how crucial the stage of her game of backgammon, would hurry to his side. With his eyes closed and with his notoriously restless body temporarily still, he would lie listening to her sweet, mellifluous voice. 'If he had so much as a few free moments between conferences and appointments, he came to spend them with Josephine,'[15] says Claire de Rémusat. He loved to watch her at her dressing table. Absorbed, he would study the way her hair was being done or her face painted. Sometimes he would rearrange the flowers which she invariably wore in her hair. Hortense, whom he would summon to admire the effect, could not help laughing at the extreme seriousness with which this great man, this master of France, devoted himself to his wife's coiffure.

At other times Napoleon's behaviour was less sensitive. He would come charging over to Josephine's dressing table, tipping out her jewel cases, upsetting her scent bottles, overturning trays of laces and feathers. He would subject her bare shoulders to vicious 'love pats', stinging enough to bring tears to her eyes. Yet her only reproach would be a softly drawled 'Enough, Bonaparte, enough!'

Her tears (and Josephine's powers of weeping have become legendary) seldom failed to move him. He would take her on to his knees, cover her face with kisses and, in his half-serious, half-bantering way, coax a smile out of her. 'What more do you need to make you happy?' he once asked teasingly. 'You have a husband who is no worse than average, two children who are a credit to you in every way. There! You were born with a silver spoon in your mouth!'

'You're right,'[16] she answered, rewarding him with one of her tremulous, tight-lipped smiles.

Sometimes, after dinner at the Tuileries, as Hortense sat talking to Napoleon's aides-de-camp and young generals, she would watch her mother and stepfather walking arm-in-arm, up and down the great room, their voices low, their heads tilted lovingly towards each other. That Josephine still had the power to enchant Napoleon there can be no doubt.

But what, exactly, was the nature of this power? Laure Junot supplies one explanation. 'Josephine's hold over Napoleon was firmly established, and there was more to their relationship than mere force of habit,' she claims. 'It was her essentially bland personality, her gentle and tender nature which, for a man like Napoleon – constantly agitated, harried by the intensity and immensity of his thoughts – provided an Eden, a sanctuary of repose.'[17]

In short, it was for her negative, rather than for her positive qualities that Josephine retained Napoleon's affections. For a man whose mind was always in such a ferment, whose body was so racked by tensions, whose temperament made him incapable of relaxation, Josephine provided an aura of sweet serenity. Hers was an unchallenging, undemanding, almost vacuous presence. The shallowness of her mind was the perfect foil for the depth of his; the langour of her attitudes a soothing balm for the restlessness of his spirit. Only in scalding hot baths, sometimes two or three a day and sometimes for as long as two hours at a stretch, could Napoleon find a comparable solace for his taut nerves.

But there was more to it than this. Claire de Rémusat, an even closer observer of the couple, touches on yet another facet of Napoleon's character which linked him to Josephine: the romantic, dreamy, almost mystical element. 'When I first knew him,' she writes of those early days of the Consulate, 'he was immensely fond of everything that led to a state of reverie. Ossian, dim light, melancholy music. I have known him delight in the murmur of the wind, speak enthusiastically of the roaring of the sea ... When, on leaving his study in the evening, he would come into Madame Bonaparte's drawing room, he would sometimes have the candles covered with a piece of gauze and enjoin complete silence ... then he would listen to soft and slow pieces of music performed by Italian singers accompanied only by a small number of instruments that were touched very lightly. Then we would see him fall into a reverie, which we were all so anxious not to disturb that we dared not move or stir ... On coming out of this condition, he was usually more serene and communicative.'[18]

Not only did these sessions induce in him the state of tranquillity which Josephine was always able to induce but he felt, apparently, that she was somehow part of this mysterious world. A visitor to Malmaison tells of the effect upon him of certain sights and sounds: how moved he would be by the glimpse of women in white dresses walking under the trees at dusk; as Josephine invariably wore white and was often to be seen under the trees at

Malmaison, it is hardly surprising that the difference between the real and imagined Josephine became blurred in his fervent imagination.

'With,' as one of his biographers only a shade too fancifully puts it, 'that flowing grace of limb and voice, that dulcet manner [Josephine] was a means through which he sensed some hidden harmony, some synthesis of eternal values.'[19]

What brought him down to earth were her debts. They were, at this stage, the only thing they quarrelled about. Napoleon, who had lost no time in reorganising France's chaotic finances, stood helpless in the face of his wife's extravagance. 'Josephine's mania for spending was almost the sole cause of her unhappiness,' noted Bourrienne. 'Her creditors were grumbling, and this brought about a highly unfavourable reaction in Paris.'[20] Nothing that Napoleon could do, by way of pleas, explanations or violent scenes, could convince Josephine that she must pay her bills and curb her spending.

Most of the money went on clothes and jewellery. She would buy thirty-eight hats in a single month. She had innumerable cashmere shawls, velvet wraps, chiffon stoles, satin shoes, lace *peignoirs*, gold-embroidered gowns, all in white or pastels – the colours Napoleon preferred. One dress would be entirely covered in white feathers, each tipped with silver; another would be sewn all over – at the last possible moment by a bevy of frantic needle-women – with real pale pink rose petals. Even the simplest-looking, short-sleeved and high-waisted shift would, in fact, be a skilfully cut and steeply-priced creation by her favourite *couturier*, Leroy.

Napoleon, who greatly appreciated his wife's elegance and who expected her to look impressive on gala occasions, could never make her understand that this could be achieved without blithely paying the inflated sums demanded by her milliners and *couturiers*. Visiting Josephine at the Tuileries one day, Laure Junot heard Napoleon instruct his wife to appear at her 'dazzling best in jewellery and costume' on some forthcoming occasion.

'Do you hear me, Josephine?' he demanded when she did not answer.

'Yes,' she replied, 'but then you will reproach me, or even go into a tantrum and refuse to approve payment of my purchases.'

Josephine pouted, says Laure Junot, 'but prettily, like a little girl, and with the utmost good humour. She looked at him so sweetly, approached him with such grace, the desire to please him shining so unmistakably bright in her eyes, that he must have had a heart of stone to have resisted her.

'Napoleon, who loved his wife, drew her close and embraced her. "If I sometimes refuse to pay your bills, my darling, it is because you are so often imposed on by your tradesmen that I cannot conscientiously sanction these abuses. But there is no inconsistency in my urging you to look magnificent on state occasions. One interest must be weighed against the other, and I merely try to maintain the balance, equitably but strictly." '[21]

But by this stage Josephine's extravagance, and her determination to keep the truth about this extravagance from her husband, was so ingrained that she invariably resorted to lying about her purchases. The couple had hardly moved into the Tuileries before Josephine paid the huge sum of a quarter of a million francs for a pearl necklace that had once belonged to Queen Marie Antoinette. Too afraid to admit to buying it, she did not dare wear the necklace. But eventually, with vanity overcoming caution, she decided to sport it at an important evening reception. Taking Bourrienne into her confidence, she begged him to back her up in her story that she had had the necklace 'for ages'.

'How lovely you look tonight!' exclaimed Napoleon on going to her apartment to fetch her. 'But aren't you wearing a new ornament? I don't think I have seen those pearls before.'

'Good heavens, Bonaparte,' she answered airily, 'it is the necklace given to me by the Cisalpine Republic years ago. Ask Bourrienne, he will tell you.'

'Well then, Bourrienne,' asked Napoleon, 'do you remember having seen these pearls before?'

'Yes, General, I remember seeing them,' answered the secretary.

He could say so, claims Bourrienne, without 'violating the truth, since Josephine had previously shown them to me.'

Josephine's debts, during this early Consular period, were worse than even Napoleon suspected. By a rough conversion, they would have equalled, today, over half a million pounds sterling or almost a million dollars. When her creditors' insistence on being paid became too clamorous to be ignored, Napoleon instructed Bourrienne to give an exact accounting of what she owed.

'No, no!' cried Josephine when faced with Bourrienne's

demand. 'No, I cannot admit to the full amount – it's too tremendous. He would make a terrible scene. I shall admit to only half of it.'

'Madame,' replied Bourrienne, 'your husband knows you owe a large sum and is prepared to pay it. As for the scene, it will be just as terrible for half the amount as for the whole.'

'No,' she insisted. 'I can never bring myself to tell him. I owe, as best as I can determine, some 1,200,000 francs. You must not mention, however, more than 600,000 – that's enough for the moment. I'll pay the rest gradually, out of my savings.'

'Madame,' repeated Bourrienne, who knew perfectly well that she would never have any savings, 'it is my opinion that the Consul will be as outraged at the 600,000 as at the 1,200,000, so why not get it over with now, once and for all?'

'I dare not,' protested Josephine, 'he is so violent! I know him, Bourrienne, and I cannot stand up under his rages.'

So Bourrienne was obliged to tell his master that Josephine owed 600,000 francs. 'Take the 600,000 francs,' growled Napoleon, 'pay off her creditors, and let me hear no more about it.'

An inspection of Josephine's bills astonished Bourrienne. 'The over-charges were fantastic,' he says. 'A system of highway robbery prevailed throughout.' By a show of firmness he was able to get the creditors to agree to accept half the figure of their original statements; even then, he claims, they were making a handsome profit. In the end, all claims were settled for 600,000 francs.

Unfortunately, sighs the secretary, Madame Bonaparte 'soon relapsed into the same reckless squandering.'[22]

And when one remembers that Bourrienne himself had what Napoleon calls a 'magpie's eye' and was busily embezzling money, one can appreciate the First Consul's exasperation.

12

The Consular Court

TO consolidate his recently won and still precarious power, the First Consul needed to assert French military supremacy. So, in the spring of 1800, Napoleon made his celebrated and imaginative crossing of the still snow-bound Alps to attack the Austrians in northern Italy. Here, by the narrowest of margins, he won the Battle of Marengo. ('My first laurel must be for my country, my second will be for you,'[1] he wrote exultantly to Josephine.) Another French victory, in Germany – in which Napoleon did not take part – forced the Austrians to sign the Treaty of Lunéville in February 1801. By this treaty, Napoleon gained for France those natural frontiers which Julius Caesar had once given to Gaul: the Rhine, the Alps and the Pyrenees.

By October the First Consul had concluded an armistice with France's other chief enemy, Britain, and in March 1802 the Peace of Amiens was signed between the two countries. For the first time in ten years, Europe was at peace.

This peace, uncertain though it might have been, allowed Napoleon to turn his attention to his mammoth task of reorganising the State. With the constitution placing all effective power in his own hands, he was able to force through his various reforms with speed, efficiency and ruthlessness. There was no aspect of national life on which he did not leave his imprint: the central administration, the judicial system, the army, the police, education, finance. The welter of previous laws were reorganised into the more coherent *Code Civil*, afterwards renamed the *Code*

Napoleon, which still forms the basis of most modern European systems of civil law. It has become one of Napoleon's most enduring, and admirable, memorials.

For practical rather than for any strongly held religious reasons, he signed a Concordat with Pope Pius VII in July 1801. This meant that throughout France the churches, cleansed both of the decadence of the *ancien régime* and the anti-Christian travesties of the Revolution, were reopened for worship. France was again a Catholic country, but on Napoleon's terms.

By the summer of 1802 France, and indeed all Europe, stood amazed by the achievements of this dynamic thirty-two-year-old. By a combination of talent, energy, determination and shrewd publicity, he had established himself as a modern hero: a soldier-philosopher, a Byron in uniform, a romantic figure in whose honour Beethoven was to compose the 'Eroica' Symphony.

Before the end of that summer, a nation-wide plebiscite resulted in an overwhelming vote in favour of making Napoleon First Consul for life, with the right to choose his successor. What Napoleon had been given, in fact, was unbridled power.

Unbridled power was all very well but it made Napoleon's position more vulnerable than ever. One assassin's bullet, bomb or knife thrust could bring down everything he had so efficiently built up during the last year or two.

Already there had been one serious attempt on his life. On Christmas Eve 1800, Haydn's *Creation* was being performed at the opera house in Paris. Josephine, with her daughter Hortense and Napoleon's youngest sister Caroline, was dressed and ready to go to the performance when Napoleon, dozing in front of the fire, announced that he did not feel like going out. Josephine urged him to come. 'It will amuse you,' she coaxed, 'you are working too hard.'[2] When he persisted in staying at home, she offered to stay with him. As she had foreseen, Napoleon would not hear of it and, not wanting to deprive her of her evening's entertainment, agreed to accompany her.

He set off first in his own carriage. As Josephine, with Hortense and Caroline, was about to set off in hers, an aide-de-camp suggested that Josephine re-arrange her shawl in the new 'Egyptian' style. Never one to spurn the opportunity for an enhancement of her appearance, Josephine allowed the young man to drape the shawl around her head and shoulders. Because of this delay, their carriage set off three minutes after Napoleon's.

As it was Christmas Eve, Napoleon's coachman had drunk rather too much. With a troop of mounted grenadiers clattering ahead, he drove the carriage at full speed across the Place du Carrousel. In the Rue Saint-Nicaise, the coachman saw a cart partly blocking the way. Instead of slowing down, as he might have done if sober, he dashed through the narrow opening and turned into the next street. As he did so, there was the most violent blast behind him: the cart in the Rue Saint-Nicaise had exploded. Had Napoleon's coachman not driven so quickly and had Josephine's coach been immediately behind, as it should have been, they would all have been blown to pieces.

In the event, Josephine and her party were shocked rather than injured. 'It's an attempt to kill Bonaparte!' screamed Josephine. She could not be calmed until she had been told, by one of Napoleon's escort who had come galloping back, that he had escaped the explosion. She was ordered to continue on to the opera by another route.

Arriving at the theatre, the distressed Josephine was surprised to find Napoleon apparently unconcerned. 'What is the matter? What has happened?' he said calmly. 'A mere nothing.' His whole manner, says Hortense, 'was as cool as though he had not realised that an attempt had been made on his life.' But when, later, he heard about the extent of the devastation – nine people dead, twenty-six injured and entire houses shattered – he lost his composure. 'How ghastly to make so many people perish because one wants to get rid of a single man,'[3] he exclaimed.

It was at first assumed that the assassination attempt had been a Jacobin plot. This assumption gave Napoleon an excuse to rid himself of some of his Jacobin opponents. But it was later discovered that the royalists had been responsible. The men who set off the bomb were sentenced to death but the royalist ringleaders, safely out of the country, lived on to make, in time, yet another attempt on his life.

It is significant that, in the *Code Civil*, Napoleon revealed his essentially Corsican view of women: fathers, as heads of their households, were invested with full authority over their wives and children. 'The wife owes obedience to her husband,' reads Article

213 of the *Code Civil*. Women were not even allowed to buy and sell their own property without their husband's permission. These articles certainly mirrored Napoleon's attitude towards his own wife. Never for a moment, and not even if she had been a more politically informed woman, would Napoleon have considered consulting her about affairs of state. 'Only in unimportant matters,' as Hortense puts it, 'did Josephine have any influence over her husband.'[4]

Yet there were, during these Consular days, a few ways in which Josephine made a valuable contribution to his schemes. In the first place, she was an ideal consort for the new Head of State. It was not only that she always looked *soignée* or that she exuded a whiff of the *ancien régime*, but that she had all the social graces that her husband lacked. Napoleon could be charming enough when he felt that he was dealing with his political and intellectual inferiors but he had never quite outgrown the feelings of social inadequacy which had so poisoned his days at Brienne and the Ecole Militaire. Now, as then, he would take refuge in brusqueness, rudeness or unnerving silences. A gauche or tongue-tied wife would simply have worsened the situation. But the worldly Josephine was able to give the Consular court a more civilised, more sophisticated atmosphere. Those who dismissed Napoleon as a parvenu were not quite so ready to think the same about his wife.

'Josephine's was the rare talent of putting people at their ease, making each person feel that he had been singled out for the especial welcome,' writes Bourrienne. 'By the magic of her cordiality, her consistently good humour, all was gaiety and relaxation in her company. With Bonaparte's entrance, a sudden change came over the room; every eye turned anxiously to read his mood in his expression – whether he was to be taciturn or talkative, gloomy or genial. His manner was imposing rather than pleasing; those who did not know him well were overcome with an involuntary sense of awe in his presence. He possessed all the attributes for being what society terms "an agreeable man" – all save the desire to be one.'[5]

In his determination to reintroduce the brilliance and formality of a court, Napoleon was unhesitatingly supported by Josephine. Where he equipped himself with an intendant and four prefects of the palace, she was attended by several ladies-in-waiting. She cultivated the society, and sought the advice, of a handful of women who had known life at the court of Versailles: Madame Campan, Madame de la Tour du Pin, Madame de Valence and, above all, old Madame de Montesson who had been the morganatic wife of Louis XIV's great-grandnephew, the Duke d'Orléans.

One by one the old royal customs and practices were reintroduced. Tours of inspection took on the atmosphere of royal visits. For an official journey through northern France, Belgium and the Netherlands, in 1803, Napoleon ordered the Minister of Finance to supply Josephine with jewellery from the treasury worthy of her new quasi-royal status. 'Everything around the First Consul and his wife is resuming the general character and etiquette of Versailles,' reported the Prussian minister at Paris. 'Ostentatious luxury, fine carriages, liveries, crowds of servants are seen on every side. Much care is taken in the reception of foreign gentlemen; and the foreign ladies who are presented to the First Consul and his wife are announced by one of the prefects of the palace....'[6]

Napoleon even revived the tradition whereby the members of the *corps diplomatique* or ministers of state, having been formally received by him, would be ushered into Josephine's presence, in precisely the way they had been presented to the Queen after their audience with the King.

Because Malmaison was considered not nearly grand enough, the royal Palace of Saint-Cloud, in the suburbs of Paris, was brought back into use as a summer residence. It was restored at considerable expense. Within its gilded, frescoed and tapestried salons, protocol was as exacting as ever it had been at the Bourbon court. Napoleon and Josephine would hold ambassadorial receptions, dine in state, and would even – this couple to whom religion meant almost nothing – celebrate Mass with all the ceremony and solemnity of their late Majesties, King Louis XVI and Queen Marie Antoinette. At the weekly reception of senior officers and officials, held after Mass, it was noticed that Napoleon 'gave little nods to right and left, like the Pope gives benedictions.'[7]

In his memoirs, Napoleon's valet Constant describes one of Josephine's semi-regal evening receptions at the Tuileries. From eight o'clock her ground-floor apartments would begin to fill up with a host of brilliantly uniformed men and sumptuously dressed women. The effect of all these medals and orders, jewels and feathers would be, he says, 'dazzling'. Only after the assembly had been marshalled into proper order would Josephine be announced.

On the arm of Talleyrand, at that stage of his tortuous career the Minister of Foreign Affairs, she would make her entrance. Sometimes, and in contrast to the ostentatiousness of the other women present, she would wear a plain white, short-sleeved dress with a pearl necklace, and have her simply arranged hair kept in place by a tortoise-shell comb. The buzz of admiration which greeted her appearance must have been, thought Constant, extremely gratifying.

With Josephine's hand still resting on the back of his, Talleyrand would present the members of the *corps diplomatique*, not mentioning them by name but designating the courts they represented. He would then conduct her slowly through the company that filled both drawing rooms. It must have been with some difficulty that the men prevented themselves from bowing and the women from curtseying.

'People spoke as one,' claims Constant, 'of the perfect grace, the skill both natural and cultivated, which was displayed by Josephine in the salons of the Consulate.'[8]

Napoleon's entry would be altogether less regal. Unannounced, he would suddenly appear by way of his private staircase. Like Josephine, though, the simplicity of his dress would be in sharp contrast to the embroidered coats, brightly coloured sashes and glittering decorations of the assembled ambassadors and dignitaries. He would be wearing a plain uniform coat, white woollen breeches, a tricoloured silk scarf about his still narrow waist and top boots. Under his arm he would carry his soldier's black hat. Unlike Josephine, he would move swiftly through the company, stopping only to address an occasional remark here and there. Again, unlike Josephine, his conversation was anything but tactful. 'I have seen that dress before, Madame,' he would grumble, or 'Your arms, Madame, are very red.'[9]

Within minutes he would have disappeared, leaving Josephine to smooth whatever ruffled feathers he had left behind him.

An equally valuable service rendered to Napoleon by Josephine concerned his so-called policy of 'fusion': the integration of the old nobility and aristocracy into the new post-Revolutionary society. 'Josephine served as my bond with a large and important segment of society,' Napoleon said on Saint Helena. '[She] put me in touch with a whole party which was essential to the success of my policy of fusion.'[10] Indeed, it would hardly be an exaggeration to say that in the person of Josephine these two worlds seemed to blend. When set beside Napoleon's boisterous brothers and sisters, and his no less boisterous young officers and their wives, Josephine seemed like an aristocrat to her very fingertips.

In the spring of 1802 Napoleon had granted an amnesty to all *émigrés* who had fled France during the Revolution. However, official action was still necessary in order to have their names struck off the lists of 'the enemies of the Republic' and the rights to their property restored. This is where Josephine – always so good hearted and with her understandable sympathy for these dispossessed aristocrats – was able to play a part.

'Noblemen with names too proud and memories too bitter to approach the First Consul directly besieged Madame Bonaparte instead with their petitions for *radiation* [erasure of the names from the banned lists] and for restoration of property confiscated by the state,' says Madame de Rémusat. 'She received them all with the utmost courtesy and seemed never to weary of listening to their tales of woe. She served as the original link between the French nobility and the Consular government.'[11]

Letter after letter bore witness to Josephine's generous intervention. 'Madame Bonaparte has the honour to convey her compliments to Messieurs de Villeneuve,' runs one such message, 'and to inform them that they have been struck from the lists.'[12] Among the letters dealing with the more than forty thousand *émigré* families who returned to France during the Consulate and Empire, there are very few which do not show signs of Josephine's intercession.

Her sympathy for these aristocratic families led many royalists to believe that Josephine was in favour of a restoration of the monarchy. This was apparently believed by the person who would be the chief beneficiary of any such restoration – the Comte de Provence, brother of the guillotined King Louis XVI and therefore claimant to the French throne. 'The support which she gives to those of my faithful subjects who have recourse to her,' he wrote in his lordly fashion to one of his supporters, 'entitles her to the name, *Angel of Goodness*, which you have given her. Convey my regards, therefore, to Madame Bonaparte. They will not surprise her; on the contrary, unless I am much mistaken, she will be happy to receive them.'[13]

The Comte de Provence was hoping that General Bonaparte

would do for him what General Monk had done for the exiled British king, Charles II, at the end of the Cromwellian period: act as his agent in the restoration of the monarchy. But whatever Josephine's own thoughts on the matter might have been, she by now knew Napoleon well enough to appreciate that he would never contemplate any such thing. Nor was the Comte de Provence left long in any doubt. When, in June 1800, he wrote to Napoleon asking for his assistance, the First Consul's reply was unequivocal.

'You must no longer look forward to your return to France,' he wrote bluntly. 'Your path would assuredly lie over one hundred thousand corpses. Sacrifice your personal interests to the peace and happiness of France. History will record its gratitude to you for doing so....'[14]

The Comte de Provence was to have a fourteen-year-long wait before finally ascending the French throne as Louis XVIII.

As a complete contrast to the responsibilities and formalities of life in the Tuileries and Saint-Cloud, there was Malmaison. It was here that Napoleon and Josephine were seen at their most relaxed. For her, it became an almost enchanted place, what Hortense calls 'a delicious spot'; as for Napoleon, he loved Malmaison, says Laure Junot, 'with a passion'. Nowhere, as Bourrienne so curiously puts it, 'except on the field of battle, did I ever see Bonaparte more happy than in the gardens of Malmaison.'[15]

To the renovations already put in hand by Josephine, Napoleon – who was moved to improve everything he saw – added his own enhancements. Where his wife spent money on decorating the house and landscaping the gardens, he made more practical changes: extending the domain, adding farms and plantations that would pay for themselves. Gradually the Malmaison that was to be so closely identified with the Consulate and Empire took shape: the elegant château shining silver-grey in the pellucid light reflected off the nearby Seine, the clipped bay trees in their square wooden tubs, the 'English' garden with its informal grouping of trees, its sloping lawns, winding paths, trickling streams, wooden bridges, follies, temples and gliding swans. 'Nothing,' writes Laure Junot, 'was fresher, greener, more umbrageous'[16] than the grounds of Malmaison.

But the place was to become renowned, above all, for Josephine's flowers: for the exotic blooms in the conservatories, the massed rhododendrons beside the streams, the roses of every conceivable type and colour. Josephine had seeds and plants sent to her from all over the world; even when France and Britain were at war, the British, with commendable chivalry, would see to it that the packets of seeds found aboard captured French ships would be forwarded, as addressed, to Josephine.

Napoleon looked forward to his weekends at Malmaison, says Bourrienne, 'as eagerly as a schoolboy to his holidays.'[17] There was, indeed, something almost schoolboyish, and certainly very youthful, about the gatherings there. Even the oldest member of the group – Josephine – was still in her thirties in 1802; Napoleon turned thirty-three that year. All the rest of them – Eugène and Hortense de Beauharnais, the younger Bonapartes like Caroline and Jerome, the aides-de-camp and the ladies-in-waiting – were all in their teens and twenties.

More often than not, amusements were of a juvenile variety: riotous games of prisoner's base, with Napoleon running 'like a hare', knocking people down and cheating shamelessly. There would be amateur theatricals, with Hortense and Bourrienne as the stars and Napoleon as the director; his intense interest in these theatricals would have astonished the many people who had an altogether different picture of him, claims Laure Junot. Charades were another Malmaison favourite.

Napoleon loved being out of doors. When he was in the open air, he would exclaim, he felt that his ideas were 'loftier and more extended'. He had his study linked to a small private garden by a tented bridge over the dry moat; sometimes he would work in this pavilion; occasionally he would get up and stroll around his secluded garden.

'I arrived at Malmaison,' reported the urbane Talleyrand to a friend, 'and do you know what I did, and where the First Consul had established his work-room? On one of the bowling greens. They were all seated on the grass. It was nothing to him, with his military habits, his riding boots, and his leather breeches. But I, in my silk breeches and silk stockings! Can you see me sitting on that lawn? I'm crippled with rheumatism. What a man!'[18]

While Napoleon worked, Josephine and her ladies would amuse themselves by embroidering, reading the papers or chatting. Much of Josephine's time was taken up, of course, in discussion with her *couturiers*, her gardeners and her decorators. Under her expert guidance, the rooms were being entirely refurbished. Her only musical accomplishment, apparently, was playing the great golden harp that dominated the music room. Her repertoire, complained one member of the household, was limited to a single tune. Still, he had to admit that she *looked* lovely while playing it.

On warm spring and summer evenings, the company would dine *al fresco* on the lawn which stretched away from the garden façade of the house. During the meal, Napoleon would hold forth on a great range of topics: science, art, literature, the supernatural, even women's fashion. 'And after dinner,' remembered Hortense, 'the First Consul always took my mother's arm, to lead her away from the others for a long stroll in the gardens.'[19]

Into the deepening dusk they would wander, stopping here and there to admire some new planting or to gaze down some recently opened vista through the trees, so that, in the end, the only sign of the couple would be the faint glimmer of Josephine's white, gold-embroidered dress.

13

The Succession

THE proclamation of Napoleon as Consul for life was celebrated with great panache on 15 August 1802, the day he turned thirty-three. A reception at the Tuileries for the members of the various legislative bodies and foreign ambassadors was followed by a concert at which a three-hundred-piece orchestra performed. In the afternoon there was a Te Deum in the cathedral of Notre-Dame. That night Paris blazed with light. All the public buildings were illuminated; a thirty-foot star, outlined in lamps, gleamed above the towers of Notre-Dame, a forty-two-foot structure of Peace rose above the Pont Neuf, and the night sky was vivid with soaring and exploding fireworks.

Amongst all this gaiety, Josephine's melancholy, says Bourrienne, 'presented a striking contrast'. Although she received a host of dignitaries and officials with customary charm that evening, 'a profound depression weighed down her spirits.'[1] For, in addition to being proclaimed Consul for life, Napoleon had been granted the right to name his successor. This provision had emphasised the fact that he and Josephine had no natural successor. It had also encouraged Josephine's relentless enemies – the Bonaparte clan – to redouble their efforts to get Napoleon to jettison her.

Napoleon's steady rise to a position of absolute power and blinding glory had considerably intensified the Bonaparte–Beauharnais feud. Although, as always, Napoleon had showered his relations with honours, this brood of squabbling, self-seeking and pleasure-loving Bonapartes remained dissatisfied. In spite of the fact that Napoleon's older brother Joseph was now referred to as 'Monsieur Joseph', rather as, in the past, the monarch's eldest brother had always been called 'Monsieur', he complained of being denied proper respect. 'Joseph is just as disgusted as I am by the way in which [Napoleon] treats us...,' grumbled Napoleon's second brother, the recalcitrant Lucien. 'We are given no sort of precedence at table and have to sit down among the aides-de-camp; and, following the example of the Consul, ambassadors are taking the same liberties. Only recently Azara [the Spanish envoy] relegated Joseph to the end of the table, which is perfectly scandalous.'[2]

But the chief object of the family's dissatisfaction remained Josephine. Not only did they dislike her and her two children personally but, in order to safeguard their own positions, it was essential that Napoleon produce an heir. As Josephine showed no signs of presenting him with one, he must be encouraged to divorce her. As a result, Napoleon's relations never lost an opportunity to discredit Josephine in his eyes.

This family quarrel manifested itself in all sorts of ways, from the trivial to the important. It once came to a head during a visit to Joseph Bonaparte's magnificent country home, Mortefontaine. The entire family, including Letizia Bonaparte and Josephine, had been invited there for several days. The first afternoon had passed pleasantly enough with the guests strolling through Joseph's spectacular gardens, but when the host announced that he intended taking his mother in to dinner and that she would be sitting on his right, Napoleon objected. On no account would he allow Josephine – the first lady of France – to take second place. Joseph, for once, remained firm, but as he was about to lead Letizia in to dinner, Napoleon suddenly shot forward, snatched his wife's arm and pushed his way past Joseph and his mother. He sat himself at the head of the table with Josephine on his right and one of her ladies on his left.

The company, according to the lady-in-waiting, were all greatly embarrassed, particularly Joseph's gentle wife Julie who, although hostess, found herself placed near the bottom of the table. The brothers were furious, Josephine looked wretched, and the lady-in-waiting felt extremely conspicuous as Napoleon addressed not a single word to his family but spent the entire meal speaking to her.

Now and then, in an effort to placate her Bonaparte enemies,

Josephine would intervene with Napoleon on behalf of one of them. She certainly encouraged Napoleon's youngest sister, the attractive and passionate seventeen-year-old Caroline, in her determination to marry that most swashbuckling of Napoleon's companions-in-arms, the thirty-two-year-old General Joachim Murat. Napoleon was against the match. He thought Caroline could do better for herself, that Murat was too much of a womaniser and – typically – Napoleon had never overcome his resentment against Murat for once bragging that he had flirted, if nothing more, with Madame Bonaparte. Indeed, it was Josephine's ardent championing of Caroline's cause that convinced Napoleon that his wife could have no romantic interest in Murat and finally reconciled him to the marriage.

Caroline Bonaparte and Joachim Murat were married in March 1800. Caroline's appreciation of Josephine's intervention on her behalf was short lived. Before long, she would be plotting, as resolutely as most of her brothers and sisters, Josephine's downfall.

Josephine's apprehensions at not yet having produced an heir were intensified during these early days of the Consulate by the various threats on Napoleon's life, such as the bomb in the Rue Saint-Nicaise. And then there was always the chance that he might be killed on the battlefield. His death would leave a dangerous vacuum in national life; a vacuum that would lead, it was felt sure, to civil war and anarchy.

It was Napoleon's vulnerability that had given weight to a pamphlet, published in 1800, entitled *A Parallel between Caesar, Cromwell and Bonaparte*. Written before he had been proclaimed Consul for life, the pamphlet had argued that political stability could only be maintained if the office of First Consul was to be made permanent and hereditary. The anonymous author was Napoleon's second brother, Lucien, whom Napoleon had made Minister of the Interior. Lucien's proposal was made on the assumption that first Joseph and then he would inherit their brother's mantle.

Napoleon, embarrassed by this premature proposal, and not suspecting that it had been written by Lucien, instructed his Minister of Police, the astute and sinister Fouché, to uncover the author. When he learnt that it was Lucien, Napoleon was furious. Letizia Bonaparte, on hearing that Napoleon was angry with her favourite son Lucien, immediately assumed that Josephine was

beyond my power to describe' that 'At last, at last it has happened! My wife's menses have been restored!'[5] But this, as the less excitable Dr Corvisart had warned, was no guarantee of fertility.

During these visits to Plombières, Josephine would receive affectionate letters from her husband. 'I love you as on the first day,' Napoleon once wrote, 'because you are above all else kind and good ... A thousand warm greetings and a loving kiss, *tout à toi*.'[6]

And if Josephine's visit to Plombières in 1801 did not result in the longed-for heir, it did at least give birth to one possible solution to the problem: for it was here that she first conceived the idea of a marriage between Napoleon's brother Louis and her daughter Hortense.

Of Napoleon's four brothers, Louis, in Josephine's eyes, was the least objectionable. She had never trusted the smooth-tongued Joseph; the erratic Lucien had been openly hostile to her for years; Jerome, the youngest, was already showing signs of the vanity and frivolity that were to characterise him throughout his life. But the handsome Louis, who turned twenty-three in the year 1801, had always treated her with a certain civility. With his cultural interests – Louis fancied himself as a poet and a novelist and cultivated the society of other young writers – he was more introspective, less grasping than his brothers. Even Napoleon, who should have been more perceptive, once claimed that his brother Louis would have made an excellent successor to himself. 'He has none of the defects of his brothers and all their virtues,'[7] he announced.

Neither Napoleon nor Josephine suspected that Louis's apparent tranquillity masked a neurotic temperament: that he was insecure, suspicious and jealous, obsessed with his health and given to long bouts of melancholia.

The eighteen-year-old Hortense on the other hand – and not only in her mother's doting eyes – was one of the most attractive figures in Napoleon's family circle. Fair-haired, blue-eyed, fresh-complexioned, with a figure 'as slender as a palm tree', she had all her mother's grace and much of her poise. To these inherited traits, Hortense added others notably lacking in Josephine's character: intelligence, wit, vivacity and just enough malice to be amusing without ever being unkind. Where Josephine's personality was a negative one, Hortense's was more positive. By no means an intellectual, she was talented, sensible and well educated. And in spite of a good deal of unhappiness and disillusionment which she was to experience during her lifetime, she always retained a touching idealism.

For reasons that can only be described as self interested, Josephine now decided that Hortense must marry Louis. It seemed the perfect way out of her dilemma. If one Bonaparte–Beauharnais partnership could not produce a successor, then there was always the chance that another such partnership would. In this way, Josephine would become, if not the mother of Napoleon's heir, at least the grandmother. A child who was both Napoleon's nephew and her grandson would surely be the next best thing to a direct heir. And, most important, her own position would be secure.

Employing all the tact, tears and powers of persuasion for which she was celebrated, Josephine set about achieving her ambition. She won Napoleon round, claims Bourrienne, by 'the influence exerted in the boudoir . . . by her repeated entreaties and her caresses.'[8] And having been won round, Napoleon was prepared to go even further. 'I brought up Louis and look upon him as a son. Your daughter is what you cherish most on earth,' he said to Josephine. 'Their children will be ours. We will adopt them, and this adoption will console us for not having any children of our own.'[9]

What the future parents' views on this matter might have been, Napoleon apparently did not consider.

Josephine was overjoyed and set about informing Hortense. But, as in the case of her own marriage to Napoleon, Josephine could not pluck up the courage to break the news to Hortense herself. She made Bourrienne do it. In silence, the girl heard the secretary out. None of his arguments – the decency of Louis's character, the lack of other suitable suitors, the separation from her mother which a foreign marriage would bring – counted as much as his last point. Her mother's misfortune, he stressed, 'is that she can no longer hope for children. You can remedy this and perhaps ward off a still greater misfortune. I assure you that intrigues are constantly being hatched to persuade the Consul to obtain a divorce. Only your marriage can tighten and strengthen those bonds on which your mother's happiness depends.'[10]

Hortense, who had always made a point of stressing her 'aversion to marriages of expediency' and whose head was still full of romantic notions of marrying for love, was struck dumb by the proposal. She promised to give her answer at the end of the week. Her brother Eugène, the only person to whom she could have turned for comfort and advice, was with his regiment at Lyons. She must have known, though, what his answer was likely to have been. Once, when she had been bubbling on about marrying for love, he had warned her not to delude herself. The higher they rose in life, he said, the less opportunity they would have of choosing their own partners. She would have to suit Napoleon's plans; it would be best to forget her dream of an 'impossible bliss'.

Whatever objections Hortense might have had to the projected marriage were washed away by Josephine's tears. In fact, from the day that the news was first broken to Hortense until the day of her wedding – and for a few days thereafter – Josephine seems to have been in continuous tears. Now that she had achieved her object, Josephine was racked with feelings of guilt. 'You are sacrificing yourself for me,'[11] she seemed to be thinking whenever she looked at her daughter.

Once Hortense had consented to the marriage, and with Louis having raised no objections, Napoleon was in a hurry to get it over with. At the civil ceremony, held in the Tuileries on 4 January 1802, the entire Bonaparte family, with the exception of Pauline Bonaparte Leclerc, who was out of the country, bore steely witness to this flowering of Josephine's scheme. Letizia, in fact, referred to it as the triumph of a 'strange' family over her own. The fair-haired Hortense, wearing a simple white dress and a single string of pearls (at the last moment she had recoiled from the idea of wearing the elaborate dress which Josephine had given her) was married to the dark, silent and sad-eyed Louis.

The civil ceremony was followed by a nuptial mass. Napoleon, having recently come to his agreement with the Catholic Church, took this opportunity to get the marriage of Caroline and Joachim Murat blessed by the Church, their previous marriage having been a civil one only. This double wedding upset Hortense: with Caroline and her husband being so radiantly happy, she was afraid that 'all the happiness lay on one side, all the unhappiness on the other.'[12]

She was right. And Lucien Bonaparte made sure that whatever chance of happiness there might have been in the match was jeopardised by whispering to Louis that Napoleon was Hortense's lover. It was a slander which the brooding, suspicious, sexually maladjusted Louis was only too ready to believe.

*　　*　　*

Hortense's first child, a son, was born on 15 October 1802. The fact that it was born nine months and ten days after the marriage ceremony went some way towards persuading Louis that his brother Napoleon was not, as Lucien had asserted, the child's father. But it did not convince him that Napoleon had never been Hortense's lover; nor did it prevent others from believing the same thing.

How much truth is there in the charge that Napoleon had illicit sexual relations with his stepdaughter? None that can withstand any serious investigation. All of those who were in a position to know – people like Madame de Rémusat, Bourrienne and Napoleon's valet Constant – emphatically deny that there was any suggestion of sexual intimacy between Napoleon and Hortense. And this despite the fact that when their memoirs came to be written, neither Claire de Rémusat nor Bourrienne had any reason to defend Napoleon's reputation. By then Napoleon was dead; Madame de Rémusat had long since become disenchanted (or so she says) with her former hero; and Bourrienne, whom Napoleon had had to dismiss for embezzlement, had thrown in his lot with the restored Bourbons. Even the loyal Constant was not above passing on some scurrilous allegation – if only to refute it.

According to their testimony Napoleon, far from having been Hortense's lover, always treated her with exceptional respect. He held her, it was said, 'in veneration'. Claire de Rémusat claims that she often heard him say that 'Hortense forces me to believe in virtue.'[13] And to Hortense herself he once said that of all people, she was the one he held most in esteem.

Just as the birth of their first child, christened Napoleon Charles, did not allay Louis's suspicions about the nature of Hortense's relationship with Napoleon, so did it fail to bring husband and wife closer together. Day by day Louis became more difficult to live with; more jealous, more morose, more distrustful, more of a hypochondriac. Hortense, says Claire de Rémusat, 'was surrounded by spies; her letters were opened before they reached her hands; her conversations even with female friends were resented; and if she complained of this insulting severity, he would say to her, "You cannot love me. You are a woman; consequently a being all made up of evil and deceit. You are the daughter of an unprincipled mother...."'[14]

The couple began to spend long periods apart. Although they had two more sons ('I only ask one thing of you,' threatened Louis

140

before the birth of their second son, 'it is that this child shall be like me.'[15]), the marriage collapsed and they eventually separated.

Yet, in the end, Josephine's plan, which seemed at the time to have failed so dismally, succeeded triumphantly. Hortense's third son, born in 1808 and christened Charles Louis Napoleon, went on to become Napoleon's successor. Long after the First Empire had fallen and the first generation of Bonapartes (with the exception of Napoleon's youngest brother Jerome) had died, Josephine's grandson would re-establish the Empire by proclaiming himself Emperor Napoleon III.

Side by side with Josephine's fear that Napoleon might discard her because of her infertility went the fear that he might fall in love with someone else.

Pauline Fourès, whom Napoleon had set up as his mistress in Cairo after hearing of Josephine's infidelity with Hippolyte Charles, had by no means represented his only extra-marital adventure. During his second Italian campaign, in 1800, Napoleon had been greatly attracted to La Grassini, the famous *prima donna assoluta* of La Scala. He had lost no time in arranging for her to be installed in a house in Paris. When, inevitably, Josephine came to hear about *l'affair* Grassini, she was frantic. But her anguish was short lived. It had not taken the *diva* long to appreciate that an exciting affair with a conquering hero in Milan was a very different matter from life as the mistress of the First Consul in Paris. After a few months she had had enough. She exchanged Napoleon's occasional and perfunctory love making for the thrills of *la vie bohème* with a violinist named Rode.

La Grassini was succeeded by a rather less celebrated star – Louise Rolandeau of the Opéra-Comique. While Josephine was away on one of her visits to Plombières, the actress was invited, on several occasions, to entertain the company at Malmaison. Suspecting, only too vividly, what the nature of these entertainments might be, Josephine wrote to Hortense, who was acting as Napoleon's official hostess, ordering her to put a stop to the actress's visits. 'As if,' sighs Hortense, 'I had any control over the situation.'[16] The visits ceased only on the precipitate return of Josephine from Plombières.

There were times when Josephine was even suspicious of the women in her own household. Once, while Napoleon was away at camp in Boulogne, Josephine's young lady-in-waiting, Claire de Rémusat, was obliged to go to Boulogne in order to attend to her sick husband, himself a member of the First Consul's household. During her stay, the young woman spent a great deal of time, particularly the evenings, alone with Napoleon. While Madame de Rémusat listened, he held forth on a variety of topics: sometimes on the story of his own career, at others on politics or art or literature.

Inevitably, this frequent closeting together of the First Consul and the young lady-in-waiting led to gossip. 'The officers of the household could not believe that a woman could remain for hours together with their master, simply talking to him on matters of general interest,' writes Madame de Rémusat.

By the time she returned to Paris, Josephine had already heard about her evening sessions with Napoleon. When Claire, hurt by her mistress's coolness towards her, denied that anything improper had taken place, Josephine immediately relented. 'As she was very kind, and always easily touched by passing emotions, she embraced me, and thenceforth treated me with her former civility.' Madame de Rémusat then goes on to make a telling comment. Josephine simply did not understand, she says, Claire's feelings on having been falsely accused. 'There was nothing in her mind which corresponded to my just indignation; and, without endeavouring to ascertain whether my relations with her husband at Boulogne had been such as they were represented to her, she was content to conclude that in any case the affair had been merely temporary .... She had not the least idea that I could feel aggrieved.'[17]

An altogether more serious threat to Josephine was posed by Mademoiselle George, the beautiful, voluptuous, sixteen-year-old actress from the Comédie-Française whom Napoleon met in the winter of 1802–3. Josephine very soon discovered, through what Claire de Rémusat calls 'her household espionage system', that Mademoiselle George was paying clandestine visits to Napoleon's apartments in the Tuileries. She immediately tackled her husband about it. When he thundered back at her she resorted, as always, to tears. Madame de Rémusat, displaying a wisdom beyond her years, urged her mistress to keep calm.

'For I had quickly perceived,' she writes, 'that if the First Consul loved his wife, it was because her normal sweetness and gentleness provided him repose, and that she would lose her hold over him if she began to agitate him.'

Her sensible advice was lost on Josephine. The betrayed wife was incapable of ignoring her husband's infidelities. And so the 'stormy scenes' continued. Although Napoleon and Josephine still shared the same bed, she understood, only too well, why he was coming down so late each night: at the end of his evening's work in his study, Napoleon would spend some time, in a nearby room, with Mademoiselle George before rejoining Josephine. She found these long evening waits almost unbearable.

Yet for all the reality of Josephine's anguish, there were times when the affair led to situations of the broadest farce. One night – or, to be precise, at one o'clock in the morning – when Josephine and Madame de Rémusat had been sitting waiting for Napoleon, Josephine suddenly sprang up.

'I cannot endure it another moment,' she exclaimed. 'Mademoiselle George must be up there with him. I am going to surprise them together.'

In vain, the lady-in-waiting tried to dissuade her from this foolhardy action.

'Follow me,' snapped Josephine. 'We'll go upstairs together.'

Again, Claire tried to dissuade her. It would be foolish enough for Josephine to disturb the lovers; but for a lady-in-waiting to do the same thing would be 'intolerable'. But Josephine would not listen. She begged the younger woman to accompany her and, as few could resist Josephine's entreaties, Madame de Rémusat agreed.

Up the dark, narrow, spiral staircase to Napoleon's apartments they went: Josephine 'in extreme agitation' ahead, Claire, with a lighted candle in her trembling hand, behind.

'Halfway up, a noise, muffled but distinct, reached our ears, stopping us in our tracks,' writes the lady-in-waiting.

'It must be Roustam, Bonaparte's Mameluke, who guards his door,' whispered Josephine. 'That devil is capable of slitting both our throats.'

That was all Claire de Rémusat needed to hear. Candle in hand, she turned and rushed down the stairs, leaving poor Josephine alone in the dark. Her astonished mistress joined her a few moments later. 'But when she caught sight of my face and the terror written on it, she burst out laughing and I with her, and we renounced our enterprise.'[18]

Another incident concerning the affair was even more farcical. One night, just as Napoleon's love making to Mademoiselle

George had reached the critical point, he suddenly fell back unconscious and went into a violent convulsion. He was clearly suffering an attack of what was often, wrongly, described as epilepsy but was more likely to have been *petit mal* or a 'black-out'.

Mademoiselle George lost her head completely. Not only did she tug frantically at the bell rope beside the bed but she screamed as only an actress of the Comédie-Française could scream. When Napoleon came to, it was to find, not only Josephine but a dozen or more members of the palace staff crowded around his bed. Mademoiselle George, of course, was still in it.

That was the last of her. The actress's short reign was over; not merely because Josephine had discovered Napoleon *in flagrante delicto* but because, almost above all else, he hated being made to look foolish.

14

———⬥⬥⬥———

Napoleon as Lover

H OW much truth is there in the belief that Napoleon was one of history's great lovers? It has been taken for granted, by many people, that his prowess in the boudoir mirrored his prowess on the battlefield. Few are prepared to believe that someone of his immense drive, overweening vanity and domineering personality could be anything other than a rampant womaniser. Ambitious men, successful men, men of exceptional achievement are often sexually hyperactive. Lust is simply another manifestation of their abundant energies.

At first glance, Napoleon would seem to be a perfect example of the type. He had two wives; a string of mistresses, ranging from women like Marie Walewska with whom he was associated for years, to others whom he knew for a few weeks only; and innumerable 'actresses' who were brought to the Tuileries or Saint-Cloud to spend a single night with him. Several books have been devoted to his relationships with women. On Saint Helena he read a pamphlet about his alleged love life which even he, who was by then given to boasting about his many conquests, had to admit was exaggerated. It made him out to be, he protested, 'a Hercules'. It was widely assumed that, given all his opportunities for sexual gratification, he readily availed himself of them; that his sexual appetites were as insatiable as those of his Bourbon predecessors on the French throne.

At the height of Napoleon's liaison with Mademoiselle George, Josephine – in, admittedly, a highly agitated state – once

145

railed to Madame de Rémusat against her husband's sexual depravity. 'To hear her tell it,' writes the ostensibly shocked lady-in-waiting, 'he had no moral principles whatsoever, and he concealed his vicious inclinations only for fear that they would damage his reputation; if he were permitted, however, to follow his bent without restraint, he would gradually abandon himself to the most shameful excesses. Had he not seduced his own sisters, one after the other? Did he not consider himself specially privileged to satisfy all his inclinations?'[1]

Nor was Madame de Rémusat Josephine's only confidante in these matters. Hortense admits that, in her jealous fits, her mother would regale all her attendants with stories of her husband's licentiousness, calling him a seducer and the 'most immoral' of men.

Napoleon's outraged reaction to Josephine's accusations of immorality seemed merely to confirm these accusations. 'I am not a man like other men. The laws of morality and of society are not applicable to me...,'[2] he would thunder. 'I have the right to answer all your objections with an eternal I.'[3]

Yet this is not proof that Napoleon was an ardent womaniser. From the memoirs of Mademoiselle George, for instance, he emerges as many things – playful, jealous, charming, proprietorial – but not sexually passionate. On the first two evenings that they were together, in a huge bedroom at Saint-Cloud into which Constant had ushered her, Napoleon respected her prettily expressed reservations and did not force himself on her. Not, apparently, until their third meeting did they go to bed together. Although the actress gives no intimate details, one is left with the impression that the relationship was not intensely physical. On one occasion she has him ripping her veil and shawl to shreds, and grinding a ring and necklace to dust, not in a paroxysm of desire but because they had been given to her by a previous admirer. On another, she shows him hiding under a heap of cushions until his schoolboy laughter gives him away; on yet another he is prancing comically about the room with her wreath of white roses on his head. Nowhere, from her memoirs, does he give the impression of being a hot-blooded seducer.

Napoleon did not, in fact, even like women very much. There was certainly no touch of French gallantry in his dealings with them. Claire de Rémusat went so far as to say that Napoleon 'despises women; and contempt cannot exist together with love.'[4]

She had seldom heard him say an amiable word to any of the ladies of the court. On the contrary, he invariably went out of his way to be rude to them. At receptions he would criticise the women's dresses and hairstyles, ask if they had yet found husbands and, if so, why were they not pregnant. 'Goodness,' he once exclaimed to some poor girl on her first appearance at court, 'I had heard that you were *pretty*.'[5] Women, he would scoff, were 'mere machines to make children'; their duties were submission and dependence.

It was this disdain for womankind that gave Napoleon's liaisons a certain sterile quality. With the possible exception of Marie Walewska, he certainly felt no love for any of his mistresses. Why, he once asked Claire de Rémusat, should Josephine distress herself over 'these innocuous diversions of mine which in no way involve my affections?'[6]

Stendhal who, as Henri Beyle, had first met General Bonaparte in Italy in 1796, gives a telling description of Napoleon as lover during the days of the Empire. 'The Emperor,' he writes, 'usually seated at a small table, his sword at his side, would be signing his endless decrees. When a lady was announced, he would request her – without looking up from his work table – to go and wait for him in bed. Later, with a candlestick in his hand, he would show her out of the bedroom, and then promptly go back to his table to continue reading, correcting and signing those endless decrees.

'The essential part of the rendezvous had not lasted three minutes.'[7]

Sometimes things did not even get that far. Acting on Napoleon's instructions, Constant once brought Mademoiselle Duchesnois, another of those Comédie-Française actresses, into a private room at the Tuileries. Mademoiselle Duchesnois no doubt hoped that the patronage of the all-powerful Napoleon would further her career. As Napoleon was busy working in his study, Constant knocked at the door to announce the arrival of the actress.

'Tell her to wait!' shouted Napoleon.

Mademoiselle Duchesnois waited. After two hours Constant went again to his master's study to remind him that she was still there.

'Tell her to get undressed,' ordered Napoleon.

Mademoiselle Duchesnois undressed. For another hour she

waited, this time naked. So, for a third time, Constant went to Napoleon's study.

'Tell her to go home,'[8] snapped Napoleon.

Her dreams of powerful patronage shattered, the actress dressed herself and went home.

Even Napoleon's admiring and painstaking biographer, Frédéric Masson, has to concede that his relations with women were 'brutally abrupt'.

Napoleon's behaviour, then, was hardly that of a voluptuary or a lecher. No man who really enjoys love making, no man of strong sexual appetites would be content with this sort of bleak, mechanical exercise. Several of his mistresses complained of his perfunctoriness; one of them called his love making 'furtive'. There was a strange timidity, says Masson, in Napoleon's intimate relations with women. Napoleon himself, on Saint Helena, admitted to one of his companions to his 'feebleness in the game of love; it did not amount to much.'[9] Far, indeed, from being a great lover, Napoleon was a man of weak sexuality.

General Louis de Caulaincourt, who was closely associated with Napoleon throughout his career and the recipient of many confidences, claimed that 'It was rarely that he felt any need of love, or indeed any pleasure in it. The Emperor was so eager to recount his amorous successes that one might almost have imagined that he only engaged in them for the sake of talking about them.'[10]

Napoleon liked, in other words, to be thought of, and talked about, as sexually virile and all conquering. That his name was linked with many women is undeniable; so many, in fact, as to be almost suspect. Were his innumerable liaisons mere boosters of his ego: simply ways of making a public display of his irresistibility? Did he use them to assert his superiority, to bolster his self confidence? Constant, who knew his master very well, once gave one of those summarily ordered actresses a significant piece of advice. 'Go on looking frightened,' he told the nervous girl, 'because he'll like that.'[11]

Napoleon's inadequacies as a lover were echoed by his inadequacies as a procreator. His apparent impotence was freely and frankly discussed within his family circle and, of course, his – or Josephine's – infertility bedevilled the whole question of the succession. Napoleon is claimed to have fathered three children during his lifetime: one from his second wife, the Empress Marie Louise, one from Marie Walewska and a third from a mistress named Eléonore Denuelle. But there could be no absolute certainty that he was the father of the sons of Marie Walewska or Eléonore Denuelle, and the – admittedly bizarre – theory has been advanced that the Empress Marie Louise was artificially inseminated.

A form of artificial insemination had been carried out as early as the mid sixteenth century (it had been practised in horse breeding by the Arabs even earlier than that), and by the last decade of the eighteenth century, the Scottish surgeon, Dr John Hunter, had successfully carried out the experiment. (If *he* had been the woman's husband, wryly remarked one French specialist on hearing of Dr Hunter's success, he would be very interested to know exactly 'what kind of syringe'[12] the Scottish doctor had used.) With his keen interest in medical science, and given the imperativeness of producing an heir, it is not impossible that Napoleon would have agreed to the procedure being carried out on Marie Louise. Although Napoleon and Marie Louise lived together for four years, she bore him no more children; whereas she did have children by her second husband.

It did not take long for gossip about Napoleon's lack of sexual potency to spread, not only through France, but throughout Europe. When, having decided to divorce Josephine, Napoleon approached the Russian imperial family about the possibility of marrying a young grand duchess, the Dowager Empress would not hear of it. Napoleon, she asserted, was 'not as other men'.

What, she exclaimed, should she allow her daughter to marry a man who could be husband to nobody? Another man would then come into her daughter's bed if they wanted her to have children.

To back up her claim, the Dowager Empress commissioned her son-in-law, Prince Frederick Louis of Mecklenburg-Schwerin, to investigate the matter more fully at the French court. His findings confirmed her assertions. Josephine, he reported, always discussed her husband's inadequacies in the most indelicate manner. Napoleon might look like other men, she maintained, but then so did a famous contemporary *castrato* tenor, and he could produce *nothing*. Napoleon was *no use at all* and was likewise able to produce *nothing*. It was Josephine who gave substance to the widely repeated little quip, *Bon-a-parte est bon-a-rien*.

In his revealing diary, kept on Saint Helena, Count Bertrand tells the story of one of Napoleon's mistresses who exclaimed, with the crudeness so prevalent at the imperial court, that the Empress Josephine had said that her husband's semen was 'no use at all; that it's just like so much water.'[13]

One must always remember, though, that in encouraging the theory of Napoleon's impotence, Josephine was lessening the chances of his jettisoning her for a more fertile bride.

In recent years, yet another theory about Napoleon's sexuality has been put forward. In his study *Napoleon: Bisexual Emperor*, Dr Frank Richardson argues that Napoleon 'possibly lived in the ill-defined territory between the sexes.'[14]

Physically, Napoleon was certainly not a prime specimen of full-blooded manhood. In his account of the post-mortem examination, carried out on Saint Helena, the British army surgeon, Walter Henry, noted that Napoleon's 'skin was noticed to be very white and delicate, as were the hands and arms. Indeed the whole body was slender and effeminate. There was scarcely any hair on the body, and that of the head was fine and silky. The pubis much resembled the *Mons Veneris* in women. The muscles of the chest were small, the shoulders were narrow and the hips wide.'[15]

The use of the word 'slender' is unexpected, as everyone on Saint Helena, including Dr Henry himself, claimed Napoleon to have been very fat at the time of his death. One must assume that the doctor meant his term to imply 'small' or 'small-boned' or even to reinforce his description of the body as 'effeminate'. Dr Henry might well have been trying to belittle Britain's fallen enemy.

But Dr Henry was not the only one to comment on the effeminacy of the Emperor's body. Napoleon himself was proud of his almost womanish appearance. He was always drawing attention to the smallness, smoothness and plumpness of his hands. He loved to joke, claimed his secretary Méneval, about the 'fatness of his breasts'.

'See, doctor,' he once cried out to his fellow Corsican, Dr Antommarchi on Saint Helena, 'what lovely arms, what smooth white skin without a single hair! Breasts plump and rounded – any beauty would be proud of a bosom of mine. And my hand – how many amongst the fair sex would be jealous of it.'[16]

With this feminine-looking body went an almost feminine charm. 'He had, when he wanted,' wrote his confidant Caulaincourt, 'something seductive, persuasive, in his voice and manner ... no man ever had more charm.'[17] Another of his brothers-in-arms, General de Ségur, put it more strongly. 'When he wanted to seduce, his manner was one of ineffable charm, a kind of magnetic po... 'r. The person he wishes to attract seems to lose control of himself. In these moments of sublime power [Napoleon] no longer commands like a man but seduces like a woman.'[18]

And Napoleon himself once admitted a very curious thing to Caulaincourt. His friendship with men, he said, usually began with physical attraction; an attraction which manifested itself in a very strange way. 'He told me that for him the heart was not the organ of sentiment; that he felt emotions only where men experience feelings of a different kind: nothing in the heart, everything in the loins and in another place, which I leave nameless.' This feeling – in, one must assume, the penis and the anus – Napoleon described as 'a sort of painful tingling, a nervous irritability.'[19] The significance of this hardly needs stressing.

Throughout his life, Napoleon formed close male friendships. For the most part they were with comrades-in-arms and, for a man who spent so much of his time on campaign, such friendships were perfectly understandable and in no way exceptional. But his obsession with the young, handsome and golden-haired Tsar Alexander I, with whom he had his first meeting on the raft in the River Nieman at Tilsit, is less easily explained. 'It is Apollo!' exclaimed Napoleon on seeing him, and to Josephine he afterwards wrote, 'If he were a woman I would make him my mistress.'[20] During the time that the two men spent together, their friendship deepened into what Napoleon's secretary called 'an affectionate intimacy'. Napoleon, he says, 'truly loved the Emperor Alexander, and was charmed by his wit, grace and affability.'[21] One must always make allowance, though, for Napoleon's snobbishness: he must have been highly gratified to be meeting the Tsar on equal terms.

Both in the field and at home, Napoleon was attended by a cohort of pages, valets, footmen and mamelukes. Josephine's maid, Mademoiselle Avrillon, writes about Napoleon's 'predilection for handsome men'. He particularly liked good-looking youths, she says, and was always commandeering Josephine's best-looking pages. Napoleon's most famous valet, Constant, describes how, soon after joining Josephine's service, he found himself at dinner one evening being stared at from head to foot by the First Consul. Napoleon then invited him to join him on campaign. Constant's place was eventually taken by young Louis Marchand who Napoleon often playfully addressed as 'Mamzelle Marchand'.

Napoleon's sudden promotion of good-looking young soldiers did not go unremarked. One such was the Chevalier de Sainte-Croix. 'I often saw him at the Emperor's headquarters,' writes Constant, 'a slightly built, dapper little fellow, with a pretty, smooth face more like a girl's than that of a brave soldier which he certainly was. His features were so delicate, his cheeks so pink, his fair hair so curly, that when the Emperor was in a good humour he always called him "Mademoiselle Sainte-Croix".'[22] And Laure Junot tells how Napoleon, having had a short conversation with a handsome sixteen-year-old drummer boy, promptly made him into a subaltern in the Consular Guard.

All these young men, whether they be long-serving attendants or unknown soldiers on parade, would be subjected to Napoleon's violent slappings, pinchings and tuggings of ears, noses and hair. The more perceptive among them, like young Marbot, appreciated that this rough handling was 'a kind of caress'. He referred to Napoleon's painful ear-pulling as 'the flattering caress which he always employed to persons with whom he was pleased.'[23]

But not every caress was necessarily painful. The Emperor, says his secretary Méneval, would 'come and sit on the corner of my desk, or on the arm of my armchair, sometimes on my knees. He would pass his arm around my neck, and amuse himself by gently pulling my ear, or tapping me on the shoulder or on the cheek....'[24]

None of this is meant to prove, or even claim, that Napoleon was homosexual, although it might help to explain Josephine's accusations that he 'concealed his vicious inclinations only for fear they would damage his reputation.' If he were permitted, she added, 'to follow his bent without restraint, he would gradually abandon himself to the most shameful excesses.' Josephine could hardly have been referring to his womanising, for few of his contemporaries would have thought any the less of him for that. Nor could she have meant his supposed 'seduction' of his sisters. Not only was the situation highly unlikely (there was no reason why these adult, married sisters should have agreed to it) but Josephine's accusations of his 'following his bent without restraint'

152

and of 'gradually abandoning himself to the most shameful excesses' make no sense in the context of incest already committed.

One must, of course, always make allowance for Josephine's
distressed state of mind when she levelled these accusations, or
for the fact that Claire de Rémusat exaggerated, or even invented,
the conversation. But there is a strong possibility that Napoleon's
sexual orientation – emotionally at least – was not entirely straightforward. Elements of maleness and femaleness, in varying proportions, are present in all human beings. There is, to a greater or
lesser extent, a certain amount of homosexuality in all men. The
celebrated psychologist, A. C. Kinsey, divided men into seven
groups – from the exclusively heterosexual Group 0 to the exclusively homosexual Group 6. Dr Richardson, in *Napoleon:
Bisexual Emperor*, puts Napoleon at the centre of this seven-point
scale.

It is quite possible, of course, to be bisexual without giving
way to, or even being fully conscious of, the homosexual element
in one's makeup. This may well have the case with Napoleon.
But, whether one is inclined to believe that Napoleon was bisexual
or not, there is no doubt that his sex life was unsatisfactory,
unfulfilled and unresolved.

Perhaps a key to the conundrum lies in one of the findings in Dr
Henry's report on Napoleon's autopsy. 'The Penis and Testicles
were very small,' noted Dr Henry, 'and the whole genital system
seemed to exhibit a physical cause for the absence of sexual desire
and the chastity which had been stated to have characterised the
deceased.'[25] What the doctor refers to as 'the absence of sexual
desire and the chastity' on the part of Napoleon must have applied
to his time on Saint Helena only; no one, during Napoleon's years
of power, ever thought of him as chaste.

But about the size of Napoleon's genitalia, Dr Henry, in his
memoirs, was even more explicit. Discreetly couched in Latin,
his report reads: *Partes viriles exiguitatis insignis, sicut pueri,
videbantur* – 'The private parts were seen to be remarkably small,
like a boy's.'[26]

At the simplest level, it might have been the smallness of
Napoleon's genitalia that accounted for the timidity, 'furtiveness'
or what he himself called the 'feebleness' of his love making.
But combined with his womanly body, with – as he aged – his

'eunuchoid' appearance, it could have contributed towards his sexual ambivalence.

The psychologist, Alfred Adler, has claimed that the possession of any kind of organic deficiency leads, almost inevitably, to a sense of inferiority – the familiar 'inferiority complex'. This, in turn, can lead to over compensation. Such people 'wish to surpass all others and to accomplish everything alone . . . ,' argues Adler. 'Insatiable and lusting after the semblance of power, they demand proofs of love without ever feeling satisfied.'

In a case such as Napoleon's, his 'organ inferiority' could have prompted in him an exaggeration of all masculine traits. 'With occasional variations,' says Adler, a person suffering from such a deficiency 'regards the following as masculine: strength, greatness, riches, knowledge, victory, coarseness, cruelty, violence and activity; their opposites being feminine. He seeks triumph in every human relation.'[27]

As a portrait of Napoleon, this could hardly be bettered.

Indeed, it might not be too much of an overstatement to claim, with Dr Richardson, that 'organ inferiority' was 'the spur which drove Napoleon to play the part of a great lover and seducer, which is the role many people believe he did play.'[28]

Nor would it be any more of an overstatement to claim that some of the world's greatest soldiers, statesmen, empire builders and dictators have been sexually maladjusted men.

15

————⟡⟡⟡————

Towards the Throne

ONE day early in 1803 Napoleon, in conversation with his brothers Joseph and Lucien, mentioned a subject which had been bothering him. Touchy, by now, about his humble Corsican origins, he wanted Joseph to tell their mother, Madame Letizia, not to go on calling him *Napolion*.

'It's a name that doesn't sound well in French,' he explained. 'Besides, it's an Italian name. Let Mama call me *Bonaparte* like everyone else – above all, not *Buonaparte*, that would be worse than *Napolion*. But no, let her say the First Consul, or just the Consul. Yes, I like that best. But *Napolion*, always this *Napolion* – it irritates me.'

'All the same,' argued Lucien,'*Napolion* in French, *Napoleon*, is a very fine name. There's a grandeur about it.'

'You think so?'

'Something imposing,' continued Lucien.

'You think so?'

'Even majestic.'

'Indeed,' agreed Joseph.

'You think so too?' asked Napoleon. '*Enfin*, it is my name. I admit that it has more solemnity than Bonaparte . . . and Napoleon has the advantage of being new.'

'If you'll allow me,' maintained Lucien, 'I stand for the name Napoleon. A new great man, and a new great name!'[1]

Whether this account, written by Lucien, is accurate or not, it was at this stage of his consulship that Napoleon adopted the royal practice of using his Christian name only. In March 1803 he ordered new coins to be struck bearing his effigy and the old monarchal motto, 'God defend France'. His birthday, 15 August, became a new religious holiday, the Feast of Saint Napoleon – a saint conveniently unearthed by the Pope as soon as the First Consul became a good Catholic. In imitation of the honorific orders of the old regime, he created the Légion d'honneur, with the cynical observation that it was by baubles such as this that men were led.

With something almost indistinguishable from a royal court already having been established at the Tuileries and Saint-Cloud, he set about transforming Paris into a more imposing royal capital. He was to be responsible for inspiring some of its more enduring glories: the Arc de Triomphe, the Vendôme column, the Rue de Rivoli and the Louvre Museum. Throughout France he inaugurated a programme for the building of new harbours, new canals and new roads. He even ordered that all roads be planted with trees; the poplar-lined roads of contemporary France are one of Napoleon's most lasting legacies.

His progresses through the country took on all the dignity and splendour of royal tours. In Normandy the cities of Rouen, Le Havre and Dieppe greeted him as enthusiastically as ever they had previously greeted kings. In northern France and Belgium (which was now under French control) he drove through cheering streets under a hail of flowers and attended numberless galas, banquets, receptions and Te Deums.

'On the evening of the same day we arrived at Amiens, where we were received with an enthusiasm impossible to describe,' writes one member of his entourage. 'The horses were taken from the carriage by the inhabitants, who insisted on drawing it themselves...the joy of the inhabitants of Amiens, the garlands that decorated our route, the triumphal arches erected in honour of him who was represented on all these devices as the Saviour of France, the crowds who fought for a sight of him, the universal blessings which could not have been uttered to order – the whole spectacle, in fact, so affected me that I could not restrain my tears. I even saw Bonaparte's own eyes glisten for a moment.'[2]

Beside Napoleon, on all these triumphant travels, was Josephine. Not only by her attractiveness and her chic (greatly enhanced by the jewels which had once belonged to Queen Marie Antoinette) but by her unfeigned charm, was Josephine able to add immeasurably to the success of these tours. In Dieppe, for instance, one of her spontaneous gestures won immediate approval. A little girl, having presented her with a posy, was rewarded by having a bracelet slipped on to her arm; ingenuously, the child held up her other wrist. Josephine unhesitatingly took off one of her own expensive bracelets and clasped it on to the outstretched little arm. The incident set a precedent. From then on Josephine always wore a small piece of jewellery which she was able to unpin and present to someone. It was the sort of warm, apparently unplanned gesture which was to win her so much popularity in the years ahead.

'Madame Bonaparte charmed everyone wherever she appeared on this official journey,' remembered Madame de Rémusat, who travelled with her to Belgium. 'When I visited these regions fifteen years afterwards, I discovered that the memory of her graciousness and kindness was still fresh in men's minds.'[3]

But for Josephine these journeys were far from being occasions of unalloyed pleasure. 'I feel that I am not made for so much grandeur,' she once admitted to Hortense. 'I would be far happier in some retreat, surrounded by the objects of my affections....'[4] For by now she knew, well enough, where all this was leading: she realised that her husband would not be content with things as they were.

One morning, says Bourrienne, while Napoleon was working in his study, 'she entered quietly, approached him in her gentle, beguiling way and settled herself on his knee, caressing him and brushing her fingertips softly across his cheek and through his hair.

'Her words came out in a tender rush: "Bonaparte, I implore you, don't go making yourself a king. It's that horrid Lucien who puts you up to such schemes. Please, oh please, don't listen to him."

'Bonaparte was not angry; he even smiled when he replied, "You must be out of your mind, my poor Josephine. Where are you hearing such wild tales as these?... But off with you now. You are interrupting me at my work, and I must get back to it." '[5]

All she wanted, Josephine admitted to Bourrienne, was to continue to be the wife of the First Consul. And Claire de Rémusat once deplored the fact that Josephine seemed 'indifferent to the national destiny'. Her reactions to political developments, complained the lady-in-waiting, 'were purely personal; her only concern was for their effect on her.'[6]

This was true. For Josephine knew, claims Bourrienne, 'that every step the First Consul took towards the throne was a step away from her.'[7] Napoleon's assumption of a crown would bring the question of the succession into even sharper relief. And if, as well as not presenting him with an heir, she were to lose his love, what hope would she have of remaining his wife? Can one wonder that she was so constantly racked by anxiety, that she was so often in tears?

Yet there were times when everything seemed golden. Sometime in 1803 Napoleon paid a visit to the Channel coast and from there wrote to Josephine. Although his letter has been lost, her reply survives. It is one of the few of her letters to Napoleon to have come down to us: in grace and poignancy it could hardly be surpassed.

'All my cares have vanished in reading your wonderful and touching letter, your expression of your feeling for me. How deeply grateful I am for the time you took to write at such length to your Josephine. If you could only know how deeply, you would feel rewarded for the effort and gratified at the power you have to bring so rapturous a delight to the woman you love.

'A letter is the portrait of the soul, and I clasp this one of yours to my heart. It does me so much good; I shall treasure it forever. It shall be my consolation when you are away from me, my guide when you are near. For I want always to be, in your eyes, as you desire me – your "sweet and tender Josephine", her life devoted solely to your happiness. Whether you are touched with joy or sorrow, may it be upon the breast of your devoted wife that you seek solace and happiness. There is no emotion which you might experience that I would not share with you.

'These, then, are my desires and fondest hopes, all of which reduce themselves to the one hope and desire of my life – to please you and make you happy.

'Adieu, Bonaparte. I shall never forget the last sentence of your letter. I have taken it to heart. How deeply it is graven there! With what transports of joy, what ecstasy, mine has responded! Yes, oh yes, that is my wish, too: to please you and to love you – or, rather, to adore you!'[8]

Adore him she might but there were occasions when even Josephine found Napoleon's public irascibility deeply embarrassing. One day, in March 1803, before the weekly reception of the ambassadors and their wives at the Tuileries, the consular household gathered in Josephine's salon to wait for Napoleon's arrival. When he joined them, he seemed preoccupied. Without addressing a word to anyone, he prowled about the room; when Hortense's baby son held out his arms, Napoleon absent-mindedly lifted him up and carried him back and forth. No-one dared break the silence; not even Hortense, who was afraid that he might drop the child. After half an hour, when the arrival of the ambassadors was announced, Napoleon handed the boy back to its nurse and led the company into the large reception room.

While Josephine began to move slowly down the line of bejewelled and elegantly dressed women, saying a few appropriate words to each, Napoleon marched straight up to the British ambassador, the tall and coldly aristocratic Lord Whitworth. Without any preliminaries and in a voice loud enough to be heard throughout the room, Napoleon launched into a violent denunciation of what he considered to be the British failure to live up to certain conditions of the Peace of Amiens.

'So you are determined to go to war!' he ranted. 'If you wish to rearm, I will rearm too; if you wish to fight, I will fight also!'[9]

Astonished, Lord Whitworth wondered whether he should draw his sword if Napoleon actually struck him. Even more astonished was Josephine who tried, in vain, to mitigate the effect of her husband's tirade by being even more gracious than usual. Having delivered a final threat, the First Consul turned abruptly and strode out of the stunned and silent room.

On hurrying out after him, the distressed Josephine was surprised to find her husband in the best of humour. 'Well, what is the matter?' he asked laughingly. 'What has happened?'

'You made everyone tremble,' chided Josephine. 'Those ladies who didn't know you, who had been looking forward to meeting you, what must they think of you now? Instead of being kind and pleasant, you had to talk politics. It wasn't the time for that.'

He admitted that she was right. Just before coming down, he explained, Talleyrand had told him things about Britain's conduct that had annoyed him; 'and then that great booby of an ambassador came and stuck himself right under my nose!'[10]

If Napoleon's famous outburst at this ambassadorial reception did not cause the break between France and Great Britain, it certainly precipitated it. By the middle of May 1803, the two nations were once more at war. It was the beginning of a state of hostilities that was to last, almost uninterrupted, until Waterloo.

A legend, dear to the hearts of many Bonapartist writers, is that, in the spring of 1804, Josephine tried to influence Napoleon in a serious political matter.

The air, during the early months of that year, was full of talk of conspiracies against the life of the First Consul. The most serious of these was the Cadoudal conspiracy. Masterminded by the fanatical monarchist, Georges Cadoudal, a plan had been worked out whereby the assassination of Napoleon, as he drove to Saint-Cloud, would be followed by an invasion of the country by a royalist army and the restoration of the Bourbon monarchy. When Cadoudal was arrested by Napoleon's vigilant secret police, they found evidence which seemed to implicate a prince of the blood royal – the Duke d'Enghien – in the plot.

The thirty-two-year-old Duke d'Enghien was an attractive personality, son of the last Prince de Condé, living in Baden just across the Rhine. On the night of 14 March a troop of French cavalry secretly crossed the border, arrested the prince and brought him back to Paris for trial. The news – that a prince of the blood was to face trial and, quite possibly, execution – appalled not only French royalists but all monarchist Europe.

As appalled as anyone was Claire de Rémusat. Despite her admiration for Napoleon ('I believed him called by an invincible power to the highest destinies,' she gushed), she was a royalist at heart; the thought that the Duke d'Enghien might be shot filled her with horror. She begged Josephine to get Napoleon to promise that the prince would not be executed. Josephine reassured her that she would do what she could.

In the course of a tense weekend at Malmaison, the drama was played out. Through the eyes of Madame de Rémusat (who may well have played up her own involvement for the sake of her royalist readers) we get revealing portraits of both Napoleon and Josephine during these critical days. The First Consul, fully conscious of the momentousness of his decision, spent much of the time in consultation with various ministers, generals and officials. Whenever he rejoined the household, he astonished Madame de Rémusat by his apparently insouciant behaviour. Sometimes, she

says, 'he appeared serene and calm; it hurt me to look at his face.'
He would sit playing chess, his classical profile pale and self-
assured above the board.

One evening, knowing how upset Claire de Rémusat was
feeling, he called her over. 'He spoke to me with an air of gentleness
and interest that completed my agitation. When dinner was served,
he had me put by him, and questioned me on a multitude of
intimate things all to do with my family. He gave me the impression
that he was determined to divert me and prevent me from
thinking.' On this occasion, though, Napoleon's celebrated mag-
netism failed to work its magic. Claire remained agitated.

That night, the son of Hortense and Louis, the eighteen-
month-old Napoleon Charles, was with them, and Napoleon put
the boy in the centre of the dining table. His amusement, both at
the way the child scattered the china and at his pranks after dinner,
seemed to the lady-in-waiting to be forced and tactless.

Why, Napoleon suddenly asked Madame de Rémusat, was
she looking so pale? She had forgotten her rouge, she mumbled.

'What?' chaffed Napoleon, 'A woman forget her rouge! That
would never happen to you, Josephine! Women have two things
that become them: rouge and tears.'

He then started behaving in what the lady-in-waiting called
a 'garrison' fashion, 'with neither good taste nor propriety'; what
he did – or what Claire de Rémusat claims he did – was publicly
to fondle Josephine 'with more freedom than decorum'.

The next day, continues Claire, 'Madame Bonaparte, who
loved her trees and flowers, went out into the garden to supervise
the transplanting of a cyprus, throwing on several clods of earth
with her own hands so that she could honestly claim to have
planted it.'

'Mon Dieu, madame,' sighed the lady-in-waiting, 'it is certainly an appropriate tree for the occasion.'

'My profound distress troubled her,' claims Claire. 'Superficial and volatile, she was capable of strong but not sustained
emotion. Convinced that the Duke's death had been decided
upon – and, furthermore, supremely confident in the infallibility
of Bonaparte's judgement – she would have preferred to turn away
from vain regret. She did not like to dwell on unpleasant subjects,
but I held her to this one all day. I sobbed and entreated, and,
though she knew Bonaparte better than I did, she finally agreed
to make one last effort.'[11]

But unsuspected by Madame de Rémusat, Josephine made no such effort. She knew better than to badger Napoleon on a subject like this. Her pleas, in any case, would have carried little weight. In the face of the arguments of others like Joachim Murat, who claimed that clemency would be taken as weakness, Josephine's entreaties would not have stood a chance.

At dawn on 21 March, the Duke d'Enghien was executed by firing squad. Only then, on hearing the news, did Josephine show any signs of distress. She is said to have rushed, weeping wildly, into Napoleon's bedroom. 'You don't want to see me assassinated, do you?' he is reported to have said to her. 'The Bourbons must be taught a lesson; they cannot be allowed to continue to hunt me down like a wild beast. But come now, you are a child when it comes to politics. Try to rest.'[12]

Years later, in conversation with Count Bertrand on Saint Helena, Napoleon claimed that the generally believed story that Josephine had begged him to spare the Duke d'Enghien's life was quite untrue. 'Like everyone else, she wept and said that she had spoken to me about it, whereas in actual fact she never mentioned the matter to me.'[13]

During dinner on the night of the Duke's execution, Napoleon sat 'plunged in profound thought.' But when the meal was over, he treated the shocked and silent company to one of his famous diatribes. Up and down, up and down the salon he paced, the short figure with the disproportionately large head, spewing out words of self-justification in a remorseless torrent. His talk ranged widely, from the monarchs of the past to contemporary military tactics. Coming closer to the topic that was in the forefront of the minds of everyone present, he cited Caesar, Nero and Frederick the Great as examples of truly great men who stood above the 'customary feelings' which ruled lesser men's lives.

'I have spilt blood, I had to; I shall perhaps shed more, but without anger and, quite simply, because blood-letting is a component of political medicine,' he exclaimed. And then, facing the word-battered company, he barked out his final pronouncement.

'I am the Man of State. I am the French Revolution! And I repeat: I shall uphold it!'[14]

It was, though, in a curious fashion that Napoleon set about upholding the French Revolution. He managed to convince his countrymen – or to browbeat them into believing – that the one certain way to safeguard the republic was to convert it into a monarchy. The Senate was coerced into entrusting the 'Government of the Republic' to a hereditary emperor. Napoleon was to become 'Emperor of the French Republic'; a combination, as Talleyrand drily put it, 'of the Roman Republic and the Empire of Charlemagne'. Only by establishing such a hereditary succession, the First Consul solemnly assured the Senate, could they render vain the efforts of any future assassins.

That was Napoleon's official reason for making himself an emperor. There were many others: egotism, ambition, social insecurity, the will to dominate, the lust for power, the craving for glory, the yearning for romance, the taste for splendour. There was also a measure of idealism. For Napoleon undoubtedly felt that some of the more admirable achievements of the Revolution would be granted permanence and acceptability by being incorporated into a monarchal system. Certainly, some years later, he was to profess himself astonished at being described, by one German subject of his Empire, as a tyrant. He had always assumed that he had been spreading, throughout his far-flung domains, many of the enlightened ideals of the Revolution.

But of the republicanism which Napoleon was ostensibly safeguarding there were precious few signs when, on 18 May 1804, the members of the Senate dutifully filed into the Gallery of Apollo at the Palace of Saint-Cloud to 'ask' him to accept the new imperial title. 'All that can contribute to the wealth of the country is essentially linked with my happiness,' he assured the assembled senators. 'I accept the title which you believe to be conducive to the glory of the nation. I submit to the sanction of the people the law of hereditary succession. I hope that France will never repent the honours she may confer on my family.'[15]

The curious title – Emperor of the French Republic – which he accepted that day was soon superseded by a more resounding one. He was to be more generally known as His Imperial Majesty, Napoleon I, Emperor of the French.

By his side stood Josephine, now the Empress Josephine. If the new Emperor, says Madame de Rémusat, appeared 'gay and serene', the new Empress had 'lost none of her easy grace and affability.'[16] He would have been wearing the high-collared, red velvet suit which he had had especially designed as his First

Consul's uniform; she would have been in one of her floating, shimmeringly embroidered dresses.

Looking at Napoleon and Josephine on that triumphant day, as with charm and self-assurance they accepted the congratulations of the senators, one would have thought that they had been born to their new imperial state. Just over twenty-five years before, they had been two unknown, insignificant, almost penniless arrivals in France. Now they stood on the threshold of their years as the leading, most spectacular monarchal couple in the world.

18   'Napoleon decorating the artists.' The Emperor, watched by the Empress, presents awards.

19   A military review in the Place du Carrousel, outside the Tuileries.

17   (*Previous page*) David's famous painting of the Coronation in which Josephine, by one of her 'little intrigues', is pictured as the centre of attention.

20   Canova's famous representation of Princess Pauline Borghese as 'Venus
Victorieuse'.

21   Napoleon and Josephine, in full imperial splendour, at the wedding
of Jerome to Catherine of Württemberg.

22　The Empress Josephine in the gardens at Malmaison, by Prud'hon.

23   The Emperor Napoleon in his study, by Delaroche.

24 The flamboyant Jerome, King of Westphalia.

25 Napoleon's second wife, the Empress Marie Louise.

26 Napoleon, with the King of Rome on his knee, surrounded by his nephews and nieces.

27   Josephine at Malmaison after the divorce.

28   (*Overleaf*) Napoleon, aboard the *Bellerophon*, on his way into exile.

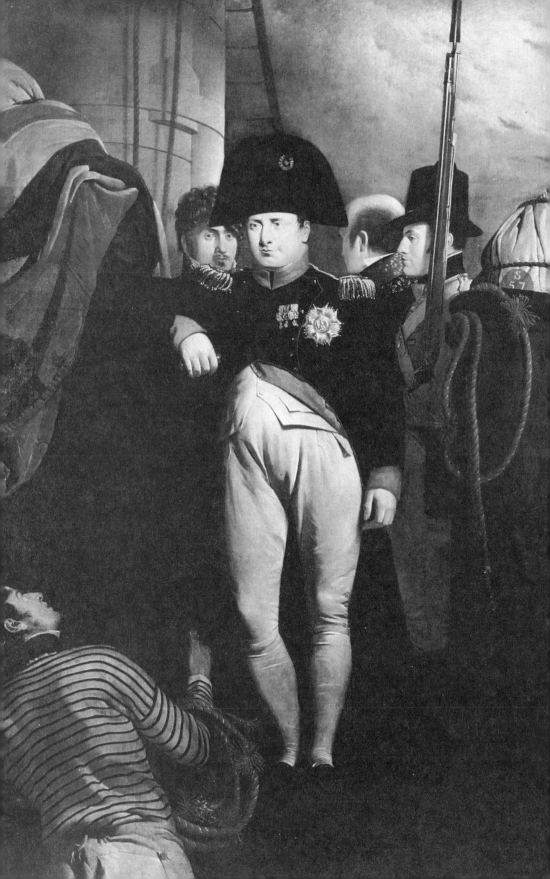

Part Four

EMPEROR AND EMPRESS

16

The Dynasty

FROM the day that Napoleon and Josephine had been proclaimed Emperor and Empress of the French until their coronation six months later, the Bonaparte family was in a state of almost continuous ferment.

The chief cause of their agitation was the question of the new imperial titles. In accordance with Napoleon's decrees, his eldest brother Joseph and his third brother Louis were created princes of the Empire. This meant that their wives, Julie and Hortense, automatically became princesses. Napoleon's two other brothers, Lucien and Jerome, were denied any such titles. Both were out of favour with the Emperor for having contracted unsuitable marriages.

The headstrong Lucien, whose humbly born and sweet-natured wife Christine had died in 1800, had since fallen in love with a married woman named Alexandrine Jouberthon. Only after she had borne him a son, in May 1803, did he marry her. The marriage was kept secret for two very good reasons: Napoleon would not have approved of it, and no one was quite sure whether Alexandrine's husband was alive or dead. But, as chance would have it, Napoleon chose this very moment to suggest a spectacular marriage for his brother Lucien: to the newly widowed and incredibly ugly Queen of the Italian kingdom of Etruria. Understandably, Lucien gave an evasive answer.

When, in time, Napoleon discovered the reason for his brother's evasiveness, he was furious. The marriage was a crime

167

against France, he ranted; Lucien's child was a bastard; he would have the marriage annulled. 'What!' he shouted to Hortense and his sister Caroline when he heard that they had received Lucien's wife. 'I try to restore morality, and a woman like that is brought into my family!'[1]

The affair climaxed in a blazing row between Napoleon and Lucien at Saint-Cloud one night in the spring of 1804. As no family quarrel could be complete without a thrust at Josephine, Lucien asked if all women who bore the name Bonaparte conferred as much honour on it as did his wife Alexandrine? Although Josephine was, in fact, pleading Lucien's case, Napoleon remained adamant. Lucien must renounce Alexandrine or leave France. To his credit, Lucien refused to break with his wife. Within days, he left for Italy.

'It's all over!' announced Napoleon to Josephine. 'I've come to a final rupture with Lucien and ordered him from my presence.'

When Josephine tried to soothe him, he took her in his arms and, resting his head on her shoulder ('that elegant coiffure of hers making a strange contrast to his sad, grim visage', writes the watching Madame de Rémusat), he said, 'It's hard to meet such opposition in one's own family ... Must I rely on myself alone? Well, I will suffice to myself alone – and you, Josephine – you will console me for all the rest.'[2]

He was equally incensed by the marriage of his youngest brother, the flighty Jerome. While on naval duty in the Atlantic, Jerome had visited Baltimore in North America and had fallen in love with a girl by the name of Elizabeth Patterson. The couple were married on Christmas Eve 1803. On hearing the news, from the anguished French consul-general in Washington, Napoleon's reaction was very much to the point. Jerome was to be refused any money whatsoever; he was to be put aboard a French frigate as soon as possible; the 'young person' with whom he had 'connected' himself was to be forbidden access to the ship; and, in the event of her managing to get aboard, she was not to be allowed on French soil. He refused, in fact, to recognise the marriage.

This refusal on the part of Napoleon to acknowledge Jerome's wife who, unlike Lucien's wife Alexandrine, was a young girl of good family and spotless reputation and whose marriage had been conducted by no less a cleric than the bishop who afterwards became the Primate of the Catholic Church in America, was an example of his increasing snobbishness and arrogance.

But with Jerome refusing to obey Napoleon's commands, he – like Lucien – was refused any imperial title.

Napoleon's middle sister, the lovely and flirtatious Pauline, had also recently married without his permission. When her first husband General Leclerc died of yellow fever during a campaign on the island of San Domingo, Pauline had accepted a proposal of marriage from Prince Camillo Borghese. Even Napoleon could not cavil at this choice. Borghese might have been almost completely uneducated but he was unbelievably rich. The trouble was that Napoleon, with his new-found passion for public decency, had recently revived the pre-Revolutionary regulation imposing one year and six weeks mourning for the death of a husband; Pauline, unable to wait that long, had married Prince Borghese in secret several months before the prescribed period was up. There was not a great deal that Napoleon could do to punish Pauline for her disobedience. He could not even deny her the title of princess as, by her marriage, she had automatically become a *principessa*.

His two other sisters, the pretentious Elisa and the ambitious Caroline – married, respectively, to the dough-like Felix Bacciochi and the flamboyant Joachim Murat – were outraged to discover that they were to be given no titles. In the course of a violent quarrel with Napoleon, they demanded to know why they were being condemned to obscurity while strangers (by whom they meant Josephine's family) were being loaded with honours. Napoleon, who was quite capable of shouting even his sisters down, assured them that he was master and that he would distribute honours as he pleased.

'To listen to you,' he bellowed at the almost hysterical women, 'one would think that I had robbed my family of the heritage of the late King, our father.'[3] At this Caroline, overcome with rage, fainted.

A few days later, Napoleon relented. He agreed that Elisa and Caroline would henceforth bear the title of 'Imperial Highness'.

Allied to this question of titles was the question of the succession. But even this was far from straightforward. The Senate decree stipulated that, in the event of Napoleon producing no direct, legitimate heir, the succession would go, first to Joseph Bonaparte and any male descendants, and then to Louis Bonaparte and his male descendants. But this right of succession could be exercised only after Napoleon had exercised another right: the right of 'adoptive succession', whereby he could adopt any of his nephews.

At the thought that one of their sons might one day outrank them (and even though Joseph had no sons as yet), the two brothers were appalled. They seem to have forgotten that had it not been for their brother Napoleon's stupendous achievements, they would probably have ended up as a couple of provincial lawyers.

Louis was particularly incensed. 'How have I deserved to be disinherited?' he demanded of Napoleon.'What will my position be when this child, having become yours, considers himself next in line to you, thus outranking me? No, I shall never give my consent to the adoption.'[4]

What infuriated the Bonapartes most of all, though, was the new status of their arch enemy, Josephine. Just the sight of her, looking so at ease in her position, was enough to set their teeth on edge. They were determined that, although she had been proclaimed an empress, she would not be crowned one. From now on they were untiring in their efforts to get Napoleon to discard her before the coronation – set for 2 December 1804. At best, advised Joseph, she should simply be a spectator.

'The question of divorce came up again at this period,' writes Hortense. 'A family council was convened, but the virulence of the Emperor's brothers was so pronounced, in the midst of what had been intended as a discussion of topics of general interest, that the Emperor could not fail to recognise his family's relentless animosity towards the Empress.'[5]

And, at one stage during the last two months before the coronation, it looked as though the Bonapartes had succeeded.

In a final desperate attempt to 'cure' her infertility, the forty-one-year-old Josephine travelled to the spa of Aix-la-Chapelle in the summer of 1804. The choice of watering place could hardly have been more appropriate. It had been at Aix-la-Chapelle that the Emperor Charlemagne – whose Empire Napoleon was busily emulating – had been crowned. Josephine travelled very much *à l'Impératrice*, in great state and with a suite of over a hundred. Napoleon, in the meantime, had set off on a tour of the Channel bases with a view to deciding, once more, whether or not he should launch an invasion of Britain. He decided against it. From Boulogne he wrote his usual affectionate letters.

'I am longing to see you, to tell you all that you inspire in me, and to cover you with kisses,' reads one of them. 'This bachelor life is wretched; and nothing can equal the worth of a wife who is good, beautiful and tender.'[6] Yet the couple had hardly returned to the Tuileries before Josephine noticed the tell-tale signs indicating that Napoleon had a new romantic interest. Since the proclamation of the Empire the court had been considerably expanded, and amongst the new, more aristocratic ladies who had been assigned to the Empress was a certain Madame Duchâtel. It appears to have been Caroline Murat, beginning now to reveal all the characteristics of selfishness, spitefulness and downright treachery for which she would become notorious, who introduced Adele Duchâtel into the court. As Madame Duchâtel was not only young, attractive and ambitious but had a look of Josephine about her, Caroline hoped she would supplant Josephine in Napoleon's affections.

Although the Empress suspected that Madame Duchâtel had become Napoleon's mistress, she had no proof. Madame de Rémusat, her usual confidante, advised her against looking for any. To antagonise Napoleon would be to play right into Caroline Murat's hands, she argued. But Josephine lacked the necessary subtlety for this sort of situation. When next she noticed that both her husband and Madame Duchâtel were absent from her salon, she rushed out after them. Her suspicions were confirmed. The dishevelled state of both Napoleon and his mistress – when eventually he opened the door to his wife's frantic knockings – told Josephine all she wanted to know. Napoleon was furious. Madame Duchâtel fled the room leaving Josephine, who had quickly been reduced to tears, to face her husband's anger.

Striding up and down the room, swearing at her, threatening her, smashing the furniture to pieces with savage kicks, he shouted that he was sick and tired of her spying, that he was determined to throw her out, that he was going to marry a woman capable of giving him children. She was to leave the palace immediately. Sobbing, she fled downstairs.

Napoleon then sent for Eugène de Beauharnais. He told him that he intended divorcing his mother and that Eugène was to take her away at once. He would compensate him, he said, for his loss of position. The upright Eugène refused Napoleon's offer and said that he asked for nothing more than to be allowed to devote his life to looking after his mother. He would always sacrifice his own opportunities for her comfort, he claimed.

As always, when confronted by members of the Beauharnais family – be it Josephine, Eugène or Hortense – Napoleon was disarmed by their unselfishness and their pliancy. None of them had ever asked any favours of him; none had opposed his wishes. They were so utterly different from his own grasping, carping, ambitious brothers and sisters. Napoleon listened to Eugène's resolution in silence and then dismissed him.

In the meantime, Josephine had sent Madame de Rémusat to break the news to Hortense. Hortense took it very well. 'I cannot interfere in any way,' she told her mother's lady-in-waiting, 'My husband has expressly forbidden it. My mother has been imprudent. She will lose a crown – but at least she will have peace and respite. Ah, believe me, there are women to be more pitied than she.'7

Claire de Rémusat knew what Hortense meant. Her own marriage to Louis Bonaparte was desperately unhappy. Hortense was, says the lady-in-waiting, 'the most unhappy person of our time, as she least deserved to be so.'8 Yet she never complained.

'Besides,' continued Hortense, 'if there is any chance at all of a reconciliation between the Emperor and his wife, that chance lies in the influence she exercises over him by means of her sweet and gentle nature and her tears. It would be fatal for anyone to interfere. The two of them must be left absolutely alone to work it out for themselves....'9

Hortense was right. Josephine's tears again won the day. 'I haven't got the courage to come to a final decision,' sighed Napoleon to his wife, 'and if you let me see that you are too deeply afflicted, if you refuse to act except in obedience to my command, I know I shall never be able to bring myself to issue it.' But he went on to warn her that she might yet one day be obliged to give way to the 'national interest'. If so, she should be the one to withdraw and, in this way, save him the pain of 'forcing the issue'.

'So, with an adroit and tender sweetness, taking the attitude of an unresisting victim,' says Claire de Rémusat, 'she succeeded in parrying the blow the jealous Bonapartes had aimed against her. Sad, complaisant, completely submissive, but shrewd enough to take advantage of her influence over her husband, she reduced him to a state of agitation and uncertainty from which he could not extricate himself.'10

One day, a few weeks before the coronation, Napoleon

summed up his attitude to these family squabbles in his usual frank and staccato manner. 'They are jealous of my wife, of Eugène, of Hortense, of everyone about me,' he said. 'Well, my wife has diamonds and debts, that's all. Eugène has not twenty thousand francs a year. I like those children because they're always eager to please me. If a gun is fired, it's Eugène who goes to see what's happening. If I have a ditch to cross, it's he who gives me a hand... I love Hortense; yes, I love her. She and her brother always take my side, even against their mother, when she flares up over a wench or some such trumpery. They say: "Well, he's a young man! You are in the wrong. He has plenty to put up with. We have plenty to thank him for." If Hortense were to ask for me while I was in council, I should go out and see her. If Madame Murat were asking for me, I shouldn't go. My wife is a good-natured woman who does them no harm. All she wants is to play the Empress a little, to have diamonds, handsome gowns, the trumpery of her age. Yes, she shall be crowned!'[11]

When, in his brusque way, Napoleon came to tell Josephine that she, as well as he, would be both crowned and consecrated by the Pope and that she had better prepare herself for the great day, her relief and joy were boundless. This, surely, would secure her position; it would be impossible for Napoleon to divorce her now.

But there was still one gap in Josephine's defences and, as it was a huge one, she lost no time in closing it. She and Napoleon had never been married by the Church. Although he had insisted on religious as well as civil ceremonies for his sisters' weddings, Napoleon had never suggested that his own marriage be blessed by the Church. Josephine had always assumed that he hoped thereby to be able to divorce her more easily.

And so, when Pope Pius VII arrived at Fontainebleau a few days before the coronation (what better imprimatur could a brand new monarch hope for than to be crowned by the Pope?), Josephine arranged to see him privately. With a becoming show of distress, she confessed to the irregularity of her marital status. His Holiness was appalled. He could hardly be expected to anoint and consecrate an emperor and empress who were living, as far as he was concerned, in sin. They must be properly married immediately.

Reluctantly, Napoleon agreed. He dare not face the risk –

and the ridicule – of the Pope refusing to play his part in the forthcoming ceremony.

In greatest secrecy, on the evening of 1 December 1804, an altar was set up in Napoleon's study. Cardinal Fesch, Napoleon's always obliging uncle, performed the marriage ceremony, in the presence of two witnesses. Taking no chances, Josephine afterwards demanded a certificate of legality from the Cardinal.

It was no wonder that Talleyrand, on once being asked if the Empress Josephine had been a woman of intelligence, wryly replied that no one had ever managed as brilliantly, as had she, without it.

'In splendour,' pronounced Napoleon to Josephine, the forthcoming coronation 'will surpass that of any of the Kings of France.'[12] He was as good as his word. With his genius for organisation and his ability to concentrate his mind on the smallest detail, the Emperor set about staging a ceremony that would dazzle, not only his countrymen, but all Europe.

Turning his back firmly on the atheism of the Revolution, he had asked the Pope to come to Paris 'to give, in pre-eminent measure, a religious character to the anointing and crowning of the First Emperor of the French.'[13] Pope Pius VII's presence would put the seal, not only on Napoleon's own assumption of the purple but on his recent Concordat with the Church. The parvenu Emperor took great care, though, to avoid taking second place to the Pope. He arranged that their first meeting should be, as though by accident, in the forest of Fontainebleau. Napoleon, in simple green hunting costume, halted the papal cortège and forced the Pontiff, in his white robes and silk shoes, to clamber out of his coach into a sea of mud. Together, as equals, they drove on to the palace in one of the Emperor's carriages, but with Napoleon taking care that he occupied the seat of honour, on the right.

Having rejected Les Invalides as not being grand enough for the ceremony, Napoleon decided on the Cathedral of Notre-Dame. Adjacent buildings were torn down to clear the entrance, a new wooden porch and covered way were erected, the painter Isabey was commissioned to prepare seven elaborate drawings showing various stages of the ceremony, and the painter David was to transform the interior of the Cathedral into something not unlike a magnificent stage setting.

Two great thrones were set up under a gilded triumphal arch for Napoleon and Josephine. A more modest throne was erected, by the high altar, for the Pope. No effect that could be achieved with paint and plaster, silk and velvet, deep-pile carpets and crystal chandeliers, gold-fringed banners and glowing tapestries was spared. A small fortune was spent on the newly designed regalia alone. A great golden coronation coach, surmounted by a crown and four eagles, was especially built for the occasion.

At noon on 2 December 1804, Napoleon and Josephine entered the Cathedral. The imperial family was led by Marshal Murat, bearing the imperial crown on a velvet cushion. Behind him walked Josephine. The forty-one-year-old Empress, her face expertly enamelled by Isabey and her hair a mass of curls, looked, it was generally agreed, no more than twenty-five that day. Her dress and train were of white satin richly embroidered in gold and silver; on her head she wore a glittering pearl and diamond diadem. Her crimson velvet, ermine-lined mantle, embroidered with golden bees – the emblem which Napoleon had adopted to replace the fleur-de-lis of the Bourbons – had been the object of one of those celebrated family rows.

Napoleon's intention had been for Josephine's mantle to be carried by the various Bonaparte women – his sisters Elisa, Pauline and Caroline and his brothers' wives, Julie and Hortense. His sisters had refused to do any such thing. How could Napoleon expect them – princesses themselves – to demean themselves by carrying the detested Josephine's train? His brother Joseph had been especially incensed. Rather than let his wife Julie subject herself to 'a duty painful to a virtuous woman', he threatened to give up everything and retire to Germany. One sharp word from Napoleon quickly changed his mind. The protesting sisters would only consent to carry the train if they, in turn, could have their own trains borne by their respective chamberlains and if the phrase 'bear the cloak' was substituted for 'carry the train'. This Napoleon allowed. But it was a very disgruntled little group who trailed in the wake of the smiling, *soignée*, slowly pacing Empress.

Napoleon walked behind, followed by his brothers Joseph and Louis. He was dressed in a long white satin garment, embroidered with gold; over this he wore, like Josephine, a crimson velvet, ermine-lined mantle sewn with golden bees and bordered with an intricate pattern of olive, laurel and oak leaves. On his head he wore a wreath of gold laurel leaves, like a Caesar's crown.

Notable by their absence from this triumphant family parade were Napoleon's brothers Lucien and Jerome, as well as his mother Letizia who had accompanied her favourite son Lucien into exile.

The length of the coronation ceremony seemed to tire the notoriously impatient Emperor. Several times he was caught stifling a yawn. When the Pope solemnly anointed him on the head and the hands, the watching Madame Junot was convinced that his only thoughts were of wiping off the oil. When it came to the moment of crowning, Napoleon, by previous arrangement with the Pope, placed the imperial crown upon his own brow. Although the crown suited him no better than his cumbersome robes, he looked, says Madame Junot, 'really handsome and his countenance was illuminated by an expression almost impossible to describe.'[14] As he placed the crown on his head, a little stone, no bigger than a nut, fell down from the roof and bounced off his shoulder. But by no change of expression or movement of his body did he reveal that he had felt it strike him.

It was now Josephine's turn to receive her crown. As no queen had been crowned in France for two centuries (the last had been Marie de Medici and that was because of the likelihood of her becoming regent), it was indeed a triumph for Josephine. 'A general movement of admiration was noticeable at the moment when the Empress was crowned,' writes Madame de Rémusat. 'She was so unaffected, so graceful, as she advanced towards the altar; she knelt down with such simple elegance, that all eyes were delighted with the picture she presented.'[15] 'I have had the honour of being presented to many real princesses...,' agreed another spectator, 'but I never saw one who, to my own eyes, presented so perfect a personification of elegance and majesty.'[16]

Josephine knelt before Napoleon. By now, of course, there were tears in her eyes. Napoleon took her small crown, placed it first on his own head, and then set it upon hers. As he crowned his wife, his manner seemed almost playful. He placed it very carefully over the diadem which she already wore, then took it off, and then replaced it. It was as if he were trying to tell her that she should wear it gracefully and lightly. The two of them seemed 'to enjoy one of those fleeting moments of pure felicity which are unique in a lifetime; and serve to fill up a lustrum of years.'[17]

Josephine's felicity was short lived. As she turned from the altar to go back to her throne, the three Bonaparte sisters, livid with a combination of rage and envy, refused to lift her train. The unexpected weight of velvet dragging at her shoulders caused her to stumble, and although she quickly regained her balance, she was unable to move forward. Napoleon, noticing this, rapped out a few sharp words to his sisters and they hurriedly lifted the mantle and moved forward.

As the Emperor and Empress regained their thrones, the Cathedral echoed and re-echoed with magnificent *vivats*.

At the close of the ceremony, Napoleon, walking in solemn procession towards the door of the Cathedral, suddenly wanted to attract the attention of one of the cardinals preceding him. Impatiently and quite unselfconsciously, he prodded him in the back with his sceptre.

That evening the Emperor was in the best of spirits. He and Josephine dined alone together, with Napoleon insisting that she wear her crown throughout the meal. Time and again he complimented her on the grace with which she wore it.

The transient glories of that day were captured for posterity by Jacques-Louis David in his famous painting, *Le sacre de Napoleon*. The vast canvas could, with more accuracy, have been titled 'The Coronation of Josephine' for it depicts, not the most significant moment of the day's ceremonial – the placing of the crown on his own head by Napoleon – but the less important gesture of his crowning of Josephine. This was her doing; what Napoleon afterwards called 'one of Josephine's little intrigues.'[18] She apparently talked her friend David into composing a picture in which it would be made irrefutably clear that she had been crowned Empress of the French.

For all the submissiveness of Josephine's pose, and the self-assurance of Napoleon's, it is she who is the centre of attention. All eyes, including those of the Emperor, the Pope and the massed Bonapartes (even those of Napoleon's absent mother, whom David was asked to paint in), are either on Josephine or on the crown which Napoleon is about to place on her charmingly inclined head.

What more convincing proof could there be of her right to remain forever by Napoleon's side as his lawful wife, his crowned consort, his consecrated empress?

17

————⬥⬥⬥⬥⬥————

The Empire

OF the many reasons for Josephine's continuing hold over Napoleon, one given by Claire de Rémusat was especially valid. 'He became accustomed to associate the idea of her influence with every piece of good fortune which befell him,' she explains. 'This superstition, which she kept up cleverly, exerted great power over him for a long time; it even induced him more than once to delay the execution of his project of divorce.'[1]

Certainly, in the period of good fortune which followed his coronation, during which – by his military successes – he made himself the undoubted master of Europe, Napoleon seems to have put aside all thoughts of divorce. By virtue of their new elevated status, which brought with it the loneliness inseparable from sovereignty, the couple were drawn closer together. Josephine was the only one left who could *tutoyer* him and call him Bonaparte; she was the only one who could still tell him the truth, as opposed to those who told him what they thought he wanted to hear.

To the chagrin of the Bonapartes, Napoleon continued to favour the Beauharnais. The first to benefit was Eugène. At the imperial court, few young men were more popular than the Emperor's twenty-four-year-old stepson. Eugène de Beauharnais, says one of Josephine's ladies, 'did not lack personal attractions. His figure was graceful; he was skilled in all bodily exercises; and he inherited from his father that fine manner of an old-fashioned French gentleman ... To these advantages he added simplicity and kind-heartedness; he was neither vain nor presumptuous; he was

178

sincere without being indiscreet, and could be silent when silence was necessary.' On the other hand, she continues, he 'did not have much natural talent; his imagination was not vivid, and his feelings were not keen. He was always obedient to his stepfather....'[2]

In a flowery announcement, the Emperor now promoted Eugène to Vice-Chancellor of State. The young man had proved himself worthy, declared Napoleon, of 'emulating and of one day surpassing the examples and lessons that we have given him.' That the sunny, complaisant, well-intentioned Eugène would try his best to emulate his stepfather was quite likely; that he would ever surpass his 'examples and lessons' was extremely doubtful.

Napoleon was equally kind to Hortense. He appreciated the fact that she never complained about her disastrous marriage to his brother Louis. He saw to it that her second son, Napoleon Louis, born just before the coronation, was baptised by the Pope himself and he always treated her eldest son, Napoleon Charles, with conspicuous favour. He would seat the three-year-old on his lap and treat him to sips of wine and helpings of lentils from the table. To the annoyance of his sister Caroline Murat, who was always forcing her own two little sons on the Emperor, Napoleon would make no secret of his preference for Hortense's eldest boy.

'Take my advice,' Napoleon once said to the child whom he had just assured would grow up to be a king, 'if you want to live, never accept anything to eat from one of your cousins.'[3]

In the spring of 1805 came further honours for Josephine and her family. The republic which Napoleon had created in northern Italy transformed itself into a monarchy and invited him to be their king. At first the Emperor offered the Italian crown to his brother Joseph but, as this would have meant giving up his own claims to the French succession, Joseph refused. Napoleon then tried to get his brother Lucien to abandon his second wife, Alexandrine, and accept the crown, but Lucien was not to be tempted. Exasperated, Napoleon accepted the crown for himself. He and Josephine travelled to Milan where, amid scenes of acclamation in the Duomo, Napoleon placed the ancient iron crown of Lombardy on his own head.

That Josephine was now the Queen of Italy as well as the Empress of the French was a bitter enough pill for the Bonapartes to swallow; more bitter still was the fact that Napoleon proclaimed Eugène Viceroy of Italy. In the following year he formally adopted him as his son. Eugène became an imperial and royal highness, taking precedence over Joseph and Louis, and was designated successor to the throne of Italy, after Napoleon.

Josephine was enjoying some more intimate triumphs as well. In spite of the fact that Napoleon still indulged in the odd loveless sexual adventure (Madame Duchâtel had been superseded by a Mademoiselle de Lacoste who was, in turn, replaced by a Signora Gazzani), the Emperor, says Madame de Rémusat, 'suddenly returned to terms of the fondest intimacy with his wife.'[4]

Napoleon's valet Constant has left a description of his master's visits to Josephine's apartments in the palace of Saint-Cloud. Wearing a dressing gown and a Madras headcloth, and preceded by Constant carrying a lighted candelabra, the Emperor would walk the length of a corridor and up a flight of stairs to Josephine's rooms. Between seven and eight the following morning, Constant would enter the Empress's bedroom to serve Napoleon a cup of tea or a tisane of orange flowers. Having drunk it, the Emperor would get up immediately.

'Must you go already?' the Empress would complain smilingly, 'Stay a little longer.'

'But I thought you were going back to sleep,' he would tease. Then, tucking the covers back around her, he would give her a playful pat on her naked shoulder and kiss her goodbye.

'I am late rising this morning,' the gratified Empress would explain to her ladies-in-waiting, rubbing her hands together glee-fully. 'But then, you see, Bonaparte has spent the night with me.'[5]

But no number of nights spent together or gallons of spa water consumed or bizarre treatments administered by Dr Corvisart could bring forth an imperial heir. And so one day, early in 1805, before he had accepted the crown of Italy for himself and made Eugène his viceroy, Napoleon summoned Louis and Hortense. It was imperative, he told them, that he formally adopt their eldest son Napoleon Charles, and crown him King of Italy.

Louis would not hear of it. For the same reason that he had objected to Napoleon's plans of 'adoptive succession' (whereby the Emperor was entitled to adopt, and name as his successor, any of his nephews), Louis now objected to this latest scheme: 'he would never consent to his son holding a higher rank than his own.'[6] To the other advantages, or disadvantages, for his son in the proposal, Louis seems not to have given a thought. Throughout what developed into a violent argument between the two brothers, Hortense said nothing. She knew that in the end it was always her mother, Josephine, who suffered from these scenes. 'The Emperor's constantly impatient manner seemed to reproach her with the misfortune of her childlessness,'[7] she wrote.

It was at about this time that Napoleon suggested that Josephine should feign pregnancy and acknowledge a child, whom he would father by some other woman, as her own. The whole Machiavellian scheme was to be carried out in the strictest secrecy. Ready to grasp at any straw, Josephine agreed. Only Dr Corvisart's refusal to have anything to do with the dishonourable project forced the couple to drop it. But it was not until years later, after the divorce of Josephine and the birth of Napoleon's son by his second wife, that Corvisart repeated the story.

Yet there were times when Napoleon seemed almost to have resigned himself to the fact of his childlessness. He knew that, in the end, he could always override his brother Louis's objections to the adoption of young Napoleon Charles and that, by adopting him, his nephew and Josephine's grandson – their own flesh and blood – would be the next Emperor of the French. And why should he rid himself of this wife whose soothing, malleable, soft-voiced presence was such a balm to his own restless spirit? She was his good genius; while he remained married to her, his luck would hold.

But at other times Napoleon's failure to produce an heir filled him with an overwhelming sense of despair. 'To whom, then,' he one day sighed to his valet Constant, 'am I going to leave all this?'[8]

In the summer of 1805 Napoleon, having once again abandoned the idea of an invasion of his implacable enemy Britain, marched his *Grande Armée* away from the Channel coast and east towards the Danube. He was about to do battle against a new Austro-Russian coalition. As always, he struck swiftly and ruthlessly. He defeated the Austrian army at Ulm in October, and in November entered Vienna in triumph. On 2 December, the first anniversary of his coronation, he beat the combined Austro-Russian army at Austerlitz. Not even the destruction of a Franco-Spanish fleet at Trafalgar a few weeks before could detract from the significance of this victory. For Austerlitz did more than strengthen Napoleon's position as Emperor of the French: the subsequent peace treaty granted him the control of vast territories, so allowing him to think in terms of a great French Empire spreading throughout the Continent.

He began by setting up the Confederation of the Rhine – a conglomeration of large states and petty principalities, with himself as their Protector.

The chief beneficiaries of Napoleon's new aggrandisement were, of course, the members of his family. The first round went to the Beauharnais faction. Josephine was summoned to travel to Munich (Bavaria was about to be transformed into a kingdom within the new Confederation of the Rhine) by way of several other south German courts. She was to make her progress, he commanded, in a style befitting a 'great Empress' and, while being her usual gracious self, was to accept the homage of these lesser monarchs as her due. She was to treat them with courtesy but nothing more.

Inevitably though, it was for her charm and her elegance rather than for her hauteur that Josephine impressed the Germans. 'I win battles,' said Napoleon on hearing of her triumph, 'Josephine wins hearts.'⁹

Reunited in Munich, the couple set about realising Napoleon's latest dynastic scheme: a marriage between Eugène de Beauharnais, or Prince Eugène as he was now called, and Princess Augusta Amelia, daughter of the newly created King of Bavaria. The fact that Augusta had already been promised to the Crown Prince of Baden bothered Napoleon not at all. In a brusque letter to the unsuspecting Eugène, who was still in Italy, Napoleon informed him that he had arranged his marriage to Princess Augusta and that the news had already been announced in the press. 'The Princess came to see me this morning, and I had a long talk with her. She is very pretty. I am enclosing a portrait of her on a cup; but it doesn't do her justice....'¹⁰ Eugène was to leave Italy within twelve hours of receiving Napoleon's letter and to travel to Munich with all possible speed.

Dutiful as ever, Eugène completed the journey in four days, shaved off his newly-grown moustache and married the King of Bavaria's daughter.

The match between Prince Eugène and Princess Augusta was surprisingly successful – a *marriage de convenance* which matured into a partnership of love. Eugène 'possessed in perfection,' says Madame de Rémusat, 'those qualities that make for happiness in home life – sweet temper, and that natural cheerfulness which rises above every ill, and was perhaps due to the fact that he was never profoundly moved by anything. When, however, the indifference towards the interests of other people is also displayed in one's own personal troubles, it may fairly be called philosophy.'[11]

This happy union between Eugène and Augusta was to provide the world with several sovereigns, among them an Empress of Brazil, a Queen of Sweden and a Consort of the Queen of Portugal.

The Crown Prince Charles Frederick of Baden, having had Princess Augusta snatched from him, was now offered compensation in the form of another Beauharnais: the Empress Josephine's niece by marriage, Stephanie de Beauharnais. He was obliged to accept. Until now, the seventeen-year-old Stephanie had been something of a poor relation at the imperial court but, on being elevated to the rank of princess by Napoleon, she completely lost her head. In front of her embarrassed fiancé, she began to flirt openly with the Emperor. Only a sharp talking-to by Josephine put a stop to the girl's imprudence. The wedding was celebrated, in April 1806, with great splendour in the chapel of the Tuileries. That night the streets and squares of Paris blazed with brilliant illuminations.

By Josephine, these two Beauharnais marriages were regarded as a further strengthening of her position.

Napoleon now turned his attention to his increasingly disgruntled blood relations. His mother who, owing to her championship of the stubborn Lucien, had been ignored at the inauguration of the Empire, was given the title of *Son Altesse Imperiale Madame la Mère de l'Empereur*. From now on she was to be known as Madame Mère. But it would have needed more than a grandiose title, a magnificent house in Paris, an equally magnificent château in the country, a chamberlain bearing one of the proudest names in France, a clutch of aristocratic equerries, nine ladies-in-waiting and an enormous allowance to change Letizia from the stiff-backed and parsimonious person she had always been. Her only interest in her son's achievements was financial: her chief concern to hoard as much of the money he lavished on her as she could.

The next member of the family to be elevated was Joseph. In a terse letter Napoleon told his brother that he intended dethroning the Bourbons of Naples and offered him the crown. This time

Joseph accepted the offer and in February 1806 entered Naples at the head of a column of French troops.

For the two years that he reigned in Naples, Joseph enjoyed considerable popularity. His easy-going disposition, his courtly manners, his interest in the arts and his love of display were all very much in tune with the Neapolitan character. He retained as many of the officials of the old regime as possible and made very few changes in the day-to-day life of the people. He saw himself as the protector rather than the conqueror of the Neapolitans; he planned to rule as an Italian king, not as a lieutenant of the French Empire.

Joseph was reckoning without Napoleon. Before many weeks had passed, the Emperor was bombarding him with letters of instruction; it was a bombardment that was to be kept up throughout his reign.

There was no throne for Lucien but in June 1806 Napoleon made Louis and Hortense King and Queen of Holland. The prospect was not much to the taste of either of them: the hypochondriacal Louis feared the damp Dutch climate and was afraid that he might be denied his two-month-long sojourns at various spas; while Hortense dreaded leaving Josephine and resented what was bound to be a disruption of her quiet daily life. But Napoleon brushed aside their reservations. And so, accompanied by their little sons, Napoleon Charles and Napoleon Louis, Louis and Hortense set out for The Hague.

The Emperor's eldest sister Elisa was created hereditary Princess of Piombino. Napoleon's gift of this little principality, not far from Pisa, gratified the self-important Elisa immensely. With her husband, the simple Bacciochi in tow, she first annexed and then took up residence in the neighbouring state of Lucca. She then proceeded, with an almost Napoleonic vigour, to transform her long-neglected realm into an efficiently run country.

Pauline – the beautiful, ingenuous, sexually insatiable Princess Borghese – was given the principality of Guastella, also in Italy. Her initial delight evaporated when she learned that it was a state of six square miles with an impoverished population of three thousand. Nothing would induce her to live there. So Napoleon offered to incorporate the small state into his own kingdom of Italy and to pay Pauline six million francs for it, on the understanding that she could retain the title. She agreed and, the transaction over, resumed her sybaritic life in Paris.

The Empire

After weeks of tireless scheming on the parts of the ambitious Joachim and Caroline Murat, Napoleon gave them the duchies of Berg and Cleves. They had both hoped, of course, for more than this but were shrewd enough to accept it and begin working for something better. Murat, resplendent in furs, feathers and yards of gold braid, went clattering into his new domain while Caroline remained in Paris to exercise her considerable powers of fascination on those men of influence, like Talleyrand and Fouché, who could prove useful in the event of the Emperor being killed in battle. As Napoleon's brothers Joseph, Louis and Jerome had no influence whatsoever with the army and as Murat had a great deal, Caroline planned to have her husband proclaimed Emperor in Paris if ever news of Napoleon's death should reach the capital.

The last of Napoleon's family to be given a throne was his youngest brother, the feckless Jerome. Once the Emperor had annulled the young man's marriage to Elizabeth Patterson of Baltimore, Jerome resumed all the carefree, dissolute and extravagant habits of his bachelorhood. Notwithstanding this, and with his sense of family solidarity and dynastic pretensions overcoming his common sense, Napoleon made Jerome King of the newly created German state of Westphalia. Having given Westphalia a king, he set about bestowing upon it a queen. Napoleon chose, as Jerome's second bride, Princess Catherine of Württemberg, the daughter of the King of Württemberg – another of those south German monarchs who had recently been tucked under the French Emperor's wing.

A couple of years older than the twenty-two-year-old Jerome, Princess Catherine was a squat, plain and badly dressed young woman. Beside the vivacious Jerome (the elegance of whose satin coat and white plumed hat had once caused him to be mistaken for the Empress Josephine in a carriage procession) she was dull stuff indeed. Yet it turned out to be a happy marriage. Catherine's qualities of devotion, simplicity and sincerity were excellent foils for her husband's less dependable characteristics. From their union is descended the present Bonapartist pretender to the French imperial throne.

The French Empire, Napoleon once grandiloquently declared, would one day become the mother country of all the other monarchies of Europe. His intention was for each monarch to build himself a large palace in Paris so that, on occasions such as the coronation of the Emperor of the French, these kings could come to 'render homage' to Europe's leading sovereign.

By the year 1806, and despite the fact that there was still no direct heir to Napoleon's Empire, his vision was beginning to sound less preposterous than it might once have done.

18

The Eagle

FOR all the magnificence of his new Empire – and, during the next few years it was to become more magnificent still – Napoleon's private life was curiously simple, almost bourgeois.

His day began between six and seven when Constant brought him his tea or orange flower water. On some mornings, says his valet, 'he would rush at me with his favourite greeting of "Hullo you rascal" and pinch both my ears at once, making me scream. Not infrequently he added sundry slaps adroitly applied, whereupon I was sure to find him excellently good-tempered for the whole day – considerate and charming as he alone could be.'[1]

Putting on a dressing gown – white piqué in summer and swansdown in winter – and leather slippers, Napoleon would drink his tea, read his letters and reports and glance at the newspapers. He then enjoyed a steaming hot bath. Hot baths were one of the Emperor's chief pleasures; a relaxing hot bath was worth four hours' sleep, he would maintain. He would spend at least an hour in the bath, continually turning on the hot tap and filling the room with so much steam that Constant, one of whose duties was to read aloud the newspapers, could barely see the print.

After his bath, Napoleon put on a vest, underpants and dressing gown. His body linen, says Constant, was 'a very fine texture' and marked with a crowned N. Napoleon always shaved himself. While Roustam, the handsome, Georgian-born Mameluke who had joined Napoleon's service in Egypt, held the looking-glass, the Emperor lathered his face with herb-scented soap and shaved with a British-made, mother-of-pearl handled steel razor. British steel was superior to French, he claimed. In spite of having already spent an hour in the bath, Napoleon washed his face, neck and ears with a soapy sponge. He then picked his teeth with a polished boxwood tooth-pick and brushed them twice, first with toothpaste and then finely powdered coral. Finally, he rinsed his mouth with a mixture of brandy and water and, in contemporary fashion, scraped his tongue with a silver or tortoiseshell scraper. Taking off his dressing gown and vest, he would have eau-de-Cologne poured over his head. This he would rub briskly, with a hard bristled brush, over his chest and arms, while Constant did the same to his back and shoulders. He got through sixty bottles of eau-de-Cologne a month. Napoleon had his hair cut, very short, once a week by Josephine's hairdresser, Duplan.

Unlike the levées of the Bourbon court, at which courtiers had dressed the monarch, Napoleon used the levée to discuss the day's events with the officials who ran his court; he was always dressed by his valets. He wasted very little time, or money, on clothes. 'It is not everyone who has the right to be plainly dressed,'[2] he once murmured in an amused aside to Claire de Rémusat, on being confronted by a group of his gorgeously uniformed marshals. Napoleon often professed himself astounded at what Constant spent on clothes; if ever his valet was sporting some new garment, Napoleon would want to know what it cost. Most days he wore a linen shirt, white silk stockings, white cashmere breeches, black, gilt-buckled shoes (which had always been broken in by one of his servants), a long cashmere waistcoat, a simple muslin cravat and a dark green, unadorned frock-coat of a colonel in the Chasseurs. He always pocketed a handkerchief sprinkled with eau-de-Cologne and a snuff box containing coarse, cheap tobacco which he would sniff without inhaling.

Napoleon's sartorial unconcern was the despair of his tailors. He once astonished one of them by asking him to patch the worn seat of a pair of riding breeches. By surreptitiously getting the tailor to make each of his master's new coats an inch shorter, Constant succeeded in getting the unsuspecting Emperor into coats of a more fashionable length. He also managed to talk him into forsaking outmoded pointed-toed shoes for the more stylish *bec de canne* shape. Invariably, though, Constant's painstaking efforts to improve his master's appearance were nullified by the Emperor's unthinking habits, such as wiping his pen on his white breeches or of scratching his leg with a shoe. On campaign, or even in the palace, Napoleon would ruin his boots by stirring the burning logs with his feet; if angry, he would give the logs savage kicks.

Most mornings, while dressing, the Emperor would be visited by his personal physician, Dr Corvisart. Napoleon had great confidence in Corvisart, in spite of the fact that he had very little confidence in medicines. The best medicines, the Emperor would maintain, were chicken broth, chicory water and salts of tartar. But he enjoyed discussing illnesses with Corvisart, although strongly disapproving of the doctor's often qualified answers. 'He liked to go straight to the point in everything,' says Constant, 'and if anyone was mentioned as being ill, his first question was always "Will he die?"'[3]

Napoleon started work, each day, on the stroke of nine. His chief theatre of work was his study in the Tuileries, with its view of the Seine. He sat at his great mahogany desk for signing letters only; he preferred to pace up and down or to perch on a green taffeta settee near the fire. His secretary – Bourrienne was succeeded by Méneval, and Méneval by Fain – sat at a smaller desk in the embrasure of the window. Napoleon usually dictated but at such speed as to outrun his secretary's shorthand. His own handwriting was almost illegible, his spelling uncertain and his pronunciation idiosyncratic.

His powers of concentration were phenomenal. When he took hold of an idea, he seized it, as he himself claimed, by the neck, the arse, the feet, the hands and the head, until he had exhausted it. He would sometimes remain in his study for sixteen hours at a stretch, immersed in the myriad demands of his position, including the receiving of ministers and ambassadors. Yet he still found the time to give his full attention to some relatively unimportant detail. Was it true, he once wrote to ask from a Prussian battlefield, that the Louvre Museum had been late opening on a certain day, and that the public had been kept waiting?

On set days the Emperor presided over ministerial and state councils. Here, too, his grasp of the matters under discussion was not only exceptional but disconcerting. 'He frequently astonished his hearers by lucid and profound remarks on subjects which would have seemed to be quite beyond his reach,'[4] testifies one observer. Equally disconcerting was his unconscious habit of shrugging his right shoulder in a quick, nervous way; to those who did not know him well, it was taken as a sign of disapproval.

Napoleon usually lunched off a tray in his study but, in the evening, he would join Josephine and the household for dinner. He preferred simple food like fricassée of chicken, lentils, rice and haricot beans, and drank inexpensive wine, well watered. He sopped his bread in his gravy. Josephine always poured, sugared and tasted his coffee. After dinner the couple might attend a performance in one of the theatres which the Emperor had had built at the Tuileries and Saint-Cloud. These performances were the despair of the First Chamberlain, whose duty it was to provide amusement for the man whom Talleyrand called 'The Unamusable'.

'In vain,' wrote one member of the household, 'were the masterpieces of our theatrical repertoire performed; in vain did our best actors strive their very best to please him; he generally appeared at these [theatrical] representations preoccupied and weighed down by the gravity of his thoughts.'[5] Often he remained for one act only.

The Emperor could never appreciate that his almost permanent air of preoccupation had an inhibiting effect on others. 'It is a singular thing,' he once exclaimed during a season at Fontainebleau, 'I have brought together a lot of people; I wanted them to amuse themselves. I arranged every sort of pleasure for them, and here they are with long faces, all looking dull and tired.'

'That,' explained Talleyrand boldly, ' is because pleasure cannot be summoned by beat of drum, and here, just as when you are with the army, you always seem to be saying, "Come, ladies and gentlemen! Forward! March!"'[6]

Napoleon was no more communicative during the evenings on which no entertainment was provided. While, in complete silence, the ladies sat and the gentlemen stood, the Emperor would pace backwards and forwards, deep in thought and paying no attention to the others in the room. The ladies felt especially slighted. 'He deems us only fit to decorate a drawing room,' complained one of them. 'I really don't think he finds much difference between a fine vase of flowers and a pretty woman.'[7]

Yet when he did deign to speak it was almost worse. As he talked non-stop, it was difficult to make any reply. 'He neither knew how to put people at their ease or cared to do so,' wrote one lady-in-waiting, 'for he avoided the slightest appearance of familiarity, and he inspired all who were in his presence with the apprehension that some disparaging or unkind word would be said to him or her before witnesses.'[8]

But occasionally, and when part of a small group, the Emperor was capable of taking part in a free and easy discussion. 'I think I see him now,' remembered Claire de Rémusat of one occasion, 'in the window recess of a drawing room at Saint Cloud, astride a chair, resting his chin on the back of it. [The Empress] reclined on a sofa near him; I was sitting opposite him, and M. de Rémusat stood behind my chair.' In an intimate and relaxed fashion, the four of them had enjoyed an hour's conversation.

Everything, says Claire, 'had been very agreeable; his tone of voice, his countenance, his gestures, all were familiar and encouraging. He had been smiling, he had marked our answering smiles, and had even been amused by the remarks we made on his discourse; in fact, he had put us perfectly at ease.'

The discussion over, Napoleon rose to take his leave. In a moment, says Claire, his manner changed. 'He looked at us sternly, in a way that always seemed to increase his short stature, and gave M. de Rémusat some insignificant order in the curt tone of a despotic master, who takes care that every request still be a command.

'His tone of voice, so different from that to which I had been listening for the last hour, made me start, and when we withdrew, my husband, who had noticed my involuntary movement, told me that he had felt the same sensation. "You perceive," he said, "he was afraid that his momentary unbending and confidence might lessen the fear he is always anxious to inspire. He therefore thought proper to dismiss us with a reminder that he is the *master*."'[9]

The Emperor usually went to bed at ten as he liked seven or eight hours' sleep. He undressed quickly, scattering his things in all directions: his coat and grand cordon on the floor, his hat on to a chair, his watch on to the bed. Except in the hottest weather, his bed was warmed before he got into it. Often he would send for Josephine to read to him. 'No one acquitted herself in this task better than the Empress,' says Constant, 'in fact, he preferred her to all other readers...her special charm was the ravishing sound of her voice. How often did it happen that I, like many others, could stop short merely to enjoy listening to that lovely voice.'[10]

Josephine could soothe her husband in other ways as well. As he always bolted his food, Napoleon often suffered severe stomach ache. One evening, on being summoned to the Emperor's bedroom, Constant found him lying full length on the floor, with the Empress sitting beside him, cradling his head in her lap. 'The Emperor bore this sort of inconvenience far less bravely than the thousand ills that military life brings in its wake,' claims Constant.

As soon as Constant appeared, Josephine asked him to make Napoleon some tea. Having drunk three cups, the Emperor felt better. 'He still lay with his head in the Empress's lap. She kept stroking his forehead with her dimpled white hand and rubbing his chest, as she murmured, "Do you feel better? Would you like to go to bed? I will stay by your bedside...."'[11]

In the days when Josephine had always shared Napoleon's bed, she had been intrigued by the way, before going to sleep, he had pored over the lists of the *cadres* of the army. 'He would go to sleep repeating the names of the corps, and even of those of some of the individuals who composed them; he kept those names in a corner of his memory, and his habit came to his aid when he wanted to recognise a soldier, and to give him the pleasure of a cheering word from his general. He spoke to the subalterns in a tone of good fellowship, which delighted them all....'[12]

These nights, Napoleon slept alone in his bedroom. The faithful Roustam slept outside across his doorway; an aide-de-camp slept in an adjoining room; a quartermaster of the guard and two footmen kept guard all night at the entrance to his apartments. The Emperor's room would be warmed by a fire and scented with slow-burning perfumes.

Often, during the night, he would wake and, calling his secretary, go back to his study. The secretary, having scrambled into his clothes, would find the Emperor, in his white dressing gown and with a red Madras kerchief tied around his head, already walking up and down the study. After a couple of hours' dictation, he would send for sorbets and, refreshed, resume work. As dawn broke over the roof-tops of Paris, a light could still be seen in the windows of the Emperor's study as that vibrant, emphatic voice rattled remorselessly on.

The simplicity of Napoleon's private life was in no way reflected in the *mise-en-scène* of his public life. Here all was ostentation. His dicta, that 'sovereigns must always be on show' and that 'kingship is an actor's part' were amply borne out in his public presentation of himself. With all the resources of the state at his command, Napoleon was able to move in a splendour that not only mirrored but surpassed that of the old Bourbon regime.

That Napoleon was in a position to meet the cost of all this splendour was due to the fact that, during the Consulate, he had thoroughly reorganised France's by then chaotic finances. With his innate thrift and almost peasant-like distrust of loans and paper money, he had set the country's fiscal affairs on a sound financial footing. An efficient tax system, boosted by new indirect taxes, yielded a large and increasing revenue. To this was now being added immense war indemnities and contributions from various enemy and vassal states. This meant that Napoleon was always able to balance the national budget. And even if he did spend a great deal on the glorifying of his imperial status, he – unlike the Bourbons with their grandiose palaces and expensive mistresses – never spent more than he could afford.

Whereas, in the days of the Bourbons, life had revolved around the King's person, with the monarch eating, dressing and undressing in the midst of his courtiers, so that his bedroom became the centre of court life, Napoleon kept his public life strictly separate from his private. The throne room with its enfilade of antechambers became the most important in the palace. In fact, in both the Tuileries and Fontainebleau, what had once been the King's bedrooms were converted into throne rooms. This helped both to distance and to glorify the monarch. What Napoleon wanted emphasised was the grandeur, the magnificence and the majesty of the sovereign's official position as opposed to that of his physical person.

Under his direction, the new imperial court was established with a speed and a thoroughness that characterised all his enterprises. A bulky volume, drawn up by a special commission and titled *Etiquette du Palais Impérial*, detailed the precise rules to be adhered to, and the exact duties to be carried out, by the members of this brand new court. Chapter Two, for instance, had forty-eight densely written paragraphs on 'the Arrangement of Apartments and on the Rights of Entry into Each of Them'. Chapter Five had forty-three no less detailed paragraphs on 'The Meals of Their Majesties'.

The lavishly tapestried and freshly gilded apartments of the three main palaces – the Tuileries, Saint-Cloud and Fontainebleau – swarmed with court officials in their silver embroidered coats of violet, crimson and amaranth. The servants sported powder-blue livery with silver lace. On state occasions the Emperor and Empress were attended by the six Grand Officers who were in charge of the six services of the household – the Grand Almoner, the Grand Marshal of the Palace, the Grand Chamberlain, the Grand Equerry, the Grand Huntsman and the Grand Master of Ceremonies. One could hardly move for equerries, footmen, ushers, pages and *valets de chambre*. Josephine's ladies-in-waiting were increased from seventeen to thirty (Marie Antoinette had had only sixteen); she even had a priest-confessor, a bishop with the unmistakably aristocratic name of Ferdinand de Rohan.

'The larger the imperial court grew,' writes Claire de Rémusat, 'the stricter the ceremonial and the more impersonal and monotonous the life there became; and as the Emperor's despotism increased, so did the fear and the silence among the courtiers. All former intimacies with him ceased. We seemed, all of us, on an eternal dress parade, our sole function being to surround the throne with the appropriate pomp and splendour, in line with the Emperor's theory that luxury and glory were unfailingly intoxicating to the French.'

The palaces, which had been splendid enough under the Bourbons, now became even more splendid. Vast sums were spent on their restoration and redecoration. Not content with his three main palaces, Napoleon acquired others throughout his Empire; in time he was to make use of the Elysée Palace in Paris, the Palace of Compiègne and he even, at one stage, toyed with the idea of moving to Versailles. By 1812 he had no less than forty-four palaces at his disposal.

To the furniture, paintings and *objets* inherited from the Bourbons he added still more: Gobelin tapestries, Sèvres china, Savonnerie carpets, Thomire bronzes, Biennais silver. The walls were hung, not only with the monumental battle scenes that were as much propaganda as painting but with portraits in which he appeared as self-confident and as regal as any of the monarchs who had preceded him. Huge allegorical murals represented him as hardly less than god-like. The light-hearted furniture of the late eighteenth century was replaced by the altogether more heroic Empire style: their pastel colours and floral patterns giving way to bold reds, greens and, above all, gold. The whole effect was more military, more classical, more assertive. The new imperial emblems – the crowned Ns, the laurel wreaths, the golden bees, the eagles – were everywhere. No one appreciated better than Napoleon the potency of such symbols.

Nor did he ever forget that the real basis of all this magnificence was the army. The Imperial Guard formed a highly visible element of his court. Its four colonel-generals were part of his military household; its dazzlingly uniformed soldiers and its swaggering bands added 'incomparable glamour'[13] to the Napoleonic palaces. The Emperor's official appearances among his soldiers were always the most spectacularly stage-managed of his many public appearances. With him, militarism went hand-in-hand with imperialism: he was fully alive to the pulse-quickening effect of military parades.

On the Champs de Mars he presented the army with new colours designed by himself on the model of the Roman legions' eagle standard: 'these eagles will always serve you as rallying points,' he proclaimed, 'they will be wherever your Emperor judges it necessary for the defence of his throne and his people....'[14] With the Empress by his side ('in a cloud of pale pink tulle sparkling with silver stars...and an arrangement of diamond wheat ears in her hair'[15]), he distributed crosses of the order of the Légion d'honneur to members of the army, the government and the court.

'Napoleon had discovered,' claims Claire de Rémusat, 'that France's secret weakness was vanity, that it was difficult to prevent Frenchmen from ranging themselves on the side of glory...the avidity with which men sought the titles, badges and crosses he distributed proved that he was not mistaken.'[16]

A new imperial nobility was established; a complete hierarchy of princes, dukes, counts, barons and knights. To those die-hard Jacobins who grumbled at this revival of rank and title, Napoleon could claim that it not only associated nobility with public service (as opposed to the old hereditary feudal system) but it reconciled the old France to the new.

Not that the old France needed a great deal of reconciling. Gradually, and then in a steady stream, the ancient *noblesse* rallied to the new regime. Napoleon was sometimes seen to smile as his eye ran down the list of names of those who were suddenly anxious to be received at his parvenu court. His swashbuckling young marshals and their lowly born wives found themselves rubbing shoulders with bearers of long-established titles who, until recently, had jeered at the pretensions of the Corsican.

'I noticed at this time with some amusement,' writes Claire de Rémusat, 'as by degrees the *grands seigneurs* of former days came to court, they all experienced, no matter how widely their characters differed, a certain sense of disappointment curious to observe. At first – when they breathed once more the air of palaces; found themselves again amongst their former associates, and in the atmosphere of their youth; beheld anew decorations, throne rooms, and court costumes, and heard the forms of speech habitual in royal dwellings – they yielded to the delightful illusion. They fondly believed that they might conduct themselves as they had been accustomed to do in these same palaces, where all but the master remained unchanged.

'But a harsh word, a peremptory order, the pressure of an arbitrary will, soon reminded them roughly that everything was new in this unique court ... the arts of the courtier availed nothing with Bonaparte and so profited them not at all ... it was easier and quicker for everybody to assume the attitude of servility.'[17]

Occasionally, though, a hint of aristocratic disdain broke through this newly acquired mask of acceptance. When Madame de Chevreuse, ablaze with diamonds, came to a reception at the Tuileries, Napoleon – intending perhaps to put her in her place – asked if her jewels were real. 'Heavens, Sire, I don't really know,' she answered airily. 'But at any rate, they're good enough to wear here.'[18] And when the Emperor asked a visiting *marchese* if it were true that he was descended from some Roman general, the nobleman replied that he could not prove it: the claim had been made by his family for only twelve hundred years.

What the relics of the *ancien régime* could not approve of was the pace of the imperial court; everything was done in a rush. Ceremonies were conducted 'as if directed by the roll of a drum'. It was magnificent in its way, complained one aristocrat, but it lacked ease, it lacked dignity. The Emperor 'could never get over that precipitation which gave him an ill-bred air,'[19] agreed another.

Madame de Rémusat's description of an imperial procession certainly bears this out. A group of court ladies, with their long trains flung over their arms so as to hurry along more easily, is being urged to go even faster by the chamberlains who, nearly treading on their heels keep repeating 'Allons, allons, mesdames, *avancez donc!*' ('They ought to call us the Palace postilions,' grumbles the Countess d'Arberg, scrambling along with the rest.) All this urgency is due to the Emperor who, bringing up the rear, is impatiently prodding the grand chamberlain walking just in front of him.

The Emperor's lack of small talk was another un-royal characteristic. While Josephine made her way slowly and graciously around the circle of guests, asking, listening and nodding her head sympathetically, Napoleon would bark out a few abrupt questions and hurry on. He, who was famous for remembering the faces of his soldiers, could seldom remember those of his guests. At one Sunday afternoon reception, the well-known composer, André Grétry, who had been presented to the Emperor on countless occasions, was asked, yet again, for his name.

'Sire,' answered the composer, 'I am *still* Grétry.'

Another anecdote concerns one of those newly converted aristocrats, the Duchesse de Brissac who, resplendent in glittering gold train, came to the Tuileries to make her obeisance to the new sovereign. Being slightly deaf, the duchess memorised the answers to the three questions which the Emperor invariably asked: her name, the department from which she came, and her age.

But on this occasion, having heard her name, Napoleon changed the formula for the next two questions.

'Your husband must be the brother of the Duc de Brissac massacred at Versailles,' he said. 'Have you inherited his estate?'

'Seine et Oise, Sire,' she answered, adhering to her prepared answers.

Napoleon was astonished. 'Have you any children?' he asked.

'Sire, fifty-two,'[20] came the serene reply.

Yet in private, and when the theme interested him, Napoleon could talk with an authority and a fluency that was beyond the capabilities of any monarch born to the purple. Metternich, who arrived as Austrian ambassador in 1806, once paid tribute to Napoleon's powers of conversation.

'What at first struck me most was the remarkable perspicuity and grand simplicity of his mind and its processes,' wrote Metternich. 'Conversation with him always had a charm for me, difficult to define. Seizing the essential point of subjects, stripping them of useless accessories, developing his thought and never ceasing to elaborate it till he had made it perfectly clear and conclusive, always finding the fitting word for the thing, or inventing one where the image of language had not created it, his conversation was ever full of interest. Yet he did not fail to listen to the remarks and objections addressed to him. He accepted them, questioned them or opposed them, without losing the tone or overstepping the bounds of a business conversation; and I have never felt the least difficulty in saying to him what I believed to be the truth, even when it was not likely to please him.'[21]

19

---•◦◦◦◦•---

The Swan

SIMPLICITY was hardly the keynote of the Empress Josephine's private life. On the contrary, it was luxurious in the extreme. Yet it was a curiously sterile kind of luxury: 'she lived quietly, always kind and pleasant,' says Claire de Rémusat, 'but detached, indifferent, languid, idle. If she was not a pleasure-seeker, neither did she seek escape from boredom.'[1] Cut off from her children and grandchildren (Hortense was now Queen of Holland, Eugène Viceroy of Italy), Josephine devoted herself – when not on public display – to her appearance, her amusements and the cultivation of her gardens at Malmaison.

Woken, at the Tuileries or Saint-Cloud, at eight each morning by her two maids on duty, and having breakfasted in bed, the Empress would spend the next three hours getting dressed. After a leisurely scented bath, she would seat herself at her mirrored dressing table. Her maids could then begin the daily ritual: tinting her chestnut hair, patting on astringent, smoothing in cream, applying skin whitener, powder and rouge. As with so many women in her position, Josephine's maids were her chief confidantes. With Napoleon ordering her to cut ties with several of her former friends and to be careful in what she said to her ladies-in-waiting, Josephine was obliged to discuss her intimate affairs with her maids.

In the early days of the reign, Josephine had been delighted to find herself surrounded by so numerous and aristocratic a suite of ladies-in-waiting; even she, says one observer, had had her head turned by this bevy of 'real *grandes dames*'. But not for long. Napoleon soon put her right. 'The Empress always knew perfectly well how to preserve the supremacy of her own rank,' writes Claire de Rémusat, 'while showing polite deference towards those men and women who enhanced the splendour of her court by their personal distinction.'[2]

Once her *maquillage* had been completed and she had been helped into a lacy *peignoir*, Josephine received her ladies. They would sit about gossiping while her *coiffeur*, in embroidered coat and ceremonial sword, did her hair, and while her wardrobe mistress and assistants carried in clothes for the day's – or rather, the morning's – selection. They could hardly have carried them all in for, according to the inventory for the year 1809, there were almost a thousand dresses in Josephine's wardrobes; in that year alone she bought over five hundred pairs of shoes to add to the two hundred and fifty pairs she had purchased the year before. She changed everything, including her lingerie, three times a day. And so now, with much discussion and enormous pleasure, she would decide on what stockings, petticoats, dresses, slippers, shawls, cloaks, scarves and, finally, jewellery, she should wear.

Dressed and perfumed, she would leave her own suite – the Interior Apartment – comprising library, boudoir, bedroom, dressing room and bathroom – and enter the Apartment of Honour with its antechamber, three salons, dining room and concert room. Having taken three hours to dress, she would only just be in time for luncheon, invariably served at eleven. Occasionally Napoleon would join her and her ladies for the meal; more often, he was content to have a hastily swallowed cup of coffee with them.

If she went out driving in the afternoon, Josephine would be accompanied, not only by a couple of ladies-in-waiting, but by her equerries, an officer, a trumpeter and a troop of cavalrymen. But more often she stayed at home. As the gardens of the Tuileries were open to the public, she could hardly walk there, so she tended to remain indoors – chatting, playing cards, listening to music or doing embroidery. Often she would receive her doctor (although, apart from 'nervous' headaches, her health was good) or her librarian, Abbé Nicholas Halna.

More of a tutor than a librarian, Halna was considerably impressed by the quickness with which the Empress mastered the curriculum Napoleon had asked him to set her: a course in the history and traditions of the courts of Europe, including the genealogies of all the royal houses. The result was that, at any gathering of crowned heads, ambassadors or statesmen, the Empress Josephine never put a foot wrong; her knowledge of rank, titles and family relationships was faultless; she never committed a social or diplomatic gaffe.

Josephine wrote countless letters and notes. Usually they were on behalf of friends or relatives for whom she was trying to get posts or pensions. But there were other supplicants who, knowing something of her kind heart and inability to refuse a request, bombarded her with begging letters. She always passed them on, with a recommendation, to the appropriate quarter.

But Josephine was not quite as altruistic as she appeared. 'My dear Carnot,' she once explained to a minister who had objected to the number of her requests, 'don't pay any attention to my recommendations or my notes. People get them from me by pestering me, and I give them indiscriminately to all and sundry.'[3] Claire de Rémusat bears this out. 'She promised everything, and sent everyone away well pleased,' she writes. 'Their petitions were put aside and lost sometimes, but they brought fresh ones, and she never seemed tired of listening.'[4]

Having already changed her clothes during the afternoon, the Empress would change again into one of her most elaborate evening dresses for dinner even if she were dining, quite alone, with the Emperor. For this her resident hairdresser, Herbault, who did her hair in the mornings, would not be considered skilled enough. It called for that master *coiffeur*, Duplan. His pay was rumoured to exceed that of a brigadier-general and he was the only person to be trusted with one of those intricately flowered, feathered or jewelled evening confections.

Often, the Emperor and Empress would preside over a ball or concert in the palace. Side by side they would sit in their gilt chairs (Napoleon had decreed that only he and Josephine could have armchairs; even the other members of the imperial family had to make do with stools), with the Emperor looking on at the dancing 'with a countenance so little encouraging to gaiety, that enjoyment was out of the question.'[5]

Yet even he must have felt gratified by the brilliance of it all. The quadrilles were particularly colourful. Sixteen ladies, in groups of four, would be dressed in white, each group wearing different coloured flowers in their hair and on their dresses; their sixteen gentlemen partners would be wearing white satin coats, with scarves corresponding in colour to their partner's flowers.

The concerts in the *Salle des Maréchaux*, decorated with portraits of Napoleon's marshals, were no less impressive. The concert would be followed, first by a ballet and then by a gala supper in the Gallery of Diana. Here, says one observer, 'the beauty of the apartment, the number of the lights, the sumptuousness of the tables, the display of silver and glass, added to the elegant dresses of the guests, gave a fairy-like effect to these entertainments.'[6]

But on other nights Josephine would sit, elaborately coiffured and shimmeringly dressed, with just one or two other ladies, waiting for Napoleon to appear from his study. Sometimes he arrived late, sometimes not at all. But she never complained. Provided he were not with some other woman, she remained the perfect wife: long-suffering, sweet-tempered, boundlessly sympathetic. Her ladies might be disconcerted by her indolence and her shallowness but they understood, very well, that these qualities formed part of her attraction for her increasingly egocentric husband.

'If he was ever really stirred by any emotion,' claims one of them, 'it was by her and for her.'[7]

More, perhaps, than for her charm and her chic, the Empress Josephine is remembered for her extravagance. She has gone down in history as one of the most recklessly extravagant women in the world.

The general costs of the Empress's household were administered by the so-called Treasury of the Crown. Her personal expenditure, which was the cause of the trouble, fell under two headings: the *Cassette* and the *Toilette*. The *Cassette* enabled Josephine to contribute to numerous worthy causes, to provide for various pensions and to make special gifts to individuals in need. On the whole, the *Cassette* was ably administered by a civil servant who seldom exceeded the allotted annual sum.

The *Toilette* was a very different matter. Out of this handsome allowance Josephine was meant to contribute to more personal charities and to spend the rest on clothes and jewellery. But each year she got through about double the allotted amount, so producing a huge annual deficit. To this deficit were added the large debts accumulated during the years of the Consulate. So, all in all, Josephine's annual personal expenditure was in the region of one million francs; which, by a rough conversion, equals more than half a million pounds sterling or almost a million United States dollars.

Where did all this money go? Her charities were innumerable. She handed out money to almost anyone who asked for it. She even provided a pension for her first husband's ex-mistress, that same Madame de Longpré who had been largely responsible for the collapse of her marriage to Alexandre de Beauharnais. And in the same way that she gave money to whoever asked for it, she bought whatever was being offered to her for sale. 'She bought everything,' says Claire de Rémusat, 'and without even asking the price, and most of the time immediately forgot what she had purchased. The waiting rooms off her private apartments were always crowded with merchants and merchandise of every sort and description.'[8]

'The truth was,' concurs her maid, Mademoiselle Avrillon, 'she had an uncontrollable passion for everything beautiful. One couldn't even say that she had a special penchant for this or that, one kind of thing more than another. Everything beautiful, artistic, in good taste caught her fancy, and she simply had to have it – whatever it was, whatever it cost. Often she bought extremely expensive objects for which she had no use whatsoever, merely for the pleasure of acquiring them. No-one in the world, I might add here, had such exquisitely refined taste as she; but then, those artists and artisans who vied with one another to display their wares before her were all masters in their specialities, so all were accepted. To make it worse, she could never summon up the courage to turn away a tradesman without making a purchase of some kind.'[9]

And often, having bought something at an outrageous price, she simply gave it away. Silver boxes, gold chains, bottles of scent, baskets of sweetmeats, lengths of material, mechanical toys – monkeys playing violins, flowering trees full of singing birds – portraits and miniatures of herself painted by celebrated artists, all these she presented to friends, acquaintances and servants. Her generosity was boundless, impulsive and quite indiscriminate.

But most of the money went on personal adornment; on her clothes and her jewels. In spite of having all the crown jewels of France at her disposal, the Empress bought well over one million francs' worth of jewellery. And even this dazzling collection of diamonds, pearls, emeralds and rubies she was constantly having reset and refashioned, happily paying whatever price the gratified jewellers chose to charge for their services.

Her vast, walk-in wardrobes were crammed with clothes: with dresses in velvet, silk, muslin, voile and organdie; with lacy underclothes and frothy *peignoirs*; with chiffon scarves, cashmere shawls, fur-edged wraps; with satin shoes, kid gloves, flesh-coloured tights, feathered hats, lace parasols, artificial flowers. She never wore a pair of stockings twice. 'The quietest party, the smallest dance, was an opportunity for ordering a new dress,'[10] writes one of her ladies. One season she would be in polka-dotted turbans; in another she would be wearing lace ruffs; in a third she would be sporting fabrics shot through with gold or silver. Whether on grand state occasions, in gold-embroidered white satin, or at Malmaison in some simple shift, the Empress Josephine never looked anything less than perfectly groomed, transcendently smart, ineffably romantic.

Yet extravagant as she might have been as a woman, Josephine was not spectacularly extravagant as an empress. When set against the spending of women like Queen Marie Antoinette, the Marquise de Pompadour or Madame Du Barry (who had a diamond collar made for her dog), Josephine's extravagance seems almost bourgeois. She did not build sumptuous palaces or give outrageously expensive parties or run up vast gambling debts. Her profligacy would never have contributed, as did theirs, towards the downfall of a regime. Josephine's recklessness was that of a woman who has known poverty and was now making up for it, rather than that of a spoiled, insensitive, pleasure-seeking wastrel. She might have been self-indulgent but she was never selfish. When compared with the palaces, châteaux and pavilions built by previous French monarchs, Malmaison was a very modest home.

Not that Napoleon was prepared to see things in this perspective. So simple in his own personal tastes, so conscious of the value of money, so concerned with efficiency and economy, so determined not to be overcharged, the Emperor was in despair about the way money seemed to slip like water through his wife's fingers. In an effort to put a stop to the hoards of merchants who crowded the back corridors of Josephine's apartments, Napoleon decreed that no tradesperson was to approach the Empress directly.

The decree was soon violated. One day, on his way to see

Josephine, Napoleon passed a woman sitting on a mountain of hatboxes.

'Who are you?' demanded the Emperor.

'I am called Despeaux,' she answered.

'What do you do?'

'I am a milliner, Sire.'

Furious, Napoleon burst into Josephine's dressing room. 'I demand to know who sent for that woman!'[11] he shouted.

Poor Josephine, with the *coiffeur* dressing her hair and the pedicurist manicuring her feet, was too terrified to admit that she had sent for Madame Despeaux and Napoleon promptly ordered the woman's arrest. Only the intervention of the grand marshal of the palace saved Madame Despeaux from being hauled off to prison.

'On such occasions as these,' says Mademoiselle Avrillon, 'the Empress, groaning in silence, met the Emperor's tantrums with an unshakable sweetness and gentleness . . . But on his behalf it is only fair to say that these rages of his were of a short duration; he never harboured resentments.'

Much worse, and of considerably longer duration, were the scenes that followed Josephine's annual, and inevitable, realisation that she had exceeded her allowance. 'Then,' says Mademoiselle Avrillon, 'she had to turn to the Emperor to liquidate her debts, and though he always ended up by doing so, it was only after the most violent scenes. The Emperor raged, the Empress wept; a reconciliation invariably followed, but these altercations were so shattering to her nerves that she invariably made a resolve never again to allow herself to become so involved. But, just as invariably, her acquisitive mania won out once more over her resolve, and she was soon back at it again, running up bills with all the tradesmen of the capital. Her extravagance was the principal basis for her husband's complaints.'[12]

Yet in spite of all this, there were times when Napoleon, suddenly catching sight of his *soignée* wife, would feel almost overwhelmed by a blend of pride and affection. Laure Junot was with the Empress in the Blue Salon at Saint-Cloud one day in 1806 when the Emperor entered the room.

'Josephine was a vision in misty white *mousseline de l'Inde*, with a narrow lamé border like a rivulet of gold around the hemline of the pleated skirt, a gold-and-black enamelled lion's head at each shoulder and another as clasp for the golden belt.

Her *coiffure* was like that of an antique cameo, curls spilling out of a golden circlet, and she wore a golden serpent for a necklace, with matching earrings and bracelets. If there was a striking simplicity in her costume, it was simplicity of the most artful kind; if it was tremendously becoming, it was because Josephine always adapted the mode to her person – one explanation for her reputation as the most elegant of women.

'It was clear that the Emperor was as struck as I by her charming ensemble, for he went to her as he entered the room, kissed her on the shoulder and the brow, and led her to the mirror over the mantle so that he might see her from all sides at the same time.

'"Now, now, Josephine, I think I should be jealous. You must have some conquest in mind. Why are you so beautiful today?"

'"I know that you love to see me in white, and so I put on a white gown, that's all."

'"Very well, then, if it was to please me, you have indeed succeeded." Whereupon he kissed her again.'[13]

20

The Turning Point

CAROLINE MURAT, the most implacable of Josephine's Bonaparte enemies, proved also the most resourceful. In 1806 she came up with what she imagined would be the perfect scheme for persuading Napoleon to rid himself of his wife: his ability to procreate must be proved by means of a properly controlled experiment. Only when he knew, beyond a shadow of doubt, that he could father a child, would he consider divorcing Josephine.

Obviously, none of the succession of amoral actresses and adventuresses with whom Napoleon usually diverted himself could be considered suitable for the sort of experiment Caroline Murat had in mind. What was needed was a young woman who could be kept under strict surveillance for the necessary period of time. Caroline had the perfect candidate to hand: an attractive, seductive and sophisticated eighteen-year-old named Eléonore Denuelle de la Plaigne, whose husband had just been arrested for forgery. She would be immured in a pavilion on the Murats' estate at Neuilly and would be taken, under close supervision, to the Tuileries for regular meetings with the Emperor. No other man would be allowed near her.

As Napoleon was ready, and Eléonore Denuelle more than ready, to fall in with Caroline Murat's scheme, it was put in hand that spring. The Emperor seems, though, to have conducted this affair with even more perfunctoriness than usual; one eye, noted Eléonore, was always on the clock. The result was that Eléonore

207

quickly tired of her lover's strictly rationed love making, and found even the short periods she spent in his company too long for her liking. On one occasion, as the two of them lay on the couch in Napoleon's study, she was able to reach out behind his back and surreptitiously advance the hands of a nearby clock. 'So soon?' exclaimed the Emperor on glancing at the clock. He promptly got up and resumed his desk work.

By September that year Napoleon – and, in that whispering gallery of a court, Josephine – knew that Eléonore Denuelle was pregnant. This time the Empress said nothing. She had at last, it appears, learned resignation. 'Either that,' says Claire de Rémusat, 'or she no longer had the strength to make useless scenes. At any rate, only her air of sadness revealed her secret sorrow.'[1]

Josephine had a further cause for sorrow in that September of 1806. Napoleon was about to set off, once again, for battle. That month Prussia, uneasy at Napoleon's increasingly high-handed behaviour in Germany, threatened war unless he withdrew his *Grand Armée* beyond the Rhine. As there could be no question of that, Napoleon was obliged to take up the challenge. On his last victorious campaign he had faced the Austro-Russian armies; this time he would be fighting a coalition of Russia and Prussia. On 24 September, he left for the Rhineland.

With him went Josephine. They travelled together only as far as Mainz. Here, after three days, he left her; he was heading northeast to meet the advancing Prussian forces in Saxony.

Their parting was highly emotional. 'The Emperor held his wife for the longest time in his arms, as if unwilling to release her,' noted the watching Monsieur de Rémusat, husband of Josephine's lady-in-waiting and a member of Napoleon's household.

'It is painful indeed to leave those one loves best in the world,' sighed Napoleon.

'Then,' continued Rémusat, 'repeating his words, the Emperor gave way to tears; a sort of nervous spasm seized him, and he went into convulsions which brought on severe vomiting.'[2]

Unsuspected at the time, the couple would not see each other again for ten months. And when they did, the tenor of their relationship would have changed irretrievably.

Once again, Napoleon won a brilliant victory. For all its formidable reputation, the Prussian army proved to be far too cumbersome for the more supple French forces. In the twin battles of Jena and Auerstadt, fought on 14 October 1806, the French smashed the Prussians to pieces. Within three weeks all Prussia was conquered and the Emperor of the French had made his triumphant entry into Berlin, passing under that monument to Prussia's vanished glory, the Brandenburg Gate. He slept at Sans Souci, the elegant Potsdam palace of Frederick the Great, and appropriated the late Prussian king's sword and alarm clock as spoils of war.

Flushed with his victory Napoleon decided to march into Poland to beat the advancing Russian army as well. By 19 December the Emperor had arrived in Warsaw to direct the coming battle in person.

During these weeks he had been writing cheerful letters to Josephine, still waiting in Mainz. She certainly needed cheering up. Bored, depressed, vaguely apprehensive, Josephine spent much of her time in tears. Not even the presence of her daughter Hortense, Queen of Holland, with her two little sons, or of her niece, Crown Princess Stephanie of Baden, could dispel her black mood. She attended the various fêtes and galas in her honour, she squandered money on jewellery for herself and gifts for others, she played innumerable games of solitaire. But she remained low spirited.

'I don't know why you should be weeping,' wrote Napoleon from Berlin. 'I am feeling marvellously fit and well, and you have had news of my successes.'

'Talleyrand has arrived and tells me that you do nothing but cry,' he wrote on another occasion. 'But why? You have your daughter, your grandchildren, and good news from me; everything to make you content and happy.'[3]

But the only thing guaranteed to make Josephine content and happy would be a reunion with Napoleon. She longed to join him. For not only was she by now deeply in love with her husband but, in his absence, she always felt adrift, unfulfilled, insecure. Josephine had never been self-sufficient. Without Napoleon's assured presence, she was unable to play the Empress, unable to handle her large retinue, unable to apply herself to her duties and obligations.

Throughout the months of November and December she begged to be allowed to join him, but he, for a variety of reasons, put her off. Using the weapons of affection, flattery and cajolery, he kept her at bay. Sometimes he said that she must merely postpone her departure, at others he warned her that she must not think of facing the hazards and hardships of winter travel.

Napoleon's objections to her joining him were – at this stage – genuine enough. Her presence at the front, or even in Berlin, would be too much of a distraction for a commander who had yet to face the Russian army. And she could hardly complain about the tone of his letters: they were never anything less than charming. Referring to the intervention of the redoubtable Queen Louise of Prussia on behalf of the conquered Prussians, Napoleon assured Josephine that, above all else, he hated an intriguing woman. 'I am accustomed to women who are good, gentle and conciliatory; those are the sort I like. If such ones have spoiled me, it's not my fault, but yours ... I like women who are good, simple and sweet – because only such ones resemble you.'[4]

During this anguished period of waiting, Josephine seems to have dreamed one night that Napoleon had met, and fallen in love with, a Polish beauty. He, on hearing about the dream, dismissed it as nonsense. 'Here in the wastes of Poland, one gives little thought to beauties ...,' he reassured her on 2 December. 'Besides, there is only one woman for me. Do you know her? I could describe her to you but I don't want you to become conceited; yet, in truth, I could say nothing but good about her. The nights are long here, all alone!'[5]

'Your recent letters have really made me laugh,' he wrote later. 'You overestimate the fascination of Polish ladies.'[6]

This letter was written on the last day of 1806, from Pultusk in Poland, where Napoleon's forces had just won a minor victory over the Russians. That same day brought him news of a different, and more personally significant, sort of victory as well. A courier came galloping into headquarters with a letter from the Emperor's sister Caroline Murat. It told him that Eléonore Denuelle had given birth, on 13 December, to a male child.

That was one blow for Josephine. The next week brought another. For on 7 January 1807 Napoleon met, as Josephine had dreamed he would, a Polish beauty. Her name was Marie Walewska.

The couple met at a reception given in the old palace of the Polish kings in Warsaw. The twenty-year-old Countess Walewska was one of the crowd who had assembled in the brilliantly lit ballroom to greet the man whom the Poles regarded as the liberator of their country. For years poor, dismembered, Poland had suffered at the hands of Russia, Prussia and Austria. Now, into their lives had come a saviour whose enemies were their enemies, and who was said to be thinking in terms of re-establishing an independent kingdom of Poland.

Of that roomful of Polish patriots gathered to pay homage to the Emperor, few were more patriotic than Marie Walewska. And, by now, all her fervent patriotism was concentrated on the figure of Napoleon. His portrait had pride of place among those of the Polish heroes that adorned her walls; his writings and pronouncements had become gospel to her. Now, on actually being presented to her hero, she felt as though a dream were coming true.

Napoleon's interest in her was distinctly less elevated. '*Ah, qu'il y a de jolies femmes à Varsovie*'[7] he exclaimed as Countess Walewska, in her pale blue velvet dress, dropped her curtsey. She was the sort of young woman he would not mind seeing again, in private.

But Marie Walewska was a far cry from the sort of adventuress with whom Napoleon was usually associated. Although only twenty, she was married to a seventy-year-old, twice-widowed Polish nobleman and was known to be modest, chaste and devoutly religious. With her curly blonde hair and bright blue eyes she was an undoubted beauty but it was to be for her other qualities – her charm and her gentleness – that Napoleon would find her so enchanting. She was, in temperament, a carbon copy of Josephine; one of those 'good, simple and sweet' women Napoleon preferred.

Unlike Josephine, though, Marie Walewska was not sexually compliant. Napoleon soon discovered that it would need more than a simple invitation to get her into his bed. The more resolutely she resisted, the more ardently he pursued. He wrote her impassioned letters, he sent her expensive gifts, he tried emotional blackmail. 'Think how much dearer your country will be to me if you take pity on my poor heart,'[8] he argued. In the end, it was a plea by her friends that she 'surrender' herself in the all-transcending cause of Polish independence (a plea in which her old husband fervently joined) that finally won her round. For Poland, Marie Walewska made the supreme sacrifice. Or so she protests.

211

Writing, with all the fervour of the Romantic Movement, she shows us the 'wild' Emperor flinging his watch to the floor and swearing that if she persisted in refusing him her love, he would grind her people into dust, like the watch under his heel. In the face of threats like this, she felt obliged to succumb. But she did not do so, she assures us, until the second night.

Marie's claim that she fainted dead away at the moment of the consummation of her sacrifice might explain – if one were feeling generously disposed – why Napoleon, years later, said that she did not struggle 'overmuch'. But it is quite possible that, in giving herself to Napoleon, this normally chaste young woman was both swept away by her patriotism and bedazzled by his reputation. 'The dove,' as she quotes him as saying, could not escape the 'swooping eagle'.

Having swooped, the eagle promptly fell in love with his prey. That his love for her was, in her own words, 'transitory' made it no less genuine. Of the dozens of women with whom Napoleon was extra-maritally involved, Marie Walewska was the only one towards whom he displayed any tenderness, the only one with whom he was prepared to spend more than just an hour or two at a time. Napoleon loved her, not only for her youth and her Josephine-like sweetness and docility, but for her burning love of her homeland. 'Little patriot' or 'You who so dearly love your country' is how he would begin his letters to her.

Their idyll was interrupted in February 1807 when Napoleon was obliged to face the advancing Russians. The battle of Eylau, fought on 8 February in a blinding snowstorm, was one of the most appalling, and inconclusive, of Napoleon's career to date. Casualties on both sides were enormous, with the French losing nearly a third of their deployed strength. Although the Emperor presented it to his countrymen as yet another great victory, he was obliged to withdraw into winter quarters. He could only hope to inflict a more decisive defeat on the Russians in the spring.

Whatever hardships might have been endured by the French troops in the wastes of East Prussia were not shared by their Emperor. He had established himself in the comfort of the fortified Schloss Finckenstein. It was, he wrote to Josephine, 'a fine château in the style of Bessières. There are many fireplaces which is very pleasant seeing that I rise often during the night. I love to see a fire.'[9] What he did not tell Josephine was that with him, in this richly furnished and well-heated castle, was the delectable Marie

Walewska. For almost two months – April and May – Napoleon and Marie were closeted together. By now, Napoleon was beginning to refer to her as his 'Polish wife'. Even his valet Constant, who adored Josephine, had to admit that the love of this 'angelic woman, with her sweet, unselfish nature'[10] was of the deepest, most disinterested kind.

The Emperor's only disappointment was that his mistress, whom he had known since January, was showing no signs of pregnancy. She had, after all, already borne her seventy-year-old husband a child. During the same period Napoleon received reports, from his ever-vigilant secret police in Paris, that his sister Caroline's experiment had not been as watertight as he had assumed. Eléonore Denuelle seems to have shared her favours with Caroline's lusty husband, Joachim Murat. The child could just as well have been Murat's so Napoleon was still not convinced that he could father a child.

Nor did Marie Walewska's 'sacrifice' bear fruit of another sort. Her only desire, she had claimed on agreeing to give herself to Napoleon, was the 'renaissance' of Poland. In this she was to be disappointed. Napoleon, always conscious of the fact that the Bourbons had done themselves incalculable harm by building too many palaces and giving their mistresses too much say, was resolved to do neither. So in spite of all his promises or half-promises to Marie Walewska on the question of restoring Polish independence, he had no intention of doing any such thing. It would only lead to future entanglements with Russia and Austria. He was to make a few gestures towards Polish independence – mainly through the creation of the puppet state of the Grand Duchy of Warsaw – and left it at that.

Although Marie Walewska's feelings towards Napoleon were always to remain affectionate, the same could not be said of the majority of her fellow patriots. 'He thinks of nothing but himself,' scoffed the national hero Kosciuszko. 'He detests every great nation, and he detests even more the spirit of independence. He is a tyrant.'[11]

And all the time Josephine was waiting to be reunited with Napoleon. From Mainz she wrote again and again, begging to be allowed to join him. Whatever his reasons might have been for refusing her request in the past, they were now quite obvious: he did not want his idyll with Marie Walewska disturbed.

'The weather is too bad, the roads are unsure and atrocious, the distances are too great for me to permit you to come here where my business keeps me,' he wrote firmly from Warsaw in January.'It would take you a month to get here. You would arrive ill; possibly you would have to return at once; it would be folly. Your stay in Mainz is too depressing; Paris calls you; go there, such is my will...'[12]

But still she lingered in Mainz, hoping against hope that he might send for her. But in every letter he instructed her to return to Paris. Finally, towards the end of January, she yielded and, forcing herself to be gracious during the receptions that greeted her *en route*, arrived back in Paris at the end of the month.

She was hardly back before she heard, 'from several Polish ladies then resident in Paris'[13], about Marie Walewska. Afraid to tackle Napoleon head-on about the affair, Josephine would hint at it in her letters to him. He tried to allay her suspicions with jokes and evasions. 'Put no faith in the evil rumours which may be spread about,' he wrote. 'Never doubt my feelings towards you, and have no uneasiness.'[14]

'I don't understand what you say about women who are corresponding with me,' he wrote on another occasion. 'I love only my little Josephine, kindly, sulky and capricious, who can quarrel as gracefully as she does everything else; she is always adorable – except when she is suspicious; then she becomes a regular devil.'[15]

He was not too busy calming her fears, however, to forget to send her a list of instructions on how to deport herself. 'Grandeur has its price,' he lectured, 'an Empress cannot live like a private citizen.'[16] She was to behave exactly as though he were there. At the end of April she must leave the winter palace of the Tuileries for the summer palace of Saint-Cloud. She could go to Malmaison for weekends but, as her stay there was informal, she must never receive ambassadors or strangers. He was pleased to hear that she had resumed her formal weekly receptions, that she had attended fêtes in her honour and that she had visited the opera. She could go to one of the four principal theatres but she must never patronise the small theatres of which she was so fond, nor must she ever sit in anything other than the imperial box. She must extend dinner invitations only to those already on their guest list and he forbade her, 'absolutely', to have anything to do with her great friend of those devil-may-care Directory days, Thérèse Tallein. 'She used to be a nice enough trollop,' he wrote, 'she has become a horrible, infamous woman.'[17]

One of the parties which Josephine was permitted to attend was a fête given in her honour by her sisters-in-law, Pauline Borghese and Caroline Murat. A comedy was enacted in which the two princesses, dressed as shepherdesses, not only recited verses in praise of the Emperor and Empress but sang – excruciatingly out of tune. Claire de Rémusat admitted to being greatly amused by the 'mutual spitefulness' of the two princesses and claims that Josephine was completely unimpressed by the 'insincere homage' of her sisters-in-law.

Separated from her husband, cut off from her old friends, obliged to keep aloof from her ladies-in-waiting, Josephine took comfort from her correspondence with her children, Eugène and Hortense – the former in the Vice-regal Palace in Milan, the latter in the Royal Palace in The Hague. Her chief complaint was that she saw so little of them.

Yet when she next saw Hortense, it was under the most tragic circumstances. Early in May 1807, Hortense's eldest son, the four-and-a-half-year-old Napoleon Charles, died of croup. Hortense was desolate. Josephine was hardly less upset. Napoleon, on hearing the news, dashed off letters to both Josephine and Hortense, begging them to moderate their sorrow.

'My daughter,' he instructed Hortense, 'all that I hear from The Hague tells me that you are not being sensible; however legitimate your grief, it must have limits. Do not injure your health; seek some distractions, and realise that life is strewn with so many dangers, and is the source of so many ills that death is not the greatest of them.'[18]

Was Napoleon thinking, perhaps, of those thousands of other grieving mothers whose sons had been sacrificed in the furtherance of his own ambitions?

Only after they had been given the Emperor's permission to leave their respective capitals could mother and daughter console one another. They met in yet another of those many palaces which now belonged to Napoleon: the Château de Laeken, near Brussels. Josephine was shocked at Hortense's condition; she was in a state of stupor. Dr Corvisart, who had accompanied the Empress, prescribed a trip to the Pyrenees. Hortense's husband, the normally irascible Louis, was so alarmed by his wife's condition that he not only gave her permission to go but later joined her there.

A brief spell of harmony followed and, sometime during that summer, a third son was conceived. Born the following year, and named Charles Louis Napoleon, he was to become the Emperor Napoleon III.

But, of course, in May 1807, the Empress Josephine could foresee none of this. For her, the death of her eldest grandson, Napoleon's favourite nephew whom he had always intended to adopt as his heir, came as a terrible blow. She knew, by now, that Eléonore Denuelle had given birth to a son and that Napoleon was involved in a serious love affair with Marie Walewska. Would the death of the little boy who might have been his successor finally make up Napoleon's mind to divorce her and to marry some young princess capable of bearing him an imperial heir?

Never, indeed, did Napoleon's Empire stand more in need of a direct heir. For in the weeks that followed the death of little Napoleon Charles, Napoleon achieved some of his greatest imperial triumphs.

At the battle of Friedland, fought against the Russians on 14 June 1807, the French at last won a decisive victory. 'Only one line, my love,' scrawled Napoleon to Josephine on that triumphant night, 'for I am very weary after many days bivouacking. My children have this day worthily celebrated the anniversary of the Battle of Marengo. The entire Russian army is in flight. Friedland is a victory worthy of her sister victories Marengo, Austerlitz and Jena, a name to become equally famous and glorious among my people....'[19]

Just over a week later the two emperors – the victorious Napoleon and the defeated Alexander – met on a tented and beflagged raft moored in the middle of the River Nieman, at Tilsit. To the sounds of trumpets, drums and cannon, the Emperor of the West and the Emperor of the East were rowed out simultaneously from opposite banks for half an hour's talk on the floating pavilion. They took to one another immediately; 'each of them seeing the other's greatness' as one of Napoleon's biographers has put it, 'as a reflection of his own.'[20] Napoleon was particularly impressed by the good-looking young Tsar; he later claimed that if Alexander had been a woman, he would have made him his 'mistress'.

In the course of a series of meetings, the two emperors negotiated a peace settlement. The result was the Treaty of Tilsit from which Napoleon emerged more triumphant than ever. Prussia, in spite of all the efforts of the beautiful Queen Louise, was reduced to the status of a second-rate power. Large parts of her territory went to the new kingdom of Westphalia (to be ruled by Napoleon's youngest brother Jerome); to the Grand Duchy of Berg (ruled by his brother-in-law Joachim Murat); and to make up, as that hollow gesture to Polish nationalism, the Grand Duchy of Warsaw. Russia was obliged to concede only minor possessions and to agree to join Napoleon's so-called Continental System – the blockade of Continental ports against British commerce.

Although Napoleon's Grand Empire was to become even grander the following year by the acquisition of Spain and Portugal, Tilsit marked, in many ways, the apogee of his achievements. He was now thirty-eight years old. The haggard young soldier described by Laure Junot had given way to the plump, self-assured, stern-eyed, balding, cameo-complexioned conqueror of Europe. A lady-in-waiting to the Queen of Prussia, who met him at Tilsit, talks of his excessive ugliness, his swollen face, his corpulent body, his great gloomy eyes and his severe features. He looked, she claimed, like 'the incarnation of fate'; but then she, like all the Prussian court, hated him.

A distinctly more flattering picture is painted by Count Molé in his memoirs. 'Napoleon's face, seen at such close quarters, struck me even more forcibly than the idea I had formed of it. I have always believed in faces. His was in keeping with his whole history. His head was superb, and unlike any other. In the depth of his skull, the formation of his splendid forehead, the setting of his eyes, his sculptured lips, the droop at the corner of his mouth, the beautiful proportions of his face, and the regularity of his features, but above all in his glance and his smile – in all this I thought I could recognize all the qualities which raise a man above his fellows, and make him fit to rule over them.'[21]

Whether Napoleon was, in fact, so fit to rule over his fellow men is a matter of conjecture but that he did rule over them there is no doubt. His vast domains were administered either by himself or by satellite sovereigns whose power was strictly limited to the carrying out of his orders. It was no wonder that, on his arrival back in Paris after ten months away, on 27 July 1807, he awarded himself with the title of Napoleon the Great. Or that his arrival ushered in a month-long series of balls, fêtes, receptions and military parades. His birthday, by now named 'The Feast of Saint Napoleon', was celebrated with a mass in the Cathedral of Notre-Dame.

'Sire,' fawned the President of the Senate in his official address to the returning hero, 'these are miraculous achievements for which probability would have asked centuries, and for which a few months have sufficed Your Majesty ... It is impossible worthily to praise Your Majesty. Your glory is too great. One has to place oneself at the distance of posterity to become aware of your immeasurable elevation.'[22]

By the Emperor's side, throughout all these triumphant festivities, stood his Empress. 'On rejoining his wife,' noted one of her ladies, 'he again felt for her the kind of affection with which she always inspired him, and which often made him uncomfortable, because it embarrassed him when he grieved her.'[23]

For in spite of all her failings – her debts, her jealousies and, most important, her childlessness – Josephine suited him so well. He realised that no legitimate empress, queen or princess in Europe at that time could match the parvenue Josephine in charm and elegance. And Napoleon, to whom an outward show meant so much, appreciated these qualities afresh each time he returned to her. Talking one day to Hortense about the beautiful Queen Louise of Prussia, Napoleon claimed that 'she does not compare with my Josephine'.[24]

21

━━━◆◆◆◆━━━

The Beginning of the End

IN the autumn of 1807 Napoleon moved his court to Fontainebleau for several weeks. This huge Renaissance palace, mirrored in its lake, was one of the Emperor's favourites: 'a real home of kings, the residence of the ages',[1] he would call it. Staying at Fontainebleau enabled him to associate himself even more closely with the previous reigning houses of Valois and Bourbon (he was by now blandly referring to Louis XVI as his 'uncle') and to hunt in the surrounding forests in which they had once hunted. This did not stop him, though, from leaving his own stamp on the palace. He spent millions of francs on introducing an Empire decor, including a throne room with a domed canopy of swagged red velvet embroidered with golden bees and supported by imperial standards, and a study rich in the bronze sphinxes and griffins that were all part of the distinctive imperial style.

To the hunt, too, Napoleon introduced new fashions. He commanded Leroy to design special hunting costumes. For the men, there were green coats decorated with gold or silver lace; each of the imperial princesses was obliged to dress her household in a different colour – pale blue for Hortense, pink for Caroline, lilac for Pauline. The Empress and her household wore amaranth, embroidered with gold. 'These brilliant costumes, worn either on horseback or in carriages, and by a numerous assemblage, had a charming effect in the beautiful forest of Fontainebleau,'[2] writes one member of the court.

Napoleon enjoyed hunting for the exercise which it obliged

him to take rather than for the pleasure of the chase itself. 'He did not follow the deer very carefully,' writes one observer, 'but, setting off at a gallop, would take the first road that lay before him. Sometimes he forgot the object of the hunt altogether, and followed the winding paths of the forest, or seemed to abandon himself to the fancy of his horse, being plunged the while in deep reverie. He rode well, but ungracefully.'[3]

Josephine enjoyed hunting even less. Although she dutifully followed the hunt, on set days, in her elegant calèche, she was far too soft hearted to relish the prospect of deer being hunted to death. On one occasion a terrified stag, to escape its pursuers, rushed under her carriage and was trapped there. Moved to tears by the animal's plight, she begged Napoleon to let it go free. He agreed. Josephine arranged for a silver collar to be put around the stag's neck, both to mark its deliverance and to save it from other huntsmen.

Josephine was able to give comfort of another sort at Fontainebleau that season: to the young, attractive and affable widower, Prince Frederick Louis of Mecklenburg-Schwerin. The prince had come to France to ask the Emperor if he would consider withdrawing the occupying French garrisons from his states. As the young man could get no definite answer from Napoleon, he appealed to Josephine. As always, the Empress listened to him with sympathy and patience. 'The unfailing kindness that distinguished Josephine, her sweet face, her lovely figure, the suave elegance of her person,' writes Claire de Rémusat, 'were not without their effect on the Prince. We saw, or believed we saw, that he was captivated; she laughed and was amused.'[4]

The twenty-nine-year-old Prince Frederick Louis was so captivated, in fact, that, after Josephine's divorce from Napoleon, he was to propose marriage to the forty-seven-year-old Empress. She would not hear of it.

Josephine, Claire goes on to say, 'was entirely devoid of coquetry; her manner was perfectly modest and reserved; she never spoke to a man except to find out what was going on.'[5]

For the Empress, this particular season at Fontainebleau was anything but relaxing. Napoleon, fresh from the arms of Marie Walewska, felt none the less compelled to chalk up yet more conquests ('But *no one* is supposed to refuse His Majesty *anything*!'[6] exclaimed Pauline Borghese on hearing that one of her ladies had rebuffed the Emperor's advances) and, as always, the

Empress soon knew all about it. But by now she had learned to hold her tongue. 'No more jealousy, no more scenes,'[7] as she put it in a letter to Eugène.

Infinitely more distressing for Josephine was the renewed talk of divorce. The air, that season at Fontainebleau, was thick with speculation on the subject. But for Napoleon, contemplation of divorce was always easier out of Josephine's presence than in it. Faced with her – looking so sad, so sweet, so *soignée* – he simply could not bring himself to broach the subject directly. So he would do so obliquely.

Talking on one occasion of the death of Hortense's eldest son, he manoeuvred the conversation to mention that 'perhaps one day' he might be forced to take a wife capable of giving him children. 'If such a thing should happen, Josephine, it is you who will have to help me make the sacrifice. I shall count upon your love to save me all the odium of a forced rupture. You would take the initiative, wouldn't you?'

But Josephine, whose attitude towards the divorce had always been one of passive resistance, refused to fall into his trap. 'Sire,' she answered calmly, 'you are the master, and you shall decide my fate. When you order me to leave the Tuileries, I will obey instantly, but the least you could do would be to order it in a positive manner. I am your wife; I have been crowned by you in the presence of the Pope. Such honours at least demand that they should not be voluntarily renounced. If you divorce me, all France will know that it is you who are driving me out....'[8]

The quiet dignity of her answers would touch him; they even, on occasions, reduced him to tears. But out of his presence she was much less controlled. She confided to Madame de Rémusat her fears that Napoleon might one day try to do away with her altogether. He might, she implied, have her poisoned. The lady-in-waiting, who was by now thoroughly disillusioned with Napoleon, none the less protested that he would never have entertained such an idea.

A few days after this conversation, the Empress one morning sent for Claire de Rémusat's husband. He found her 'half-undressed, pale and in great agitation.' Josephine showed him a letter which she had just received. It was from Fouché, the sinister Minister of Police. In it, Fouché urged her, at great length and with considerable skill, to grant Napoleon a divorce. 'The political future of France,' he claimed, 'is compromised by the want of an heir for the Emperor.'

Suspecting that Fouché had been primed by Napoleon (few of the Emperor's ministers acted independently of their master), Josephine was in a quandary. 'What shall I do?' she asked Rémusat. 'How shall I avert this storm?'

He advised her to go straight to the Emperor. This she did and Napoleon, protesting innocence in the matter, calmed her fears. It had been an 'excess of zeal' on the part of Fouché, explained Napoleon. 'We must not be angry with him for it; it is quite enough that we are determined to reject his advice, and you know well that I could not live without you.'

As though to emphasise these sentiments, Napoleon again began paying his wife 'nocturnal visits'; visits, says Claire de Rémusat, 'far more frequent than at any time in the recent past. Genuinely distressed, he clasped her in his arms, wept and vowed undying devotion.'[9]

Napoleon might not, in fact, have instigated Fouché's letter. Another Bonaparte – Josephine's enemy Caroline Murat – might well have been behind it. Fouché, by this stage, was fascinated by the lovely Caroline and she was using her powers of fascination to get him to encourage Napoleon to think about a divorce. By making use of his secret police, Fouché was able to get the subject of the necessity for an imperial heir discussed in cafés and brought up at public gatherings. This police-induced talk Fouché then repeated to Napoleon, leaving the Emperor with the impression that the public was far more concerned with the matter than was actually the case. Divorce was nothing like the 'national wish' that Fouché claimed it to be.

That the Emperor was truly torn between his love for Josephine and his need to father an heir for his ever burgeoning Empire, there is no doubt. 'Were I to divorce my wife,' he said one day to Talleyrand, 'I would be giving up all the charm she has brought to my private life. I would have to start all over again to learn and have to accommodate myself to the tastes and habits of a new and possibly very young wife. This one adjusts herself to mine and understands me perfectly. Then, too, I would be displaying ingratitude for all she has done for me. I am not actually beloved by my people. Divorce from a beloved Empress would not enhance my popularity....'[10]

To the Count de Champagny, who succeeded Talleyrand as

Minister of Foreign Affairs that year, Napoleon said much the same thing. 'Were I to have the misfortune to lose Josephine, reasons of state would compel me to remarry; but I would only be marrying a womb. Josephine alone would have been my choice as life companion.'[11]

Knowing all this, the Empress behaved with extreme circumspection. 'My only defence,' she wrote to Eugène, 'is to live in such a way as to leave myself open to no reproach. I no longer go out, I have no pleasures. People are astonished that I can endure such a life as I am leading, accustomed as I have been to greater independence of action and to a large society. I console myself with the thought that it represents my submission to the Emperor's wishes . . . .'[12]

What astonished Claire de Rémusat was the fact that the Empress should wish to 'cling so tenaciously to so precarious a royal position.' She was equally astonished by that very tenacity; by the way in which Josephine stood up to the pressure exerted by the all-powerful Napoleon. For although apparently docile and submissive, Josephine had a curiously negative strength: the proverbial strength of the clinging vine.

The Empress was also genuinely unsure about her husband's true feelings. Did he really want to rid himself of her? Sometimes she thought that he was merely feigning indecision; at others that he was trying, by tormenting her, to turn her against him; and, at yet others, that by his vacillations, he was hoping to break her down completely.

But there were occasions when his distress at the thought of losing her rang profoundly true. One night at the Tuileries, in the spring of 1808, when the Empress was dressing for a gala reception of 'princes, ambassadors and courtiers', she was summoned to the Emperor's apartment. She found him in bed, suffering from 'severe stomach spasms and in a dreadful state of nerves.'

At the sight of her he burst into tears and, heedless of her elaborate dress and carefully coiffured hair, dragged her down on to the bed beside him. Clutching her in his arms, he kept repeating, 'My poor Josephine, I shall never be able to live without you.'

'Sire, calm yourself,' she replied, 'make up your mind what you want to do, and let us put an end to these devastating scenes.'

But her words only agitated him still more. Finally, she urged him to cancel his scheduled appearance at the reception and to go to bed. Only, he begged, if she would come to bed with him. So

Josephine had to take off her shimmering gown and climb in beside him. But not even this was able to stem his floods of tears. 'I am surrounded by people who torment me, and make my life hell,' he sobbed.

Josephine remained with him all night. 'It was a night of love, interspersed with intervals of restless sleep,'[13] she afterwards reported.

But by the following morning the Emperor was his old imperious, assured, egotistical and offensively sharp-tongued self.

'Ambition is never content, even on the summit of greatness,'[14] Napoleon had once written. This was certainly true of him by the year 1808. For his ambition was about to lead him to still higher summits of greatness and, as always, it was his undeserving family that would reap many of the rewards.

In an effort to coerce Portugal into complying with his blockade of British goods, Napoleon had already sent his troops into Lisbon. Portugal's reigning family, the Braganzas, fled to Brazil ('Not so fast,' said the Queen to the coachman as they drove towards the port, 'people will think we are fleeing.'[15]) and Napoleon offered the now-vacant Portuguese throne to his estranged and recalcitrant brother Lucien, then living in Italy. But Lucien remained estranged and recalcitrant. Considering Napoleon's stubborn insistence that he repudiate his wife to be too high a price to pay for the Portuguese throne, Lucien refused it.

The next throne to become vacant was the Spanish. When the slow-witted King Charles IV abdicated in favour of his son, who became Ferdinand VII, Napoleon saw an excellent opportunity of getting rid of all the Spanish Bourbons. With Machiavellian cunning he enticed ex-King Charles IV, his Queen, their son King Ferdinand VII and the Queen's lover Godoy, to Bayonne for a 'conference'. Once this unprepossessing group had gathered together, Napoleon, by alternately bullying and coaxing, forced them to pass the Spanish crown to him. They were then rewarded with handsome pensions and sumptuous houses of exile. The throne could now be presented to one of Napoleon's relations.

With Lucien no more likely to accept his brother's terms for the Spanish throne than he had for the Portuguese, Napoleon offered it to Joseph. Joseph, perfectly happy in Naples, refused. Napoleon then tried Louis. Louis, if not exactly happy at The

Hague, hotly resented the idea of being shifted around like an official. As King of Holland his place was with his Dutch subjects and that was where he intended to remain. So Napoleon was obliged to turn once more to Joseph. This time he all but ordered him to accept the Spanish crown. And Joseph, ever submissive, fell in with his wishes. On 6 June 1808, Napoleon declared his brother Joseph King of Spain and the Indies.

On the family chequerboard, this left the thrones of Naples and Portugal vacant. The obvious candidate was Napoleon's brother-in-law, his sister Caroline's husband, Joachim Murat. Murat was given a day to choose between Naples and Portugal. Choking back his disappointment at not being given Spain, Murat chose Naples. In August 1808, this handsome and power-hungry couple took possession of their new kingdom.

Napoleon's Empire, in that summer of 1808, was at its zenith. He ruled over almost all of Western Europe. The territory over which he exercised control stretched, in one direction, from the sunlit Tagus Estuary in Portugal to the icy wastes of the Russian frontier in the far north-east. In the other direction it extended from Hamburg and the North Sea to the toe of Italy in the Mediterranean. It covered a population of seventy million. Some of these territories were regarded as part of France (even Rome, even Dalmatia on the Adriatic, were deemed to be French); most of northern Italy made up Napoleon's own Italian kingdom, which he ruled through a viceroy, his stepson Eugène; the rest were vassal states, either ruled by members of his family, like the kingdoms of Spain, Naples, Holland and Westphalia, or by puppet sovereigns, like Bavaria, Württemberg and Saxony.

But it was Napoleon, backed up by his powerful army, that controlled the destinies of these seventy million people. Monarchs and prefects alike were simply there to carry out his will; he alone managed foreign policy and decreed the principles of administration and finance. Whether pacing up and down his study at the Tuileries or huddled over a camp fire on campaign, the Emperor dictated hundreds upon hundreds of letters, applying himself to every aspect of the running of his huge Empire.

No subject was too immense, or too trivial, for that exceptional mind. He passed laws, he issued decrees, he ordered reforms, he erected new buildings, he inaugurated roads and canals, he restored historic monuments, he replanned cities. At one moment he would be setting up a new kingdom; at another he would be instigating enquiries on whether or not some impecunious forestry official had bought his new home out of forestry funds.

The trouble with all this was that the Empire depended, almost entirely, on the Emperor. Napoleon's lavishly uniformed courtiers were not the only ones to remain edgy until he returned home safely from battle. If he were to die on campaign, the whole elaborately constructed imperial edifice would come crashing down.

For some years now Napoleon had been convinced that his powers would wane after forty. Already he was getting fat and sluggish; at thirty-nine, he felt that time was running out. This was why it had become essential, by the year 1808, for the Empire to have a legitimate, acceptable, generally recognised heir. The adoption of one of the Emperor's nephews was not really a satisfactory answer. The only solution would be for him to marry a princess of some firmly rooted royal house and to establish a dynasty. There was no other possible way of perpetuating his magnificent achievements.

Between Napoleon and the fulfilment of his ambition stood the slight, poignant figure of Josephine.

More and more, during this anguished period, did Josephine devote herself to the one place she loved above all others – Malmaison.

In contrast to the palaces of the Tuileries, Saint-Cloud and Fontainebleau, with their grandiose salons, traditional furnishings and inherited treasures, Malmaison was intimate and personal; the entire estate bore Josephine's stamp. It was she who was responsible for the house's fashionable decor. The white marble entrance hall with its full-length windows overlooking the park, made the perfect, neo-classical setting for receptions. The Emperor's rooms were consciously masculine: mahogany bookcases, Pompeian frescos, olive-green fabrics for the study; striped material, hung to resemble a military tent and supported by pikes, *fasces* and standards, for the council chamber. Napoleon slept, not in one of those massive, heavily curtained four posters in which his Bourbon predecessors had slept, but in a low, simple bedstead under a light silk canopy. The Empress's apartments were even more imaginatively furnished. Her bedroom was particularly impressive. Her bed, decorated with the gilt swans that were her emblem, was surmounted by a red velvet canopy; the walls were hung with a matching red fabric.

To house her ever-increasing collection of paintings, Josephine had a hundred-foot-long gallery added to the château. Although her own taste was for *le style troubadour* – the then fashionable romantic idealising of the medieval period – and for sentimental pastoral scenes, she managed to amass a collection of much more important paintings than these. Some of these pictures were presented to her: others had been commandeered by her all-conquering husband. She owned paintings by every leading European artist from Hans Memling to David, including Leonardo, Titian, Raphael, Van Dyck, Holbein, Rembrandt and Rubens. Had her paintings not been dispersed, they would have constituted one of the great European collections.

Josephine enjoyed having her own portrait painted. From full-length portraits to miniatures, her features were reproduced hundreds of times; Louis-Bertin Perant alone produced over fifty cameo portraits of her. She gave away these likenesses to anyone she thought might want them, whether they be kings or chambermaids. To her collection of paintings were added other treasures – tapestries, carpets, vases, urns, china, busts, inlaid cabinets, console tables, assorted *objets* in crystal, ivory, mother-of-pearl, bronze, gold, silver and silver-gilt.

It was Napoleon rather than Josephine who was responsible for the library at Malmaison. She seldom read anything other than light novels or the great folios produced by her botanical experts, and books were the one commodity on which she did not squander great sums of money. Napoleon, on the other hand, read avidly. He particularly enjoyed narrative history ('history is for men,' he would say), poetry and, later, novels. He preferred a novel with an heroic theme and a tragic ending. If ever he caught his valets reading a light novel as they sat waiting for him to come to bed, he would fling the book into the fire. 'Let the filth burn,' he would exclaim, 'That's all it's fit for.'[16] He would do the same with any book by an author he disliked. Madame de Staël's *Allemagne* was similarly tossed into the flames. Like Josephine's pictures, Napoleon's extensive collection of books was dispersed after his fall.

The gardens were the Empress's special pride. Overriding, for once, Napoleon's preference for gardens laid out in the formal French style, Josephine insisted on a romantically landscaped

'English' garden. Trees and shrubs were picturesquely grouped. On ornamental lakes floated the graceful white swans with which she had come to be synonymous. At every turn along those meandering paths one could come across some imported ruin or antique statue: a Grecian temple, a marble obelisk, a broken column, an entire thirty-six-foot-high Gothic chapel of the Carmelite order.

On one occasion Josephine was strolling in the park with an earnest German prince who – assuming, quite correctly, that every carefully constructed grotto and mock-antique pavilion had been built to enhance the view – asked solemn questions about each of them. And what, he asked, pointing to the distant aqueduct of Marly erected decades before to carry water to the lakes and fountains of Versailles, was that? 'Oh that,' said Josephine smilingly. 'Just a pretty little thing Louis XIV ran up for me.'[17]

No more a botanist than an art expert, Josephine had a passion for flowers. From all over the world hitherto unfamiliar plants were brought to Malmaison. During the years that she lived there, almost two hundred species new to France flowered there. Napoleon once sent her eight hundred plants from the Schönbrunn Palace in Vienna; she was known to pay as much as three thousand francs for a rare bulb.

Although Josephine's name has been so closely associated with roses, this did not come about until after her death when her protégé, the artist Pierre-Joseph Redouté, published his famous work *Les Roses*. The Empress preferred tulips, hyacinths and carnations. None the less, there were nearly two hundred varieties of roses in her special experimental garden. With the help of the famous botanist Aimé Bonpland, she was able, by crossing a cabbage rose with a China rose, to produce a tea rose which bloomed for weeks rather than days. From Josephine's tea roses was to develop the hybrid perpetual – the rose most frequently seen in today's gardens.

Another of Redouté's productions, which Josephine did not live to see published but helped to finance, was the two-volume, superbly illustrated *Jardin de la Malmaison*. A book with the same title was produced by yet another distinguished botanist, Etienne Pierre Ventenat, who held the post of 'Botanist to Her Majesty'.

'You have gathered round you,' wrote Ventenat in dedicating his book to the Empress, 'the rarest plants growing on French soil. Some, indeed, which never before had left the deserts of Arabia or the burning sands of Egypt have been domesticated through your care. Now, regularly classified, they offer to us as we inspect them in the beautiful gardens of Malmaison an impressive reminder of the conquests of your illustrious husband and a most pleasant evidence of the studies you have pursued in your leisure hours...'[18]

The largest of the Malmaison conservatories could be compared with those at Kew in London or Schönbrunn in Vienna. In the heart of this great glass palace was a salon, richly furnished with carpets, statuary, vases and 'antique-style' furniture, from which one could gaze out at the profusion of lush ferns and exotic blooms that stretched away on either side. Strolling through her hot houses, with the sound of water splashing in her ears and the sweet smell of flowers in her nostrils, Josephine spent some of the happiest hours of her life. 'The last week has passed very rapidly and very agreeably,' she once wrote to Hortense. 'I spent it at Malmaison, in the midst of the work going on there, and this employment has completely restored me.'[19]

But by the year 1808 it would have needed more than a stay at Malmaison to restore Josephine's spirits. Laure Junot, who had brought her little daughter to visit the Empress one day that summer, describes a pathetic scene that took place in the famous conservatory.

Despite the steamy, almost tropical atmosphere under the glass dome, Josephine shivered and seemed unable to focus her attention on her beloved plants. 'It's very cold,' she remarked to her visitor, drawing her shawl closer. It was, realised Madame Junot, 'the chill of grief creeping about her heart, like the cold hand of death.'

When the little girl had gone scampering off among the bright banks of flowers, Josephine suddenly took hold of her guest's hands and exclaimed, 'Madame Junot, I beg you to tell me all that you have heard relating to me. I ask it as an especial favour – you know that they [Napoleon's family] all desire to ruin me and my Hortense and my Eugène. Madame Junot, I again beg as a favour that you will tell me all you know.'

Laure Junot, in spite of being a member of Napoleon's mother's household, knew nothing. She assured the trembling Empress that, on her honour, she had not heard the word 'divorce' uttered by either Napoleon's mother or his sisters. At the mention of the dreaded word, Josephine burst into tears. 'Madame Junot,' she said, her lovely voice choking with sobs, 'remember

229

what I say to you this day, here, in this hothouse – this place which is now a paradise but which may soon become a desert to me – remember that this separation will be my death, and it is they who will have killed me.'

At this moment the little girl came running back and the weeping Empress gathered her in her arms 'with an almost convulsive emotion'.

'You have no idea how much I have suffered when any one of you has brought a child to me!' continued Josephine. 'Heaven knows that I am not envious, but in this case I have felt as though a deadly poison were creeping through my veins when I have looked upon the fresh and rosy cheeks of a beautiful child, the joy of its mother, but above all, the hope of its father! And I, struck with barrenness, shall be driven with disgrace from the bed of him who has given me a crown.

'Yet God is my witness that I love him more than my life, and much more than that throne, that crown which he has given me!'[20]

22

'Stress and Strain'

AN added inducement for Napoleon to think in terms of
fathering a successor was the patent unfitness of any of his
relations to fill his place. Not only were these instant
monarchs proving incompetent, they were also insubordinate. 'If
I made one of them a king,' sighed Napoleon on Saint Helena, 'he
imagined that he was king by the grace of God. He was no longer
my lieutenant; he was one more enemy to watch.'[1]

Joseph had entered his new Spanish kingdom full of good
intentions. As he had tried to be a Neapolitan king in Naples, so
would he endeavour to be a Spanish king in Spain. He was soon
disillusioned. Whereas the easy-going Neapolitans had welcomed
him, the stubborn Spaniards resisted him. Even before he set foot
in the country the people rose in revolt against the occupying
French troops. Only by force would Joseph be able to retain his
throne. This was not to his taste at all. Nor did he feel that matters
were made any easier by Napoleon's flood of instructions on how
he was to manage his rebellious subjects. Joseph maintained,
naïvely perhaps, that if only Napoleon would give him a free hand,
he would be King of Spain 'not by force of arms but through the
love of the Spaniards.' Napoleon dismissed this as both foolish
and disloyal.

The surly Louis, King of Holland, was displaying what Napoleon considered to be an equally regrettable insistence on ident-
ifying himself with his subjects. And just like Joseph, Louis very
soon came up against Napoleon's iron will. As a Constable of the

231

Empire, warned Napoleon, Louis's first duty was towards France. But unlike the more pliable Joseph, Louis took active steps to thwart the Emperor's policies. He sided with the Dutch merchants in their opposition to Napoleon's Continental blockade; British goods still seemed to find their way into Holland. Exasperated, Napoleon sent troops into the country. By the year 1810 Louis had been obliged to sign a treaty whereby his powers were curtailed and his kingdom considerably reduced in size.

Jerome, King of Westphalia, was proving no less of a thorn in the Emperor's side. Like Louis, Jerome resented having to make his country conform to Napoleon's Continental blockade, but, unlike Louis, Jerome valued his crown more than his country. When he complained to the Emperor that the French troops stationed in Westphalia were crippling the country, Napoleon instructed his brother to put Westphalia's finances in order; it was the worst managed state in the Confederation of the Rhine, grumbled Napoleon. But in spite of the fact that Westphalia was almost bankrupt, Jerome ignored his brother's advice. He continued to live in the most extravagant fashion, dedicating himself to his lavishly decorated palaces, his expensive clothes and his numberless mistresses.

The Murats – King Joachim and Queen Caroline of Naples – were proving most troublesome of all. Not only were they displaying the customary reluctance to carry out Napoleon's orders, but they were actively scheming to get their hands on his throne. Caroline was determined that, in the event of Napoleon's death, her husband Joachim should become Emperor. For her latest plot, she had secured two powerful allies. One was Talleyrand, the other was her long-standing admirer, Fouché. This astute pair, realising that the bombastic Murat would be putty in their experienced hands, had united to champion his cause. It was believed that Fouché had arranged for relays of horses to be kept ready on the road between Naples and Paris: as soon as there was news of the Emperor's death in battle, Murat – so popular with the army – would be rushed to the French capital and proclaimed Emperor.

What a shot in the eye for Caroline's long-standing *bête noire*, Josephine, that would be.

Can one wonder that Napoleon was so often exasperated by his relations? Or that on one occasion, when all three of his sisters – Elisa, Pauline and Caroline – were in the room, he should give vent to this exasperation? 'I don't believe any man in the world is more unfortunate in his family than I am,' he exclaimed. 'Suppose we sum up. Lucien is an ingrate. Joseph is a Sardanapalus. Louis is a paralytic. Jerome, a scamp.

'And as for you, ladies,' he said, lowering his eyes and dropping his voice, *'you know what you are.'*[2]

'You will appreciate to what stress and strain I have been subjected,' wrote the Empress Josephine to Eugène from Saint-Cloud in September 1808. 'I have paid for it with excruciating headaches. But the Emperor proved his attachment by the concern he manifested, getting up as often as four times a night to come and see how I was feeling. For the last six weeks he has been simply perfect to me. Thus when I saw him leave this morning it was with sadness at the parting, but with no disquietude as concerns our relations.'[3]

Napoleon was on his way to Erfurt in Germany for a meeting with his new friend, the young Tsar Alexander I. 'I wish my journey to be brilliant,' he kept saying while the preparations were being made. 'I wish to astonish Germany by my splendour.' And indeed, surrounded by a glittering retinue of subservient kings, princes and dukes of his Empire, Napoleon at this meeting was his usual impressive self. But, on this occasion, the Tsar was somewhat less impressed. Although as cordial as ever, Alexander was evasive: evasive about promising Russian support in the event of a war between France and Austria, and evasive about Napoleon's other request – the hand of one of his sisters in marriage.

For, unbeknown to Josephine, Napoleon had already decided to divorce her. As early as August the year before, he had had a list of eligible princesses drawn up, classified according to age, religion and country. The complete list totalled seventeen, ranging from the twelve-year-old Grand Duchess Anna Pavlovna of Russia (Tsar Alexander I's youngest sister) to the twenty-nine-year-old Princess Sophia Fredericka of Saxe-Coburg.

Of these seventeen, the two most likely candidates were the nineteen-year-old Grand Duchess Catherine Pavlovna, another of the Tsar's sisters, and the sixteen-year-old Grand Duchess Marie Louise, daughter of the Emperor Francis I of Austria. These two were undoubtedly the most important princesses on the Continent.

Among the many reasons for Napoleon's decision to divorce Josephine, not the least potent was his desire to ally himself to one of the great royal houses of Europe. With each passing year he was becoming more of a snob. Where, at the beginning of his reign, he had welcomed members of the old aristocracy to the Tuileries for mainly political reasons, he now welcomed them for social ones. 'I will not deny,' admits his secretary Méneval, 'that the Emperor had a penchant for the remaining representatives of the élite of the old *noblesse* at court... Those polite manners, the tradition of taste and urbanity which they brought to his court had an effect on his mind which he strove to conceal.'[4]

How much more of an effect then, did the members of royal families have on his mind? He, with his quick perspicacity, would have been very conscious of the air of exclusivity that characterised the European family of kings. He would have noted the self-confidence, the shared attitudes and outlook, even the inflections of voice, of this royal brotherhood. Despite the fact that he had been consecrated by the Pope and that he had reigned as Emperor for four years, there must have been times when Napoleon was very aware of his own parvenu status. Having proved himself superior to every monarch in Europe on the battlefield, he wanted to prove himself at least their equal in the drawing room.

For all the pomp with which he surrounded himself ('One cannot conceive all that passed through his head in reference to it,'[5] declared Madame de Rémusat), for all the rigid code he had introduced into the Tuileries, there was something missing when he set himself against these legitimate kings in their long-established courts. They might be less brilliant, they might be less powerful, but there was an indefinable aura about them which established their superiority. And to Napoleon any sense of inferiority was unbearable.

Although there was nothing that Napoleon could do about the fact of his own relatively humble birth, he could at least link himself to one of these royal houses. Such an alliance would consolidate his position among this royal freemasonry and from it would spring a line of half-royal children. Surely then he would be accepted?

But not yet, apparently. Tsar Alexander's reaction to Napoleon's request for the hand of the Grand Duchess Catherine was non-committal. There were good reasons for this. For one thing the Tsar had no intention of forcing his strong-minded sister Catherine to marry against her will. For another, Alexander's mother, the redoubtable Dowager Empress Maria Feodorovna, loathed the upstart Napoleon; she had once described her son's

Tilsit alliance as 'a pact with the devil'. But the Dowager Empress had a more intimate objection to the proposed match as well. She had been told that Napoleon was 'not as other men'; that he was impotent. Her assertion was subsequently confirmed by Prince Frederick Louis of Mecklenburg-Schwerin.

The Dowager Empress should have treated his confirmation with more circumspection. For Prince Frederick Louis had had it backed up by someone with every reason for wanting it to be believed: the Empress Josephine.

Back home in Paris from Erfurt, Napoleon could still not bring himself to say anything about a divorce to Josephine. Not only could he not bear the thought of hurting her, he could not resist her allure. In any case, he was hardly home before setting off again; this time for Spain.

Here, things had been going seriously wrong. In August 1808 a British expeditionary force, commanded by Sir Arthur Wellesley, the future Duke of Wellington, had landed in Portugal and inflicted a crushing defeat on the French. With this defeat encouraging the Spanish in their opposition to the occupying French army, Napoleon was obliged to take matters into his own hands. Acting as briskly as ever, he smashed the insubordinate Spaniards, instituted a series of political reforms and then turned his attention to the British expeditionary force. Here he was less successful. The British made a tactical retreat, so robbing the Emperor of the decisive victory he so badly needed.

Nor could he afford the time to win one. By January 1809 he had heard that the Austrians were actively preparing for war against him. He hurried back to Paris to face this fresh threat. It came, on 9 April, when the Austrians invaded Napoleon's ally, Bavaria. Within days, the Emperor was preparing to leave Paris to take command.

By now even Josephine, who had never spoken out against (or possibly not been concerned by) the repressive nature of her husband's regime, found herself seriously disturbed by the almost continuous blood-letting. 'Will you never stop making war?' she one day asked, voicing what a great many French people were thinking.

'Well,' answered Napoleon. 'Do you think that I enjoy it? Don't you think that I would rather stay peaceably where I have

235

a good bed and a good dinner instead of facing all the hardships that I have before me? You think I am made differently from other men? There! I can do other things beside wage war. But needs must. I owe a duty to France. It is not I who direct the course of events. I obey it.'[6]

Whether or not Josephine was convinced by this glib reasoning one does not know. But there is no doubt that she was by now deeply concerned, not only by this never-ending warfare but for Napoleon's safety. She could no longer bear the thought of being separated from him. When he announced that he was off to fight the Austrians, she begged to be allowed to accompany him. He would not hear of it.

According to Constant, the Emperor tried, at dawn one morning, to slip away without her; but on hearing sounds of departure in the courtyard, Josephine sprang out of bed, threw on a *peignoir* and rushed downstairs. Flinging herself into his carriage, she begged to be taken with him. Always helpless in the face of Josephine's tearful entreaties, Napoleon agreed. He gave orders for her luggage to be sent on and the two of them went rattling off in the direction of Strasbourg.

There she remained while he went to do battle with the advancing Austrians. Within three weeks he had inflicted a couple of resounding defeats on the enemy and was headquartered, once again, in Schönbrunn Palace, outside Vienna. A few weeks later, in July, he won a still more decisive victory at Wagram. By the Peace of Schönbrunn, which followed, Napoleon gained yet more territory for his Empire.

These months in the lovely summer palace of Schönbrunn (he did not leave until mid October) brought Napoleon satisfaction of another sort as well. With him during that period was Marie Walewska. Since their first sojourn together, in East Prussia, Marie had been installed by Napoleon in a house in Paris where she had had to be content with her lover's occasional visits; now their stay together was relatively uninterrupted.

Once again, the Emperor delighted in Marie's sweet, gentle, Josephine-like qualities, and this time she was able to delight him still further by revealing that she was pregnant by him. If there had been some doubt about the paternity of Eléonore Denuelle's child, Napoleon seems to have been convinced that there was none about Marie Walewska's. The news reinforced his decision to divorce Josephine.

Marie's child – a son – was born in May the following year. As she had taken advantage of her aged husband's chivalrous offer to recognise the child as his own, it was born on the family estate in Poland and given the surname of Walewski. As Count Alexandre Walewski, he was to play a prominent role in the Second Empire, under the Emperor Napoleon III.

Napoleon's other illegitimate son, by Eléonore Denuelle, was to have a less satisfactory career. Known as Count Leon, he was to develop into a profligate troublemaker whose chief activity, during the Second Empire, would be the pestering of the long-suffering Napoleon III for a yet larger pension.

Napoleon's decision to divorce Josephine was confirmed by yet another incident that happened at Schönbrunn. One day, while he was reviewing his troops in the great courtyard of the palace, a well-dressed young man approached him. He seemed to be about to present a petition. When asked by one of Napoleon's attendant generals what he wanted, he replied that he wished to speak to Napoleon. He was turned away but a few seconds later he again approached to within a foot or so of the Emperor. The general, suspicious of the young man's determined air and of the fact that he kept his right hand in his coat pocket, had him arrested. On him was found an enormous kitchen knife.

When, after the review, Napoleon was told about the youth and his knife, he asked to have him brought before him.

'What were you going to do with your knife?' asked the Emperor.

'Kill you,' answered the young man.

'Why did you mean to kill me?'

'Because you are the bane of my country.'

'Have I done you any harm?'

'Yes. Me and all Germans.'

'Who sent you? Who has encouraged you to do this crime?'

'No one,' answered the youth calmly. 'It is my deep-seated conviction that by killing you I should do the greatest service to my country and to Europe.'

Napoleon, thinking him mad, had him examined by his doctor, but the latter pronounced the youth quite sane. He was tried and shot a few days later. His last words were, 'Liberty forever! Germany forever! Death to the tyrant!'[7]

The incident seems to have disturbed Napoleon profoundly. He had always considered himself the friend of people such as this young man; he could not understand why he, who saw himself as the champion of the ordinary man, should have his life threatened by a middle-class boy like this. Had he not, throughout his Empire, abolished feudalism, established constitutions, introduced the benefits of the Civil Code, insisted on religious toleration? Had he not told his brother Jerome, on becoming King of Westphalia, that 'I want your subjects to enjoy a degree of liberty, equality and prosperity hitherto unknown to the German people'?[8]

What Napoleon never really understood was the strength of the nationalism which his conquests had helped unleash. He remained blind to all feelings of patriotism other than that of the French.

But if he was indeed so much hated by the common people of Europe whom he had sought to liberate from feudalism, might not someone else try to assassinate him? And if someone else were successful, what would become of his life's work, of his great Empire? This question was certainly in the minds of his generals. They, writes Hortense, 'alarmed at the idea of what might have happened, turned their attention once more to the absence of any direct heir to the Empire. 'They asked themselves who could possibly have been chosen had the attempt [on Napoleon's life] succeeded.' Their unanimous choice, she claims, was her brother Eugène.

But their talk, when Napoleon came to hear about it, annoyed him. It 'revived the question of divorce in his mind.'[9]

In the third week of October, Napoleon wrote to Josephine to tell her that he would be arriving at Fontainebleau within a few days and instructing her to meet him there. Because he had arrived early, she arrived late. Hurrying in to greet him, she was met with a sharp reprimand for having kept him waiting. When she started to make excuses, he cut her short and dismissed her.

Recognising his anger for what it was – a pretext to distance himself from her – Josephine withdrew. She must have known that, even now, he was incapable of withstanding her blandishments and that, later that night when they were alone, he would not be able to maintain his assumed coldness.

Her reasoning was correct. But it was confirmed in the most uncompromising fashion. When Josephine went to her apartments, she discovered, with a pounding heart, that the communicating door to his had been securely sealed. He was not going to risk a private discussion with her.

'So now we have come,' writes her maid Mademoiselle Avrillon with a fine dramatic flourish, 'to the epoch when the Empress's agony begins; her destiny must needs play itself out.'[10]

23

Divorce

FROM the day of Napoleon's arrival back at Fontainebleau, late in October 1809, until the finalisation of his divorce seven weeks later, he spent only one short period – no more than a few minutes – alone with Josephine. This was on 30 November when he finally steeled himself to tell her that he intended divorcing her.

Until then, he treated her with exceptional brusqueness. 'No more kindness, no more consideration for my mother,' says Hortense. 'He had given her up. He became unjust and tormenting. Our family seemed a burden to him and he sought the company of his own people.'[1] Chief amongst his 'own people' at Fontainebleau that autumn was his sister, Pauline Borghese. The frivolous Pauline, who devoted half her time to the perfecting of her beauty and the other to the satisfying of her voracious sexual appetites, shared the family's aversion to the Empress Josephine. She, no less than her sister Caroline, was in the habit of surrounding herself with attractive and available young women whom she knew would interest the Emperor. The bait, on this occasion, was one whom Hortense calls 'a Piedmontese lady' and whom Josephine's maid, Mademoiselle Avrillon, identifies as a fair-haired beauty named Christine de Mathis.

Night after night, the Princess Borghese would give parties in her apartments; parties from which the Empress would be pointedly excluded and at which the Emperor would be thrown into the company of the coquettish Countess de Mathis. 'This love intrigue, carried on in the very midst of our domestic life,' writes Hortense, 'added new fuel to the rumours of an impending divorce.'[2] From her windows, Josephine would be able to see the lights blazing and to hear the talk bubbling in her sister-in-law's salon. 'God knows,' writes Mademoiselle Avrillon, 'how many sleepless nights she spent peering across the shadows of the court-yard.' Which, the maid afterwards wondered, had caused her mistress the greatest anguish: the divorce itself or the 'cruelly protracted preliminaries'?[3]

For Josephine still knew nothing definite. Yet she could not bring herself to tackle Napoleon directly. In his company she became tongue-tied, tremulous, utterly lacking in confidence. Knowing, in her heart of hearts, what the final outcome would be, she none the less 'clung to the very end to some faint ray of hope.'[4]

She resorted to plying any dignitary or official with oblique questions, and they, who knew no more than she did, parried her with oblique answers. 'The Empress's obsession with her fate,' writes Méneval, 'accounted for her endless application to me for information. My role became so embarrassing that, to escape her enquiries, I had no choice but to avoid her altogether... This situation was too charged with tension to be long endurable. The constraint which His Majesty had brought about in their daily contact was a torture to them both.'[5]

For Napoleon was – in spite of his air of frigidity – hardly less anguished than she. He was ashamed, not only at having to treat her so coldly (it was the only way he knew of preparing her for the blow) but of his weakness in not confronting her. It is some measure of Napoleon's love for Josephine that he, the most ruthless and efficient of men, simply could not bring himself to get rid of this obstacle to his ambitions.

By now Hortense was equally tortured by the dragging on of the affair. 'Witness to my mother's constant tears and to the indignities that provoked them, both my heart and my pride rebelled,' she writes. 'I found myself wishing that the divorce had been pronounced.'[6]

But by the time the court returned to the Tuileries on 14 November, Napoleon had still not plucked up the courage to speak.

A week later, without Josephine's knowledge, Napoleon instructed

General Louis de Caulaincourt, his ambassador to St Petersburg, to make formal application for the hand of Tsar Alexander I's youngest sister, the fourteen-year-old Grand Duchess Anna Pavlovna.

By now the Grand Duchess Catherine, for whose hand Napoleon had made tentative approaches to the Tsar at Erfurt the year before, had married the son of the Duke of Oldenburg. At this stage Napoleon still did not know why the Tsar should have been so hesitant about agreeing to the match. Only later would he be told of the Dowager Empress's opposition to any proposed marriage between one of her daughters and the upstart, and reputedly impotent, Napoleon.

So, all unsuspecting, Napoleon had asked his ambassador to send him a report on the Grand Duchess Anna. Her ability to bear children was, he said, of the utmost importance; as she was not yet fifteen he did not want to have to wait, even six months, for her to become nubile. Caulaincourt assured him that the entire Russian imperial family was physically precocious and that the Grand Duchess was indeed nubile.

On being formally approached, Tsar Alexander proved as evasive about Anna as he had been about Catherine. Had the decision depended on him, he told Caulaincourt, he would have given his immediate consent. The late Tsar, however, had decreed that in all matters concerning the marriages of the young grand duchesses, the Dowager Empress must have the last word. And the last word, he realised, would be 'no'.

It did not take Napoleon long to appreciate, by the equivocal tone of his ambassador's letters, that his request was going to be refused. And so it was. Politely, the Emperor was told that the matter of the Grand Duchess Anna's marriage would have to wait until she turned eighteen, in three years' time.

Although Napoleon's approach had been unsuccessful, it had been – as far as Josephine was concerned – a positive step towards divorce. A few days later the Emperor took another positive step: he sent a message by semaphore to Italy to summon Josephine's son, Eugène. Napoleon could not delay the dreaded confrontation much longer.

It came on the last day of November 1809. The scene has become one of the famous setpieces in the saga of Napoleon and Josephine.

Divorce

The couple dined together, with the palace prefect, the Count de Bausset, in attendance. The Empress's face was shadowed by a wide-brimmed hat but Bausset could see the sparkle of tears in her eyes. The meal lasted for ten minutes with the Emperor and Empress barely touching their food. Nor did they say a word to each other. The only sounds to be heard were the clatter of plates as the footmen served the meal and the occasional nervous tapping of the Emperor's knife against his wine glass. At one stage Napoleon asked Bausset about the weather but ignored his answer.

The meal over, Josephine followed Napoleon into the drawing room. When a servant brought in the coffee, the Emperor helped himself to a cup, thereby breaking the tradition by which the Empress poured his coffee, sugared it and tasted it before handing it to him. Napoleon signalled the servant to withdraw. Bausset, only too happy to get away, followed him.

While he stood waiting in the adjoining ante-room, Bausset heard the Empress cry out. Napoleon flung open the door and shouted, 'Come in Bausset, and close the door behind you.'

Josephine was rolling about on the floor, moaning 'piteously'. 'No! No!' she cried out over and over again. 'No, I shall never survive it!'

'Do you think you could carry Her Majesty to her apartments?' asked Napoleon. Bausset thought that he could. He lifted Josephine who by now appeared to have lost consciousness and was like a dead weight in his arms. The Emperor picked up a lighted candle and led the way to the head of the dark narrow spiral staircase which led down to the Empress's apartments.

But Bausset soon realised that, with the unconscious Empress in his arms, he could never descend the stairway. So Napoleon summoned a guard and, telling him to go ahead with the candle, took hold of Josephine's legs.

Down the steep, winding staircase they stumbled, Bausset going backwards with his arms around Josephine's waist and her head lolling against his right shoulder, and Napoleon following, with his arms under her knees. Halfway down, Bausset almost tripped over his sword and, involuntarily, clutched the Empress more tightly around the waist.

Suddenly, at the moment when his head was bent close to hers, she whispered, 'You're gripping me too tight!'

At that moment Bausset realised that 'I need have no further alarm about her condition.'

Reaching her apartments, they laid the Empress on a sofa in her bedroom where Napoleon tugged at the bell rope to summon her attendants.

Throughout this painful scene Bausset had been so concerned with the Empress that he had hardly noticed the Emperor. But now that her women had taken over, he followed Napoleon into an adjoining room. The Emperor was in a terrible state. His eyes were brimming with tears. 'The interest of France has done violence to my heart,' he blurted out to the embarrassed Bausset. 'Divorce has become a political necessity... I am all the more distressed by the scene tonight because her daughter should have told her about my decision three days ago. I pity her with all my heart.'

So violent were Napoleon's feelings that he had to gasp for breath between each sentence. 'He must indeed have been beside himself to have taken someone like me into his confidence,'[7] comments Bausset.

Returning to his own apartments, the Emperor sent for Hortense and Dr Corvisart to go to the Empress.

Hortense found her mother in tears. Josephine explained that Napoleon had at last told her that he had decided on a divorce.

'Well, so much the better,' replied Hortense. 'We will all go away with you and you can live in peace.'

'But what will become of you and Eugène?' cried Josephine.

'We will go with you. My brother will feel as I do. For the first time in our lives, far from the crowd, we will really know what it means to be happy.'

Hortense's matter-of-fact reaction seemed to calm Josephine. When her daughter left, the Empress seemed more resigned to her fate.

Hortense then answered Napoleon's summons. Embarrassed in front of this admirable young woman whose mother he was about to discard, the Emperor affected an abrupt manner.

'You have seen your mother,' he snapped. 'She has spoken to you. My decision is made. It is irrevocable. All France desires a divorce and claims it loudly. I cannot oppose my country's will. So nothing will move me, neither prayers nor tears.'

'Sire,' answered Hortense, who had not the slightest intention of either praying or crying, 'you are free to do as you think fit. No one will try to oppose you. Since your happiness exacts this step, that is enough; we shall know how to sacrifice ourselves. Do not be surprised at my mother's tears; it would have been surprising if, after fourteen years of married life, she shed none. But she will submit, I am convinced; and we shall all go, remembering only the kindness you have shown us.'

At this Napoleon's air of reserve crumbled. In a voice thick with emotion, he begged them not to leave him. Her mother would always be his dearest friend, he claimed; her brother Eugène would continue to be like a son to him; she herself, if only for her two children's sake, must never dream of leaving him. Again and again he protested that he was divorcing Josephine for the sake of his country only; 'the only way of assuring the future peace of France was to leave his throne to his own child.'

But whether the divorce be for the future peace of France or the greater glory of Napoleon, Hortense refused to be swayed. 'Sire,' she answered, 'my duty is towards my mother. She will need me. We can no longer live near you. That is a sacrifice we must make. We are prepared to make it.'[8]

But the worst was not yet over for Josephine. By a supreme irony, the fifth anniversary of the coronation – the day on which Napoleon had crowned her as his Empress, 2 December – fell two days after he had told her she was to be his Empress no longer. To celebrate this anniversary, and his recent victories over the Austrians, the Emperor had invited a galaxy of vassal kings, princes and grand-dukes to Paris. For two weeks the capital was *en fête*; every day brought another royal procession, military parade or public ceremony. There was a Te Deum in Notre-Dame, a 'grand recep-tion' at Malmaison, a review of troops at the Tuileries, a banquet and ball at the Hôtel de Ville, and a 'formal reception' at court.

To face not only the strain of these ceremonies but the knowing stares of thousands of eyes, poor Josephine was obliged to dry her tears, put on more rouge, get into one of her white satin or silver lamé dresses, and behave as though nothing were wrong. Her gallant and, as always, impeccable public behaviour during this agonising period brought home, to those about her, the realis-ation of how much her leaving was going to mean to them. Had she not been 'Notre Dame des Victoires', 'La Bonne Josephine', the winner of hearts and bringer of good fortune?

'There is no one in the palace who will not live to rue the day she leaves,' admitted Talleyrand to Claire de Rémusat. 'She is gentle, sweet and kind, and she knows the art of calming the Emperor. She understands everyone's problems here and has been a refuge to us all on a thousand occasions. When you see some foreign princess arrive to take her place, you will see discord between the Emperor and the courtiers. We will all be the losers by it.'[9]

The Empress was considerably cheered by the arrival, on 5 December, of Eugène from Italy. He had reported first to the Emperor and the two men had then joined the Empress and Hortense in Josephine's apartments. In no time all four of them were in tears, with Napoleon even going so far as to offer to change his decision about the divorce. But his stepchildren assured him that it was too late for that; the best thing for all concerned, they maintained, would be for a complete break between the Bonaparte and Beauharnais families. 'Otherwise,' claimed Eugène, 'we would be in a false position.'

But Napoleon would not hear of it. He wanted them all, Josephine included, to retain their rank and positions and to remain part of the imperial family. He wished Eugène to continue as his Viceroy in Italy, he wanted to have Hortense and her sons – his nephews – close to him, and he intended that Josephine should retain the title of Empress and live in an appropriate style. If they were all to leave him, he argued, it would be claimed that he had had good reasons for repudiating his wife; whereas if they stayed, the world would see that she had been sacrificed for political reasons only and that, by agreeing to the sacrifice, she had proved herself even more deserving of 'the praise, love and respect of the nation.'

Against this reasoning, Eugène and Hortense were powerless. 'We were won over by the Emperor's solicitude for his wife's reputation at the very moment he was leaving her,'[10] says Hortense. For their mother's sake, they agreed to everything Napoleon suggested.

There remained only the final settlement to be worked out. This was done, two days later, at a meeting between Napoleon, Josephine and Eugène. Josephine hoped that, out of it, Eugène might get the crown of Italy. But her principled son would not even allow the matter to be discussed: he had no intention of turning his mother's misfortune to his own advantage, he protested.

The provisions granted to Josephine were very generous. She retained the rank of a 'crowned and anointed' empress, with all its honours, privileges and distinctions, and the right to be addressed as 'Your Majesty'. She could use the imperial coat of arms, dress her servants in imperial livery, retain the officers of her household and have her carriage drawn by eight horses. Malmaison – the château, the estate and its revenues – was to be hers and, in Paris, she was to have the exclusive use of the Elysée Palace. She was granted an allowance of three million francs a year, and her debts, which totalled nearly two million francs, were to be settled immediately by cash advanced out of her future revenues.

She could hardly have wished for better than that.

In the meantime, the formalities to terminate the marriage were being attended to. The civil dissolution did not present many problems. Riding roughshod over most of the stipulations of his own Civil Code, Napoleon instructed Cambacérès, as Arch-chancellor of the Empire, to prepare a suitably legal-sounding statement to the effect that both parties agreed to a civil dissolution of the marriage. This statement was to be formally signed by Napoleon and Josephine and then presented to the Senate for approval. No one doubted that it would be approved. Yet, when it was put to a secret vote on 16 December 1809, the result was less than unanimous: seventy-six were in favour of dissolution, seven against, and four blanks.

The annulment of the religious marriage was not managed quite so effortlessly. After all, the couple had been married, on the eve of the coronation, by a cardinal of the Church. Indeed, it had been the Pope himself who had insisted on the marriage; the very fact that the Pontiff had agreed to officiate at the coronation was proof of the religious validity of the marriage ceremony.

But Pope Pius VII was in no position to be approached on this matter. Outraged at the French occupation of his last temporal possessions in Italy, he had recently excommunicated Napoleon. The Emperor had retaliated by taking the Pope prisoner and holding him in the bishop's palace at Savona, in northern Italy. Quite clearly, His Holiness would be in no mood to co-operate.

Failing the Pope, what about the cardinal who had performed the marriage ceremony? Fortunately, that cardinal happened to be none other than Napoleon's uncle, the always accommodating Cardinal Fesch. What could be more proper, or profitable, than to approach him and that body of leading clergy known, collectively, as the Officiality of Paris?

The obliging Cambacérès, who had been responsible for drawing up the statement dissolving the civil marriage, now submitted his arguments to the Officiality for the annulment of the religious marriage. The Officiality neatly side-stepped the ticklish question by creating a diocesan tribunal composed of three cardinals, an archbishop and three bishops. But with Cardinal Fesch being unable to convince even this pliant body that Napoleon – the mighty conqueror of Europe – had consented to the marriage 'under duress', they agreed to the annulment on the almost equally shaky grounds that no proper witnesses and no curé of the parish had been present. Apparently, in the eyes of the Church, the Emperor and Empress of the French had been living in sin throughout their reign.

The third of these formalities was, for both Napoleon and Josephine, the most painful. This was the formal signing of the deed of separation which took place at nine o'clock on the evening of 15 December 1809 in the throne room of the Palace of the Tuileries. It was a full dress occasion, with the men in uniform and decorations and the women in court dress and jewels. In the presence of Arch-chancellor Cambacérès and Count Regnault de Saint-Jean d'Angely, secretary of state to the imperial family, the Bonapartes assembled to witness the downfall of Josephine. 'Try as they might,' says Hortense, 'they could not conceal their joy...every time they looked at us, of whom they had always been so jealous, they betrayed themselves by their satisfied and triumphant air.'[11]

Except for Joseph – desperately defending his crown in Spain – Elisa, who was pregnant, and the independent Lucien, they were all there: the parsimonious Madame Mère; the surly Louis; the skittish Jerome and his devoted wife Catherine of Württemberg; Joseph's modest wife Julie; the lovely, empty-headed Pauline; the boastful Murat and his scheming, unscrupulous wife Caroline. This was the moment towards which they had all been working for years. Eugène de Beauharnais stood beside Napoleon; he was trembling so violently that it seemed as if he must fall.

Josephine, wearing a plain white dress and no ornament whatsoever, entered on the arm of Hortense. She seated herself in an armchair in the centre of the room. She seemed quite calm.

She did not remain calm for long. As Napoleon read out his statement she became increasingly agitated. 'Only God knows what this resolve has cost my heart,' he read. 'I have found courage for it only in the conviction that it serves the best interests of France. Far from having any complaint to register, I have only gratitude to express for the devotion and tenderness of my well-beloved wife. She has embellished fourteen years of my life; the memory thereof will remain forever engraved on my heart. She has been crowned by my hand. It is my wish that she retain the full rank and title of empress; above all, that she never doubts my sentiments for her, but considers me always as her best and dearest friend....'[12]

It was now Josephine's turn. 'With the permission of my dear and august husband, I wish to declare that, devoid now of all hope of bearing children who could satisfy the requirements of his dynastic interests and the welfare of France, I proudly offer him the greatest proof of attachment and devotion ever given a husband on this earth...'

She could read no further. Sobbing, she fell back into her chair. Regnault finished reading it for her. 'Everything I possess has come to me through his bounty. It is his hand that crowned me, and as long as I sat upon the throne the French people vouchsafed me abundant proof of their love and affection. It is in recognition of these sentiments that I consent to the dissolution of a marriage which is an obstacle to the national good, in that it deprives France of the happiness of being someday governed by the descendant of the man whom Providence raised up to remedy the evils of a terrible revolution and to re-establish the altar, the throne and the social order of France... We both, he and I, stand transmuted, glorified by the sacrifice we make on the altar of the national good.'[13]

The official record of the proceedings had still to be signed. Napoleon's signature came first, then Josephine's, and then the triumphant signatures of all the other Bonapartes.

'The Emperor then kissed the Empress,' says Hortense, 'took her by the hand and led her to her apartments.'[14]

Late that night, says Constant, just after he had helped the Emperor into bed, the bedroom door was flung open and

Josephine, red-eyed and dishevelled, burst into the room. She tottered towards the Emperor's bed and, sobbing violently, threw her arms about his neck. At this he, too, was reduced to tears.

'Come, come, Josephine my love, don't give way like this,' he murmured. 'Come, you must be brave, you must be brave! I shall always be your friend.'

Choked with tears, Josephine could make no reply, and for a few minutes there was no sound other than their mutual sobbing. Suddenly Napoleon realised that the valet was still there. 'Constant, leave the room,'[15] he said thickly. The valet obeyed and withdrew to an adjoining room. An hour later he saw the Empress leave the Emperor's apartment and make her way to her own.

The Empress Josephine left the Tuileries for Malmaison the following day. That morning the Emperor, who had decided that it would be wisest to bring his secretary Méneval with him, came to bid her goodbye. He might just as well have come alone: Méneval's presence in no way inhibited Josephine from flinging her arms about Napoleon's neck and covering his face with kisses. When she appeared to faint, Méneval rang for help. Napoleon, hardly less affected, hurried away, leaving his secretary and the Empress's maids to settle her on to a sofa.

The rest of the morning was spent in packing Josephine's personal possessions, itself a mammoth task. Both Eugène and Hortense did what they could to keep up their mother's spirits: Eugène forcing himself to tell funny stories, Hortense by reminding Josephine how much luckier she was than the last consort – Marie Antoinette – to have left the Tuileries.

By the time two o'clock – the hour of departure – came round, the Empress's rooms were filled with weeping women. Heavily veiled and leaning on Hortense's arm, she made her way through the silent crowd of court officials gathered in the entrance hall of the palace. She held a handkerchief to her eyes. 'Everyone present was moved to tears as this adorable woman crossed the short distance to the carriage,'[16] says Constant.

If there was an element of comic relief in this doleful scene, it was provided by the Empress's maid, Mademoiselle Avrillon, who followed her mistress with what she calls a 'small menagerie': a parrot in a cage, two miniature German wolfhounds, and a basket containing a litter of their puppies. Once this 'menagerie' had been settled in the carriage, the coachman slapped the reins and they moved off into the rain-dark afternoon. Behind trundled several more carriages, piled high with the Empress's possessions.

'Our drive to Malmaison,' says Hortense, 'was sad and silent.' Only after they had entered the house in which Josephine had known some of the most blissful hours of her life did she speak.

'If he is happy,' she said to Hortense, 'I shall not regret what I have done.'[17]

From anyone else the observation might have sounded trite; but not from Josephine, because she made it in all sincerity.

Part Five

THE TUILERIES: MALMAISON

24

The New Empress

NOW was the time, one would have thought, for a complete
break between Napoleon and Josephine. That would certainly have been the wisest course. But she could not stop
yearning for him; and he could not keep away from her. It was
not that he was passionately in love with her; but he was fond of
her and he felt sorry for her.

Within two days of their emotional parting at the Tuileries,
they were together again. Napoleon drove over to Malmaison
from the nearby Trianon and, during the course of the following
few weeks, he either saw her or wrote to her almost every day.
But he was careful to keep the atmosphere somewhat formal and
never to be left alone with her. If the two of them sat in one of
the salons, a couple of staff officers would remain at a discreet
distance in the same room; if they strolled outside in the winter
sunshine, Napoleon would make sure that they were in full view
of the château windows. These windows would be crowded with
Josephine's ladies, all anxious to read, from the Emperor's expans-
ive gestures and the Empress's expressive face, what they were
saying to one another.

'My dear one,' wrote Napoleon after their first meeting, 'I
found you today less resolute than you ought to be. You have
shown courage, you must find more still to sustain you, you must
not let yourself give way to a fatal melancholy; you must be
contented and, above all, take care of your health which is so
precious to me. If you are attached to me and if you love me, you

must show strength of mind and make yourself happy. You cannot doubt my constant and tender affection, and you would understand very wrongly all the feeling I have for you if you imagine I can be happy and content unless you are feeling calm.

'Adieu, my dear one, sleep well; dream that I wish it.'[1]

Claire de Rémusat who, unlike some others, had remained at the Empress's side, considered the unbroken communication between Napoleon and Josephine a mistake: it was far too unsettling. Instead of getting on with her own life (according to Hortense, Malmaison was crowded with well-wishers 'from petty tradesmen to marshals of France'[2]), Josephine lived for her ex-husband's visits and letters. The tone of these letters – sometimes solicitous, sometimes self-pitying, sometimes affectionate – must have led her to believe that he loved her more than ever.

'The most ardent and devoted husband,' writes Mademoiselle Avrillon, 'could not have showered more attentions on a cherished wife than did the Emperor on the Empress.'[3] He sent her game after a day's hunting; he sorted out her typically tangled financial affairs; he gave her 'a handsome porcelain table service'; he showered her with advice and encouragement. He insisted that his courtiers go to Malmaison to pay her their respects.

She, for her part, arranged her day around the coming and going of his pages; those pages who brought his messages to her and who took hers to him. Sometimes she would climb up to a little room from which she could get a view of the high road; from its windows she would watch the Emperor's carriage taking him to and from a hunt in the nearby forest.

On Christmas Day Napoleon invited Josephine and Hortense to join him and his sister Caroline for dinner at the Trianon. It was a doleful occasion. The Emperor and Empress sat opposite each other; Hortense and Caroline – the queens of Holland and Naples – sat on either side. Although the footmen served the meals and the prefect of the palace carried out his duties as usual, the atmosphere was quite different from previous occasions. 'There was deep silence,' says Hortense. 'My mother could eat nothing and I thought she was going to faint. The Emperor wiped his eyes several times, without saying a word, and we left immediately after dinner.'[4]

Yet clutching, as always, at straws, Josephine could draw some comfort from the fact that Napoleon had seemed so upset; it was a sign, she told Hortense, that 'he shared her regrets'. His letter, written on his return to the Tuileries from the Trianon after Christmas, seemed to bear this out. 'I hated coming back to the Tuileries. This great palace echoes with emptiness, and I feel terribly alone, isolated... I am dining all alone tonight.'[5]

To her many visitors, which included the kings of Bavaria and Württemberg, whom Napoleon had encouraged to call on her, the Empress Josephine presented the very picture of broken-hearted dignity. 'She is so gentle and affectionate in her sorrow that it breaks my heart to see her,' wrote Madame de Rémusat to her husband. 'Never a word that is *de trop*, never a word of bitterness or complaint, escapes her lips. She is truly as sweet as an angel.'[6]

And Laure Junot, who hurried to Malmaison to see her, says much the same thing. 'She seemed to me, at that hour, deserving of the respect of the entire universe... She regretted all she had lost but in justice to her it should be said that what she regretted above all else was the loss of her husband.'[7]

Yet curiously enough, at the very time that Josephine was playing, so touchingly, the role of the discarded wife and empress, she was actively promoting the cause of her successor.

Napoleon had once said that what he would be marrying, as his second wife, was a womb, and Josephine decided to lend a hand in choosing this womb. Her preference was for the eighteen-year-old Archduchess Marie Louise, eldest daughter of the Emperor Francis I of Austria. When Countess Metternich, wife of the new Austrian Foreign Minister who had, until recently, been Austria's ambassador to France, visited the Empress at Malmaison, Josephine brought up the subject of Napoleon's projected marriage.

It was a question, Josephine assured Countess Metternich, that occupied her attention 'to the exclusion of all else'. Her hope was to arrange a match between her ex-husband and the Archduchess Marie Louise. She had already raised the question with Napoleon and, although he had told her that he had not yet made a choice, she believed that – given the assurance that his offer would be acceptable to Austria – he would choose Marie Louise.

The Emperor, continued Josephine, would be coming to see her again that afternoon; she would then be able to give Countess

Metternich some more definite news. 'We must try and arrange this between us,' said Josephine.

In great excitement, the Countess wrote to her husband to give him this 'extraordinary' news. Metternich's reply was equally enthusiastic. Considering Napoleon's marriage to be a matter of 'supreme importance in Continental affairs', he hoped that the Empress Josephine would persevere in her negotiations. She did, and at a specially convened meeting of grand dignitaries and ministers held at the Tuileries on 28 January 1810 to discuss the marriage, Josephine's negotiations bore fruit. Although Napoleon had still not had a firm rejection of his offer for the hand of the Grand Duchess Anna of Russia, and although some of the ministers spoke out in favour of the Russian alliance, Napoleon – encouraged by Josephine – had already made up his mind about Marie Louise.

Once Metternich let it be known that the French offer would be acceptable (and with the Tsar Alexander having finally sent what amounted to a polite refusal), Napoleon went ahead.

He instructed – of all people – Josephine's son Eugène to make a formal offer to the Austrian ambassador for the hand of the Archduchess Marie Louise. The offer having been accepted, Eugène signed the marriage contract in, as he told the ambassador, 'the name of the Emperor and with the approval of the Empress, my mother.'

Why had Josephine gone to so much trouble to foster this Austrian marriage? In royal and aristocratic circles, Austria was always regarded as France's natural ally; both Eugène and Hortense had assured Countess Metternich, in confidence, that they were 'Austrian in their souls'. But Josephine's chief concern would not have been political. She was far more interested in the social and emotional possibilities of the match. She had even gone so far as to promise Countess Metternich that she would work heart and soul to ensure that Napoleon and his new bride were happy.

Perhaps Josephine hoped that, by sponsoring the marriage she would win both Napoleon's gratitude and Marie Louise's affection. Might the inexperienced young Empress not look to her predecessor for advice, example and protection? Might the three of them not set up some sort of imperial *ménage à trois*? After all, at the Russian court, a dowager empress always took precedence over a newly crowned empress. Even if Josephine were not thinking in terms of a similar position for herself, might she not have been hoping to return to court, there to take her place at, if not the right, then at least the left hand of the Emperor? Already she was badgering Napoleon for permission to take up residence at the Elysée Palace. Here, in the very heart of the Empire, she no doubt planned to resume a full social life. For whatever Josephine might have had in mind it was not, apparently, a life of tragic seclusion.

She was brought sharply down to earth on 11 March 1810 – the very day that the proxy marriage between Napoleon and Marie Louise was celebrated in the Augustine Church in Vienna. That morning the Emperor arranged for the Château of Navarre, situated in Normandy, sixty miles north-west of Paris, to be converted into a duchy and bestowed on Josephine. Her initial delight at his generosity was considerably tempered by a letter in which he gave her what amounted to precise marching orders.

'Go take possession of your new domain,' he instructed.'You should go on 25 March and spend the month of April there.'[8]

In other words, she was to leave Paris before the arrival of Marie Louise at the Château de Compiègne, on 27 March. It was, to all intents and purposes, a banishment.

From this point on, contact between Napoleon and Josephine was chiefly by letter or through her children. He might pay her an occasional visit at Malmaison whenever she was permitted to return there but these visits were always brief and invariably upsetting. 'They embraced,' reads an account of one such meeting, 'and one could see the tears of joy flowing down the cheeks of one as much as of the other.'[9] She had had, reported Josephine to Hortense, on this particular visit 'a day of happiness ... His presence made me happy, even though it renewed my sorrows ....'[10]

One of Napoleon's chief reasons for keeping his distance was his satisfaction with his new wife, the Empress Marie Louise. From the moment that he had first set eyes on her, when he had scrambled unexpectedly into the coach that was bringing her to Compiègne, Napoleon had been delighted with her. Marie Louise was not, admittedly, a great beauty. What might have been a soft, gentle face was marred by the heavy Hapsburg jaw and the somewhat prominent teeth. Her figure, although good, was graceless; compared with the lithe Josephine, she was like a block of wood. But at eighteen years of age, she had youth on her side.

She had a big, healthy body, a mane of fair hair, bright if somewhat vague blue eyes, and firm rosy cheeks.

In the same way that Marie Louise's looks were neither good nor bad, so did her character evade definition. Hers was essentially a negative personality; she had always to be seen in relation to others; she appeared to have no mind of her own. There was an elusiveness about her, a quality of indifference; one did not know what to think of her, or what she herself was thinking. She was a simple, modest, innocent, unambitious girl, yet she remained strangely unattractive.

Her upbringing was largely responsible for her lack of character. Reared in the cloistered, formal, old-fashioned court which revolved around her father, the Austrian Emperor, her days had been carefully mapped out; she had never had to make a decision in her life. Sheltered from any contact with the harsh world beyond the palace walls (her pets were all female, even her lesson books were censored), she had developed into an unquestioning, obedient young girl, always conscious of her duty towards her all-powerful father. He was the centre of her world, the fountainhead from which she derived all benefits, the master from whom she took her commands. For Marie Louise had always to have someone to tell her what to do; like a looking glass, she could mirror but never originate an image; like the moon, her light was merely a reflection of the sun's rays.

As such, she suited Napoleon perfectly. On the day that Marie Louise left Vienna, her father had given her a final word of advice: she must do absolutely everything that Napoleon asked her to do. So when the Emperor – in spite of the fact that they were not to be married until several days later – insisted on sleeping with her on the very evening they first met, she acquiesced without a murmur. In fact, she did rather more than merely acquiesce. The disapproving Lord Liverpool might have described Napoleon's conduct that night as more of a rape than a wooing, but Marie Louise had no complaints. She asked him, Napoleon afterwards admitted, 'to do it again'.[11]

It was no wonder that when he appeared the following morning, the beaming Emperor advised one of his generals to marry a German girl: they were the best women in the world, he said, sweet-tempered, kind and as fresh as roses.

She pleased him no less out of bed than in. Napoleon, who had half expected some vain, petulant, pampered princess, was filled with admiration for this unaffected, good-natured, diligent young girl. Only just out of the schoolroom, she had not yet shaken off the habits of discipline, and certain hours of each day were put aside for her drawing and embroidery lessons and for her reading periods. Compared with Josephine, Marie Louise was extremely industrious. And in thrift she could equal any Corsican woman. It was for those qualities in which she most resembled a good housewife, reported Metternich to the Emperor Francis, that Napoleon valued his new wife most.

And she, in her dependent way, adored him. To her father she wrote, 'I can only repeat to you how happy and contented I am and, I am convinced, always shall be. You will only understand this when you come to know the Emperor personally. Then you will see how good and lovable he is in private life, and what a noble-hearted man he is. I am persuaded that you will love him too.' She had come to France expecting a monster, and had found a dumpy, affectionate, entertaining, middle-aged man instead. Marie Louise, like Josephine, had a way of not concerning herself with things which did not affect her personally, and to her Napoleon was simply a kind and attentive husband. Not long after her marriage she remarked to Metternich that she supposed some of the Viennese imagined her being subject to 'daily torments' whereas, in fact, she was not a bit afraid of Napoleon. 'But I am beginning to think,' she added, 'that he is a little afraid of me.'[12]

He was not afraid of her, of course, but he was still a little in awe of her. To Napoleon, she was still something of a symbol; she represented his ultimate social triumph. Through her he had at last achieved respectability; through her, he had related himself to almost every royal house in Europe; through her he would establish the fourth French dynasty, and thus achieve immortality.

Where Marie Louise was a disappointment to Napoleon was in public. Her shyness gave her a cold, withdrawn manner; she had no memory for names and faces; she had not the slightest idea of how to make conversation. Loathing public appearances, receptions were a form of torture to her; weighted with jewels, ill at ease in Leroy's elaborate creations, Marie Louise would move like an automaton through the great state ceremonies. Someone once claimed that, as she came up to be presented to the imperial couple, Napoleon hissed urgently to Marie Louise, '*Pleine de grace! Pleine de grace!*'

In short, in the field in which Josephine had been such a

brilliant success, Marie Louise was a dismal failure. 'Nothing,' said Constant with a wealth of meaning, 'could have been more different from the first Empress than the second.'[13] The upstart Empress knew how to dress, how to move, how to smile, how to talk; the princess of the oldest royal house in Europe was as inelegant, as stiff, as expressionless and as tongue-tied as a school-girl. Josephine seemed to have all the qualities of the aristocrat, Marie Louise those of the bourgeois.

Years later Napoleon himself summed up the differences between his two wives. 'The one [Josephine] was all art and grace; the other [Marie Louise] was all innocence and simplicity. At no moment of her life had the ways and habits of the former ever been other than pleasant and seductive. It would have been impossible to find fault with her in this respect. She made the art of pleasing her constant study, obtaining her effect while concealing her method of doing so. Every artifice imaginable was employed by her to heighten her charms, yet so mysteriously that at most one had but the merest suspicion of it. Marie Louise, on the other hand, ignored artifice and anything like dissimulation; all roundabout methods were unknown to her. The former never asked for anything, but was in debt everywhere. The latter, if in want of anything, never hesitated to ask, nor did she ever purchase anything without feeling conscientiously obliged to pay at once. Both had kind, sweet dispositions and were deeply attached to their husband.'[14]

Conscious of her shortcomings, Marie Louise wanted nothing to do with her predecessor. Josephine's hopes of befriending Napo-leon's new wife and of being welcomed back to court were soon dispelled. The Empress Marie Louise's 'disposition to jealousy', as Claire de Rémusat put it, was only too apparent. One day, as Napoleon and Marie Louise were out driving, they found them-selves in the vicinity of Malmaison. As Josephine was not in residence, Napoleon offered to show Marie Louise the house and gardens.

'She made no open protest,' reported General Duroc, 'but her eyes filled with tears, and the symptoms of distress were so unmistakable that the Emperor called off the visit.'[15]

So Napoleon was obliged to pay his ex-wife clandestine visits, and to Marie Louise, Josephine remained 'that woman at Mal-maison'.

Gradually Josephine reconciled herself to the fact that she and Marie Louise would never meet. 'It seems that the Empress

Marie Louise has no desire to see me,' she wrote to Eugène. 'On that point we are in perfect accord, for I would have consented to meet her only to please the Emperor. But it appears that she regards me with something less than benevolence, and this I do not understand, because she can know me only through the sacrifice I made for her. I desire, as does she, the Emperor's happiness; this mutually shared sentiment, if nothing else, should dispose her to be friendly towards me.'[16]

25

The Heir

THE Château of Navarre, which was Josephine's home until she returned permanently to Malmaison late in 1812, was a grandiose, cube-shaped building topped by a huge, flattened dome. Because it looked like an inverted cooking pot, it was irreverently known, by the locals, as *la marmite*. The château had been empty for many years and was in a badly neglected state: damp, cold and crumbling. The woodwork throughout the house was rotting. Many of the rooms were small and inconvenient. And although the park was magnificent, it was too 'watery' for Josephine's taste; its elaborate network of canals, waterfalls, ponds, cascades and fountains made it damp and unhealthy. Both house and grounds would need to have a great deal of money spent on them before they achieved Josephine's standards of comfort and beauty.

Adding to Josephine's dissatisfaction with her new home was the fact that so many members of her household had drifted away. Some considered Navarre too much of a backwater; others found the prospect of serving the new young Empress irresistible. Josephine was neglected, too, by many of those who had most to thank her for: Leroy the *couturier*, Duplan the *coiffeur*. She, whose circle had always been so gay and gossipy, now found herself playing tric-trac with the Bishop of Evreux in the evenings. 'He is a very pleasant man,' she reported gamely to Hortense, 'despite his seventy-five years.'[1]

'We do the same thing at the same hour every day,' complained Claire de Rémusat, who was one of those who had remained loyal, 'so that it becomes difficult to know whether it is yesterday or tomorrow.'[2]

Dreary as life at Navarre might be, it was preferable to what Josephine was beginning to fear might be her fate: permanent exile from France. 'If her earlier years had been haunted by the spectre of divorce,' writes one of her biographers, 'the spectre of exile had risen to haunt her later years.'[3] Her best defence against this possibility, reckoned Josephine, was to lie low. Knowing that the Empress Marie Louise resented her, Josephine was careful not to thrust herself forward; on the rare occasions that she was allowed to spend a few weeks at Malmaison, she would promise Napoleon that she would 'live as if I were a thousand leagues from Paris.'[4] She spent long periods at Aix-les-Bains, and in the autumn of 1810 she trailed around Switzerland, from Geneva to Neuchâtel to Interlaken to Bern. She even arranged to buy the small estate of Pregny-la-Tour, near Geneva.

In her occasional, and always respectful letters to Napoleon, in which she asked for permission to go here or there, Josephine never made a nuisance of herself. 'Your Majesty may be confident that I shall always respect your new situation, and respect it in silence,' she once wrote, 'putting my trust in the sentiments you formerly bore me, and so requiring no new proof.'[5]

But a letter from Madame de Rémusat, who had not accompanied Josephine to Switzerland in 1810, set the alarm bells ringing. In honeyed phrases Claire de Rémusat suggested that, with the Empress Marie Louise due to give birth the following spring, Josephine would be well advised to stay out of France altogether. Even Navarre, she thought, would be too close to the heart of things. Josephine, in a gesture worthy of her 'noble character', should make one more sacrifice: she should save the Emperor the embarrassment of enforcing her exile by suggesting it herself.

Whether or not Claire de Rémusat had written the letter on the Emperor's orders, Josephine did not know. But in rising panic she wrote directly to Napoleon. Casting aside the 'Sires' and 'Majestys' and third-person phraseology of her previous letters, she addressed him simply as 'Bonaparte'. He had promised her, she said, that he would never abandon her: 'I have only you in all the world. You are my only friend.'

What, she demanded, was she to do? Could she return to

France from Switzerland or must she stay away? If he wanted her to stay away, would a seven or eight months' absence be enough? She could remain in Switzerland for the autumn; she could pay a visit to Eugène in Milan in the winter; she could take the waters at Aix the following spring and summer. 'That would make a whole year of absence – a year I would be able to get through only in the hope of seeing you again at the end of it . . .

'Oh, I beg you, don't refuse to guide me; advise your poor Josephine; it will be proof of your affection and will console her for all her sacrifices.'[6]

To back up this letter, Josephine commissioned Hortense to tackle the Emperor personally. She could see at once, says Hortense on being received by Napoleon at Fontainebleau, how relieved he would be if Josephine were to volunteer to go to Italy. 'I must think of my wife's happiness,' he explained. 'Things have not turned out as I hoped they would. She [Marie Louise] resents the privileges and honours accorded to your mother and the influence your mother is known to exercise over me . . . .' If Josephine were agreeable, he would appoint her as governor of Rome, or she could establish a 'brilliant court' of her own in Brussels. But he would never force her to do anything against her will. 'I shall never forget the sacrifices she has made for me.'[7]

When he finally answered Josephine's anguished letter, it was in much the same conciliatory fashion. There were, he wrote, only two suitable places in which she could spend that winter of 1810– 11: Milan or Navarre. He was afraid, though, that she would find Navarre very boring.

Blithely refusing to take the hint, Josephine gave up any idea of wintering in Milan and returned, in high spirits, to Navarre. She went by way of the only place in which she really wanted to be – Malmaison. Napoleon, still with Marie Louise at Fontainebleau, had given Josephine permission to spend just twenty-four hours there but she, irresponsible as always, remained for over a week. Not until Napoleon, back in Paris, ordered her to leave, did she go.

One reason, perhaps, for Josephine's reluctance to leave her beloved Malmaison was that it was so redolent of the days she had spent there during the happiest period of her marriage – the Consulate. Young Georgette Ducrest, who had joined the Empress Josephine's service during her recent stay in Switzerland, realised, on seeing Malmaison for the first time, how much those days had meant to her mistress.

'The Empress's adoration of the Emperor amounted to a cult,' she wrote. 'His Malmaison apartments were preserved exactly as they were the day he left them. There was his uncurtained Roman bed, there were his guns and swords hanging on the wall; even several pieces of his clothing were to be seen scattered about on the furniture. On his desk was his world map and the pen with which he wrote the laws of Europe; on the table, a history book lay open at the page he had been reading. One expected to see him enter at any moment into that room which he had forever abandoned. Josephine seldom granted permission for a visit to that sanctuary. No one but she could touch or dust what she called her "relics".'[8]

Causing both Napoleon and Josephine concern during this period were the affairs of the King and Queen of Holland – Napoleon's brother Louis and Josephine's daughter Hortense.

In the spring of 1810, soon after his remarriage, Napoleon had decreed that Hortense must return to Holland, to reconcile herself to her morose and tormented husband. This attempt was no more successful than any previous attempt had been. Within weeks Hortense had fled to Plombières.

She was still there when, during the first week of July, she heard that Louis, unable to stand Napoleon's interference in the affairs of his Dutch kingdom a moment longer, had suddenly abdicated. This was followed by a letter from Napoleon to tell her that he intended 'annexing' Holland and that King Louis's 'latest act of folly'[9] had set her free. She could now live tranquilly in Paris.

As her two little sons were safe with the Emperor at Saint-Cloud, Hortense decided to join her mother, at that stage still at Aix. And it was here that Hortense once more took up the threads of her turbulent friendship with a young general by the name of Charles de Flahaut. The natural son of Talleyrand, the dashing Charles de Flahaut was utterly unlike his subtle-tongued, impassive-faced father. He was also unlike Hortense's husband Louis. Under the indulgent eye of the Empress Josephine, the two young people were at last able to delight, openly, in each other's company.

'For the first time since I knew that I loved him,' says Hortense, 'I now saw him constantly.'[10]

Just over a year later, in September 1811, Hortense gave birth to Charles de Flahaut's son. The affair was shrouded in secrecy. Not even Josephine knew about it. Charles de Flahaut's mother took charge of the little boy (had not her own son Charles been a love child?) and he was christened Charles Demorny – Demorny being the name of an old pensioner who had posed as the baby's father at the registration of its birth.

Forty years later, as the Duke de Morny, this child would take his place at the right hand of his half brother, another of Hortense's sons, the Emperor Napoleon III.

Earlier in 1811, the baby whom Napoleon saw as the next Emperor of the French, a future Napoleon II, was born. For on 20 March 1811, the Empress Marie Louise gave birth to a son.

From Navarre, Josephine wrote at once to Napoleon to congratulate him. 'No one can read, of course, in the closed book of a woman's heart,' says Mademoiselle Avrillon, 'but the Empress manifested the most lively and apparently the most genuine delight at the news. I could detect no affectation, and no mental reservations in the satisfaction she expressed.'[11]

'My dear,' wrote Napoleon in his own hand in answer to Josephine's congratulations, 'I have received your letter, and I thank you. My son is big and is thriving. I hope that he will do well. He has my chest, mouth and eyes. I hope he will fulfil his destiny....'[12]

Josephine was still at Navarre when, on 9 June 1811, amid scenes of great splendour, Napoleon's son was christened Napoleon Francis Charles Joseph and given the title of the King of Rome. For centuries, the heir to the Holy Roman Empire had been called the King of the Romans; Napoleon, who always thought of himself as the heir to Charlemagne and who considered Rome as the second city of his Empire, would be content with no less a title for his son.

'I envy him, for glory awaits him, whereas I had to run after it...,' said Napoleon. 'To take hold of the world, he will only have to stretch out his hands.'[13]

In all these celebrations, Josephine played no part. In fact, not until September – three months after the King of Rome's christening – was she permitted to leave Navarre and take up temporary residence at Malmaison. But even this did not mean that the Emperor could visit her openly. Nor did it mean that she could see the little King of Rome. Marie Louise would not allow it.

But, in the greatest secrecy, Josephine did one day manage to see the baby.

The Countess de Montesquiou, governess to the King of Rome, had heard, from the Emperor, of Josephine's longing to see the child.

'But that would distress the Empress [Marie Louise] so much that I cannot bring myself to give you the necessary instructions,' said Napoleon to Madame de Montesquiou.

'Let me see to it, Sire,' answered the governess. 'Just give your approval to what I intend to do.'

'Very well, but be careful how you go about it.'

So the governess sent an equerry to Malmaison to tell Josephine that she, and the baby, would be driving to Bagatelle – a small château in the Bois de Bologne – the following Sunday. They would be there at two.

On arrival at Bagatelle that Sunday the equerry, pretending that he knew nothing of the arrangement, came back to the carriage to tell Madame de Montesquiou that the Empress Josephine was inside. The governess, feigning equal surprise, replied that, as they were there, they had better pay her their respects; it would be 'unseemly' otherwise.

So the governess, accompanied by a nurse carrying the baby, went in to greet Josephine. The Empress went down on her knees, kissed the baby's hand and – inevitably – burst into tears.

'Sweet child,' she said, 'one day you will know the extent of the sacrifice I made for you. I rely on your governess to help you to appreciate it.'

After spending about an hour with the infant King, Josephine asked to meet the people who were in attendance on him that day. In her gracious way, she spoke to them all.

'My, but that one's got a kind heart!' exclaimed the nurse as they were driving away. 'She's said more to me in a quarter of an hour than the other one [Marie Louise] has in six months.'[14]

Many years later, the child who was known successively as the King of Rome, Napoleon II and the Duke of Reichstadt, would pay tribute to the Empress Josephine. With Napoleon dead and with Marie Louise long since having abandoned him, the young man was living in virtual, if gilded, imprisonment in the Palace of Schönbrunn.

'If Josephine had been my mother,' he said one day, 'my father would never have been sent to Saint Helena and I would not be languishing here in Vienna.'[15]

The End

In the bulletin which Napoleon drew up to acquaint his subjects with the disasters of the Russian campaign, the Emperor took care to announce that his own health had never been better. For it was on his life alone, he now fully appreciated, that his regime depended.

He arrived back at the Tuileries on the night of 18 December. On hearing that he was home, Hortense hurried to the palace to welcome him. She found him tired and preoccupied. Misfortune seemed to have sobered him. She asked whether the retreat had really been as bad as his despatches had led them to believe.

'I told the whole truth,' answered Napoleon.

'But we were not the only ones to suffer,' she argued. 'Our enemies must have suffered very heavily.'

'No doubt,' he said quietly, 'but that does not console me.'[4]

Throughout these momentous events, Josephine had been prey, as she put it to Hortense, 'to cruel anxiety'. She was worried, not only about Napoleon but also about Eugène who was with him, as a corps commander, in Russia. Now and then she received a hastily scrawled letter from one or other of them but sometimes weeks would go by without a word. Restlessly she moved about: from Malmaison to Milan to visit Eugène's wife and children; from Milan to Aix where she was disconcerted to find several members of the Bonaparte family; from Aix to the house she had bought at Pregny on Lake Geneva; and from there back to Malmaison – the home which she had by now been allowed to move back to permanently.

'Why does Eugène not write?' she complained in a letter to Hortense. 'To allay my fears, I try to tell myself that the Emperor has forbidden letters out of Russia. The proof is in the fact that no one receives any. I am very sad.'[5]

What would become of her if Napoleon were to be killed in battle? She depended entirely on his goodwill, and generous financial support, for her comfortable existence. It was true that she owned Malmaison and its treasures but she had no income of her own; whatever Napoleon gave her she spent. She could expect no help from the Bonapartes; certainly not from the parsimonious Madame Mère, who had been squirrelling away a considerable fortune. Nor would the Empress Marie Louise feel obliged to help her.

Equally unsettling was the fact that so many members of her household – most of them nobles of the *ancien régime*, royalists at heart – were beginning to show signs of something less than undivided loyalty to the Empire. As first rumours, and then confirmation, of the Russian débâcle came in, so they started distancing themselves from the regime; 'testing', as Mademoiselle Avrillon puts it, 'the wind and looking around for a likely port in the storm'.[6]

The composition of Josephine's household was to give rise, in the years ahead, to the 'conspiracy of Malmaison' theory: the accusation that the Empress Josephine and her circle were treasonably engaged in working for the downfall of the Empire and the restoration of a monarchy. It is true that many members of Josephine's household would have preferred the Bourbons to the Bonapartes, and that Talleyrand, that 'Prince of Weathercocks', was whispering to his great friend Claire de Rémusat about the possibility of an imminent imperial collapse, but this hardly constituted a conspiracy. Some of the men in attendance on Josephine were indeed to assume their places in a Bourbon restoration but they can hardly have been said to have helped to bring it about.

As for Josephine herself, her conduct during these uncertain days was beyond suspicion. One need only read the letters of this most transparent of women to Eugène and Hortense to appreciate that her loyalty was unquestioned. Her relief, at Napoleon's safe return, was obvious to all. The welcome arrival of his courier, to tell her that he was home safely, had another effect as well: it very speedily put an end to any royalist murmurings amongst the ladies and gentlemen of her court.

But the Empress Josephine's relief was short lived. During the following fifteen months, Napoleon's whole showy, far-flung, apparently impregnable Empire came crashing down.

By the spring of 1813 Napoleon was fighting a war on two fronts: against Wellington's forces in Spain and against a new Russian–Prussian coalition in Germany. Wellington's victory, at the Battle of Vittoria in northern Spain in June, sent King Joseph scurrying back to France. And although Napoleon had by then won some successes against the Russians and Prussians, his position was so precarious that he was obliged to agree to an armistice.

The End

During this lull, Austria – acting as an 'armed mediator' – proposed what amounted to a breakup of Napoleon's Empire. France was to return to its 'natural frontiers' and to give up most of its gains in Italy, Germany and Poland. This the enraged Napoleon refused to contemplate. So in August Austria joined Russia and Prussia against him. Hardly had Napoleon's father-in-law, the Emperor Francis of Austria, ranged himself on the side of his enemies, than the most important of Napoleon's satellite kings, Eugène's father-in-law, Maximilian of Bavaria, joined the coalition.

Napoleon faced this overwhelming Allied force at the famous Battle of the Nations at Leipzig, which lasted from 16 to 18 October 1813. It was a savage engagement at which he was roundly defeated. From this point on, everything began to crumble. As the shattered *Grande Armée* retreated across the Rhine so, one by one, did Napoleon's erstwhile allies desert him. All those puppet kings, princes and grand dukes whose domains had made up the Confederation of the Rhine joined the Allied bandwagon. His brother Jerome fled his kingdom of Westphalia even more precipitately than his brother Joseph had fled his kingdom of Spain. Murat, with the active encouragement of his wife, Napoleon's sister Caroline, started secret negotiations with Britain and Austria in an attempt to hang on to the kingdom of Naples. Even Elisa, whom Napoleon had by now made Grand Duchess of Tuscany, was preparing to throw in her lot with his enemies.

Amongst this wholesale disintegration of his Empire, the only member of Napoleon's family to stand firm was Josephine's son Eugène. When Eugène's father-in-law, the King of Bavaria, announced that he was about to join the coalition against Napoleon and suggested that Eugène – in return for the promise of the kingdom of Italy – do the same, the proposal was indignantly spurned. He would never be a king at that price, Eugène told his wife Augusta; his loyalty lay with the Emperor of the French.

The Emperor of the French, unfortunately, was beginning to suspect that Eugène's loyalty was less than absolute. He had recently been told that his stepson had been in touch with the Austrians. This was true; but the only reason for Eugène's approach to the Austrian commander in Italy had been to arrange for his pregnant wife Augusta's safety in the event of his having to leave her behind in Milan. But Napoleon, made paranoid by the desertion of so many of his allies and by the secret manoeuvrings of Joachim and Caroline Murat, remained suspicious.

This was why, when he wanted to give Eugène instructions, Napoleon resorted to the extraordinary tactic of writing, not to Eugène himself, but to Josephine. One can only assume that the Emperor imagined that whereas Eugène might defy his instructions, he would never do so if they had been forwarded to him by Josephine.

The Emperor's intention, wrote Josephine to her son, was for him to bring his French troops home by way of the Alps, leaving only Italian troops to hold Mantua and the other fortresses. 'His letter ends with the words, "France above all! France has need of all her sons." So come, come quickly, my son . . . .'[7]

Resenting this implied slur on his loyalty, Eugène wrote strong letters to both Napoleon and Josephine. 'I do not feel that I have merited this,' he told his stepfather. 'My devotion to Your Majesty and to my native land are motives strong enough . . . .'[8]

Napoleon's reply was gruff; he described Eugène's letter as 'extravagant'. 'I paid you no compliments on your loyalty,' he wrote gracelessly, 'because you only did your duty.'[9]

But by now – the early months of 1814 – Eugène's troops would have made little difference to the military situation. It was desperate. The enemy had invaded, and the 'Campaign of France', the defence of French soil, was being waged.

Before leaving the Tuileries to take command of his forces once more, Napoleon had staged a highly theatrical farewell for the benefit of the officers of the newly formed National Guard of Paris. When the officers had assembled, Napoleon, Marie Louise and the three-year-old King of Rome entered. With his son in his arms, his Empress by his side, and such of his family who were still loyal to him standing behind, Napoleon addressed the men. In a voice breaking with emotion, he told them that he was entrusting to their care the city of Paris, his wife and his child. Heartfelt shouts of *Vive l'Empereur* drowned the end of his speech, and the watching Hortense reports that many eyes were filled with tears. A few days later, she says wryly, some of these same men were heaping abuse on the name of Napoleon.

Having appointed Marie Louise Regent (a post which she was singularly ill suited to fill) and his brother Joseph Lieutenant-General of the Empire (an almost equally unsuitable appointment), Napoleon left to face the invading Allied armies. Although he fought one of the most dashing campaigns of his career, it was hopeless. Outnumbered and encircled, the French armies retreated towards Paris. By the last week of March the enemy was within sight of the capital. On 30 March, Marshal Marmont, whom Napoleon had left to defend Paris, capitulated and retired south. The victorious Allies marched into the city the following day, forcing Napoleon to headquarter himself at Fontainebleau.

He had one hope left: that the Allies would be obliged to negotiate with him, the Emperor.

Josephine, in the meantime, had fled to Navarre. She had remained at Malmaison until the end, almost. 'I can still hear her accent of distress,' remembers Mademoiselle Avrillon, 'her endless, frantic staccato questions addressed to every living soul, even the lowliest and most insignificant, who came out from Paris. "What is the Emperor doing? Where is Bonaparte now? Where is the enemy? What are people saying? Is there still hope? Still courage?"'[10]

The first definite news she had was from Hortense, on 28 March, two days before Paris fell. Hortense had been astonished to hear that the Regency Council had decided that the Empress Marie Louise and the infant King of Rome should leave Paris. That, apparently, had been Napoleon's wish. When Hortense warned the bewildered Marie Louise that her flight would lose her her crown, the Empress answered, 'Perhaps you are right, but that's what's been decided, and if the Emperor has to reproach anyone, it won't be me.'[11] Marie Louise was followed, a day later, by the rest of the Bonaparte family.

With the present Empress about to quit Paris, Hortense sent an urgent message to the previous Empress to do the same. All that night at Malmaison was spent packing. Josephine's magnificent collection of jewellery was stored in strongboxes, and her maids sat sewing diamonds and pearls into the lining of the quilted skirt she was to wear on her journey. As they could not rely on post horses *en route*, the Empress took all her carriages and horses. Although the cortège was sizeable and the carriages heavily laden, Josephine was obliged to abandon most of what she owned: Malmaison with all its valuable paintings, furniture, *objets*, statuary and hot houses. It was assumed that it would be pillaged by 'the Cossacks'. In the course of their journey to Navarre one Cossack was indeed spotted, but he quickly disappeared back into the forest of Rambouillet.

Once safely at Navarre, Josephine's thoughts were all of Napoleon, Eugène and Hortense. 'I have never lacked courage to meet the many dangerous situations in which I have found myself during my life,' she wrote to Hortense on 31 March, 'and I shall always be able to meet reverses of fortune with equanimity, but what I cannot endure is this separation from my children, this uncertainty as to their fate. I haven't stopped weeping for two days. Send me news of yourself and your children – and of Eugène and his family, if you hear from them. Let me know where you are going . . . .'[12]

Hortense was, in fact, on her way to Navarre. In defiance of the wishes of her estranged husband Louis, who threatened to take away their two sons if she did not join the Empress Marie Louise and the rest of the fugitive imperial family at Blois, Hortense and her boys went to join Josephine. They arrived at Navarre on 1 April.

And it was here that Josephine's household heard that the Allied armies had marched into Paris and that the turncoat Talleyrand, as president of the provisional government, had persuaded the Allied monarchs to depose Napoleon and to restore the Bourbon monarchy in the person of the long-exiled Comte de Provence – the eldest surviving brother of the guillotined Louis XVI – as King Louis XVIII.

Napoleon, after searching for alternatives, was finally obliged to abdicate. On 6 April, at the Palace of Fontainebleau, he signed his Act of Abdication. He was to be banished from France and to be granted the island of Elba as a sovereign principality.

The news was brought to Josephine late one night by Adolphe de Maussion, a functionary of the Council of State. Bursting into Hortense's bedroom, Josephine flung herself on to her daughter's bed. 'Oh, that poor Napoleon!' she wailed. 'He is to be sent to the island of Elba! How dreadful for him! Were it not for his wife, I would go to join him in his exile.'

'I saw how much she still loved him,' notes Hortense, 'and I thought bitterly of the courage it had taken for her to have separated herself from him. As Monsieur de Maussion gave us the details of the national disaster, it was above all the fate of the Emperor which my mother lamented.'[13]

And Josephine was very much in Napoleon's mind during these

last, tortured days at Fontainebleau. 'Eugène,' he confided one evening to Caulaincourt, 'is the only one of my family who has never given me a single cause for dissatisfaction. His mother made me very happy. Those are the sweetest recollections of my life.'[14]

For by that stage – the evening of 12 April – Napoleon seems to have given up all hope of being reunited with the Empress Marie Louise and their son. She, during the early days of the débâcle, had been only too ready to leave Blois and join him at Fontainebleau, but he, perhaps thinking that she might be useful to him as a go-between with her father, the Emperor Francis, had kept her at arm's length. By the time he was ready for her to join him, it was too late. The Allies had by then decided to keep the couple apart. They, no less than Napoleon, appreciated that his position would be greatly strengthened if he were to be reunited with his wife and son; with, in other words, the Austrian Emperor's daughter and grandson.

So poor, perplexed Marie Louise was shunted from Blois to Orléans and finally to Rambouillet where she was welcomed by that other dominant male figure in her life – her father, the Emperor Francis. She was assured that she had nothing to worry about, that she and her child would be taken care of, that there was really no hurry about joining her husband and that she should go to some spa to regain her health and calm her nerves before coming to any decision.

She, only too pleased to have her mind made up for her, agreed to return to Vienna until things had been sorted out. As far as she and Napoleon were concerned, things never were. Napoleon was never to see Marie Louise, or their son, again.

By then, the fallen Emperor had signed the Treaty of Fontainebleau which set out the terms of his abdication. Among its many clauses were some concerning his two wives. Marie Louise was to be granted the principality of Parma; there was no word about her being permitted to join him on Elba. Josephine was to be allowed to retain possession of all her properties – including Malmaison and Navarre – and to be granted an annual revenue of one million francs; a third of what Napoleon had given her.

Early on the morning of 13 April, finally convinced that Marie Louise and their son would never be permitted to join him, and overwhelmed by the hopelessness of his situation, Napoleon decided to take his own life. In his dimly lit bedroom he swallowed a powdered mixture which his doctor had made up for him during the Russian campaign. Summoning Caulaincourt to sit on his bed, Napoleon spoke to him of, among other things, his first wife. 'You are to tell Josephine,' he said, 'that she has been very much in my thoughts.'[15]

But his attempt at suicide was apparently foiled by the strength of the dose: instead of killing him, it made him vomit. Recovered, Napoleon remained at Fontainebleau for a further week, waiting for the Allied commissioners who were to escort him to Elba. On 20 April, in a moving ceremony in the courtyard of the palace, he took formal leave of the members of the Old Guard. The scene, in what was to be renamed le Cours des Adieus, has become one of the great setpieces of Napoleonic iconography: an orgy of weeping and kissing, cheering and flag-clutching. 'Farewell my children,' were the closing words of Napoleon's address. 'I should like to press you all to my heart; at least I shall kiss your flag!'[16]

When it was all over, Napoleon climbed into a waiting carriage and was driven away.

His last letter to Josephine, written four days before, struck a similarly histrionic, if self-justifying, note. But it ended with a heartfelt tribute to the loyal Eugène and with a sincerely expressed farewell to her. 'Adieu, my dear Josephine. Resign yourself, as I have done, and never forget him who has never forgotten, and never will forget, you....'[17]

Never for a moment could he have imagined that she had only six weeks more to live.

27

'*Adieu Josephine*'

NAPOLEON'S advice to Josephine – that she resign herself to the changed situation – she blithely ignored. No sooner had the Emperor abdicated than she was writing to Eugène to tell him that he was now 'free, and absolved from any oath of fidelity' to Napoleon; 'anything more that you can do for his cause would be useless,' she advised, 'act for your family.'[1]

For giving such advice, and for the way in which she subsequently fraternised with the victorious Allies, Josephine has been roundly condemned by Bonapartist historians. They have accused her of ingratitude and opportunism. And of frivolity: for, at the very time that Napoleon, at Fontainebleau, was facing the blackest days of his career, Josephine, back at Malmaison, was ordering over six thousand francs' worth of new clothes from the *couturier* Leroy.

But, as always with Josephine, her attitudes and behaviour must be seen in context. She might have been tearful and superficial but she was also realistic. It was by her ability to adapt to changed circumstances rather than because of any firmly held convictions that Josephine had managed to survive the many vicissitudes of her life. The Revolution of 1789 had put an end to the world in which she had once lived; by trimming, by adjusting, by exercising her charm and cultivating the right people, she had made her way in the very different world that had followed. Now that yet another, and for her, infinitely grander world had collapsed, she would once again have to establish herself. And she would have to do it in the only way she knew: by making use of influential friends.

During those days before Napoleon's fall, Josephine had seen, much to her chagrin, not only his old comrades but even members of his family, turn against him. Compared with such treason, her attempt to salvage what she could, after his fall, could hardly be regarded as disloyalty. Nor did it mean that she lacked sympathy for Napoleon, or that she loved him any the less. She was simply being practical. Fifty years of age, alone, accustomed to a high standard of living, Josephine had very little income other than the annual allowance once granted by Napoleon. If this were to be discontinued by the restored Bourbons (as yet, the Treaty of Fontainebleau, in which her allowance was set, had not been drawn up), she would be in a very bad way indeed. And, even more than for herself, Josephine was concerned about the futures of Eugène and Hortense.

As soon as she had heard of Napoleon's abdication, Josephine had written to Talleyrand to remind him of the settlement agreed to by the Senate at the time of her divorce. 'I wait for the Senate to act anew and I place my interests and those of my children in your hands,' she wrote. 'Counsel me in these circumstances, and I shall follow your advice with confidence.'[2]

When the Treaty of Fontainebleau fixed her allowance at one million, instead of three million francs, she had no alternative but to accept. It was still no guarantee, though, that the restored Bourbons would honour the treaty and that her allowance would be continued indefinitely.

This was why, when Josephine – still at Navarre – received a message from Tsar Alexander inviting her and Hortense to return to Malmaison and promising 'to extend them his protection as concerned their personal safety, their positions and their fortunes', she so readily accepted. On 15 April, five days before Napoleon left for Elba, Josephine returned to Malmaison.

Why should the Tsar, and indeed the other royal figures gathered in Paris, have been so attentive to Josephine? Alexander, a great ladies' man, would undoubtedly have been interested in meeting the still glamorous Josephine and her beautiful daughter. There was a great deal of curiosity, too, about this undeniably romantic figure: a product of the *ancien régime* who had survived the Terror to become 'the most glittering ornament of imperial France.'[3] The Allied sovereigns, and particularly the returning

Bourbons, were anxious to make what Hortense calls 'a clear distinction between the Beauharnais and the Bonapartes'; by treating with the utmost respect the woman whom Napoleon had rejected, they hoped to benefit from her still continuing popularity.

Josephine was hardly back at Malmaison before the Tsar called on her. Together the two of them – the strange, seductively mannered Alexander whom Napoleon had found so fascinating, and the decorative Josephine – strolled through her famous gardens. When Hortense joined them, he was even more captivated. He promised to do everything in his power to safeguard the futures of these two charming women. Again and again, during the weeks that followed, Alexander visited them at Malmaison. He also paid a two-day visit to Hortense's country home, the Château de Saint-Leu. When, in answer to Josephine's summons, Eugène arrived from Italy on 9 May, the Tsar was no less affable. Eugène need have no qualms about his future title and position, he promised.

Where Alexander led, others followed. Malmaison was soon full to bursting point with visiting monarchs, crown princes, grand dukes and assorted princelings. In her new Leroy dresses, Josephine presided over balls, receptions and dinners. It was almost as though a new, and no less dazzling, phase of her life were about to begin.

Did Josephine, during this glittering round, spare a thought for Napoleon on Elba? Apparently she did. Although so many of the Empress's memorists are unreliable, too many of them mention her continuing love for the fallen Emperor for the claim to be without foundation. Her young lady-in-waiting, Georgette Ducrest, quotes her as saying, on hearing that Marie Louise had returned to Vienna, 'It is, above all, at this moment when he has been generally abandoned that I would wish to help him bear his exile and share his grief. Even though I am no longer his lawful wife, I would go tomorrow to join him on Elba, if I did not fear to cause him embarrassment... I have suffered since the very first day of the divorce, but never more than I do today.'[4]

Her physician, Dr Horeau, afterwards told Napoleon that Josephine had said that 'had she still been Empress of France, she would have driven straight through occupied Paris... to go to you at Fontainebleau, never again to be parted from you.'

'And I believe she would have done it,'[5] commented Napoleon.

Only one of Josephine's contemporaries, the outspoken Madame de Staël, back in Paris from the exile into which Napoleon had sent her, had the impertinence to ask the Empress if she still loved Napoleon. Josephine, having become increasingly agitated by the barrage of questions which Germaine de Staël had been preparing to ask 'since the divorce', drew the line at this one. In a rare display of pique, she dismissed her visitor.

'Would you believe it?' exclaimed Josephine to another guest, 'Madame de Staël had the effrontery to ask me whether I still love the Emperor! As if I could feel less ardently for him today, in his misfortune – I who never ceased loving the Emperor in the days of his good fortune!'[6]

'She lived to please,' wrote the Bonapartist historian Frédéric Masson of Josephine, 'and died of it.'[7]

To please the Tsar Alexander during his visit to Hortense's country home in mid May, Josephine went out driving with him in an open carriage wearing one of her flatteringly flimsy dresses. She caught a chill and was obliged to remain indoors. Always animated in company, the Empress quickly became despondent when alone. It was then that all her anxieties about the future crowded in on her.

'I can't throw off this terrible melancholy,' she admitted to Hortense's secretary, Louise Cochelet, that evening. 'I'm beginning to lose hope. The Emperor Alexander's intentions are all of the best, but as yet nothing definite has been accomplished. He makes us glowing promises, but those here in Paris are unlikely to carry them out once he has departed. I have suffered enough already at the fate of the Emperor Napoleon, fallen so low, abandoned, relegated to an island far from France. Must I now see my children fortuneless wanderers?'[8]

But by the next day, back at Malmaison, the irrepressible Josephine was welcoming another crowd of guests, and that evening she appeared at dinner in full *décolletage*. She would rest, she assured her worried entourage, 'once my affairs and those of my children have been settled.' On 23 May she played hostess to King Frederick Wilhelm III of Prussia and his two sons at dinner, and the following evening the Tsar Alexander with the Grand

Dukes Constantine, Nicholas and Michael of Russia were entertained to dinner and a ball. Again, in her willingness to please and
wearing one of her gauzy creations, Josephine left the heated
ballroom to stroll with the Tsar through her sweetly scented but
treacherously chilly garden.

The walk marked the beginning of the end. Two days later
her seriously worried doctor ordered her to bed and applied
mustard plasters to her chest and throat. On the following day the
Tsar sent his personal physician; he was joined, the next morning,
by two other eminent doctors. They pronounced that the Empress
was seriously ill. (The autopsy was to report an extreme inflamm-
ation of the whole trachea; Josephine's symptoms were those of
diphtheria.)

The Empress lay dying in her canopied swan bed in her
crimson-coloured bedroom at Malmaison. She was as elegantly
dressed as ever, says the admiring Claire de Rémusat, 'in rose-
coloured satin and beribboned.'9 Josephine could hardly speak
although Hortense thought she heard her whisper the
words, 'Bonaparte . . . Elba . . . King of Rome.' On the morning of
Sunday, 29 May 1814, Abbé Bertrand administered the last sac-
raments, and at noon, in the presence of Eugène and Hortense,
Josephine went, says Eugène, 'as sweetly and gently to meet death
as she had met life.'10

For three days Josephine's body lay in state on a catafalque in the
marble-floored entrance hall of Malmaison. She was buried on 2
June 1814 in the little parish church in nearby Rueil. Her obsequies
were, in many respects, unusual. As French troops, who had only
just switched allegiance from Napoleon to Louis XVIII, could
hardly be in attendance, the route was lined by National Guards-
men and Russian Guards regiments. The funeral sermon was
preached by the Archbishop of Tours who dextrously avoided
mentioning Napoleon by name and who managed to give the
impression that Josephine's chief role in life had been the assisting
of returning royalist *emigrés*. She had not, he was at pains to
point out, ascended the throne – which rightly belonged to the
Bourbons – voluntarily. Her body was laid to rest in the crypt,
and her grave marked by a simple slab bearing no imperial symbol
whatsoever.

Napoleon was not officially informed about Josephine's

death. A servant, sent on an errand from Elba to the Italian mainland, happened to see the story in a newspaper which he sent back to the Emperor.

'At the news of this death,' recorded his valet Marchand, 'he appeared profoundly distressed; he shut himself up in his private apartments and would see no one other than his grand marshal.'[11]

28

Exile

JUST over nine months after Josephine's death, on 5 March 1815, while Hortense was out driving through Paris, a friend galloped up to her carriage and thrust his head through the window. 'Have you heard the great news, Madame?' he cried. 'The Emperor Napoleon has landed at Cannes.'[1] Napoleon, with a handful of men, had escaped from Elba and was making for Paris.

Once the first shock had worn off, Hortense's thoughts were for the safety of her two sons. She hurried home and packed them off to the country. The next few days passed in a blur of uncertainty, with dozens of conflicting rumours flooding Paris and a host of anxious Bonapartists crowding her salon. By the 10th of the month, when the news of Napoleon's amazing advance towards Paris had been confirmed, Hortense was obliged to go into hiding to escape possible arrest.

For the following nine days, while more and more Frenchmen rallied to Napoleon's standard – until the few hundred men with whom he had landed had swollen to an enormous force – Hortense remained hidden. It was only when she noticed the ultra-royalist painter who lived opposite busily dusting a full-length portrait of one of the ex-Emperor's ministers that she realised that her period of hiding was over. That evening she was told that King Louis XVIII had fled Paris the night before, and the following day she was able to return home in safety.

The Emperor, his bloodless march from the south to his

capital accomplished, was due to arrive in Paris that evening. Hortense changed into a court dress and hurried to the Tuileries. So enthusiastically was she cheered on her arrival that for a moment she imagined Napoleon to have arrived at the same time. Her sentimentality being blended with cynicism, Hortense could not help smiling at this almost hysterical reception from those who, a few days before, had not even bothered to greet her.

While the company stood about waiting for the Emperor's arrival, it was noticed that the Napoleonic bees which had once decorated the carpet in the throne room had been covered with Bourbon lilies, and that, by tugging at the superimposed cyphers, they came away, revealing the original design underneath. Immediately the entire sumptuously dressed company were crawling about on hands and knees, wrenching off the offending lilies. Within half an hour the throne room carpet was once more swarming with golden bees.

Napoleon arrived at nine o'clock. His appearance was greeted with an ear-splitting shout of '*Vive l'Empereur*'. He was wearing his old grey overcoat, and so great was the press of cheering, waving, weeping admirers that he was unable to move a step.

'For heaven's sake, get in front of him, so that he can move,' shouted someone.

Lavallette, one of his devoted officers, placed himself in front of his hero and walked slowly backwards while Napoleon, his eyes closed and his hands stretched out in front of him, moved forward as if in a dream. Lavallette, in a highly emotional state, could only keep repeating, 'It's you! It's you! It's you at last!'

The following day Hortense was able to see Napoleon alone. They spoke about Josephine, and later the Emperor asked if he could visit Malmaison. As Hortense had not had the heart to visit the house since her mother's death, it had remained shuttered and silent; now she steeled herself to play hostess to Napoleon.

He arrived early one morning. As he and Hortense walked through the empty rooms and the quiet gardens, then just coming into spring-time life, the Emperor's distress was obvious. 'Everywhere I look I seem to see her!' he exclaimed. 'I cannot believe she is no longer here.'[2]

Before leaving, he went alone into Josephine's bedroom. For a long time he stood beside the gilded and canopied bed in which she had died. What he was thinking, one cannot know. Perhaps they were the thoughts that he was to put into words, six years later, not long before his own death on Saint Helena. 'I truly loved her,' he said to General Bertrand, 'although I didn't respect her. She was a liar and an utter spendthrift, but she had a certain something that was irresistible. She was a woman to her very fingertips.'[3]

Or perhaps he was thinking that if he were still married to her, she might have brought him the luck that he was going to need during the coming months.

But, at Waterloo, he had no luck. By the morning of 21 June 1815 Napoleon was back in Paris, dishevelled, exhausted and defeated. Again Josephine's daughter hurried to see him, this time at the Elysée palace, where she found him walking alone in the garden.

'Well, what have people been saying to you?' he asked.

'That you have been unfortunate, Sire,' answered Hortense simply.

The following day he abdicated for a second time. 'My political life is over,' he dictated, 'and I proclaim my son, under the title of Napoleon II, Emperor of the French.'

Thus, on 22 June 1815, a four-year-old boy, living hundreds of miles away in Schönbrunn Palace in Vienna, became Emperor of the French. His reign was to last a few days only.

Having abdicated, Napoleon did not seem to know what to do next. Bombarded with conflicting advice by his brothers Joseph, Lucien and Jerome, he finally decided to flee to North America. Before setting sail, however, he asked Hortense if he might spend his last few days on French soil in Josephine's home.

'He arrived at Malmaison the next morning [25 June],' writes Hortense, 'and I went with a heavy heart to receive him, remarking that this same Malmaison which had seen him at the height of his glory saw him now in his ultimate disaster; thinking sadly, too, that he would no longer find there his sweet companion, all tenderness and devotion. I, her daughter, could only offer my sympathy and solicitude. I could not take her place.'

Indeed, once he was there, Napoleon's thoughts were almost all of Josephine. One morning Hortense found him walking alone in the gardens; it was a lovely cloudless summer's day with Josephine's lawns and trees and flowers looking their best. 'My poor Josephine!' he exclaimed. 'I cannot get used to this place without her! Every moment I expect to see her coming along one of the paths to pick the flowers she loved so much! Poor Josephine!'

Then, seeing Hortense's blue eyes swimming with tears, he added, 'But still, she would have been very unhappy now. We only ever quarrelled about one subject – her debts, and I scolded her a great deal about them. She was the most enchanting being I have ever known. She was a woman in every sense of the word, vivid, vivacious and so tender-hearted ....'

And on the last day of his five-day stay, Napoleon came and sat beside Hortense on one of Josephine's rustic benches. 'How beautiful Malmaison is!' he sighed. 'Wouldn't it be delightful if we could remain here forever.'[4]

But he could not. With the victorious Prussians drawing nearer to Malmaison every day, Hortense was in an agony of apprehension. There were two frigates waiting at the port of La Rochelle to convey Napoleon to America, but every day's delay lessened his chances of getting away safely. Either he would be taken prisoner by the advancing Prussians or his ship would be captured by the waiting British.

Finally, just after five on the afternoon of 29 June, he left. Having said goodbye to his assembled relations – his mother, his brothers and Hortense – and followed by a handful of officers, Napoleon walked swiftly to the gate where a coach was waiting. As he was about to clamber inside, he turned to look back at Malmaison. He then flung himself into the carriage.

The coachman slapped the reins and the coach started down the road. It was the beginning of a journey that was to end, five thousand miles away, in exile on the island of Saint Helena.

The fall of the Empire scattered Napoleon's relations. His wife, the Empress Marie Louise, after a short stay in Vienna, took up her position as the Grand Duchess of Parma. Life in provincial Parma suited Marie Louise very well; she was never cut out to be an empress. By her side was the man whom her knowing father, the Emperor Francis, had designated to watch over her after Napoleon's first abdication: Count von Niepperg. In a very short time the susceptible Marie Louise had fallen in love with the handsome, virile and masterful Niepperg. She became his mistress. Beside this new passion, her four-year-long association with Napoleon was as nothing. What she had imagined to be love for Napoleon had been little more than a schoolgirl crush; it was

Niepperg who brought her womanhood into full bloom.

Incensed Bonapartists have accused Marie Louise of having no heart, of being shallow in her affections. Nothing could be further from the truth. She loved Niepperg until the day he died. There is no doubt that, had he been exiled to some lonely island, she would have followed him without a moment's hesitation.

Her son by Napoleon, the little King of Rome, had been left behind in Vienna. Indeed, never had so small a child been so great an embarrassment. All the glories, all the menace of Napoleon's Empire were now concentrated in this little boy; while he lived, Napoleon had an heir and the system against which Europe had fought so desperately for the last fifteen years had a figurehead. What was to be done with him? Several centuries earlier he would probably have been poisoned; in these more enlightened times, a more subtle means of minimising his importance had to be devised. Luckily he was still young enough to be moulded into whatever form was considered advisable, and to this end his grandfather, the Austrian Emperor, spurred on by the shrewd Metternich, directed his energies.

Gradually, but resolutely, all traces of his French imperial past were eradicated and he was transformed into an Austrian princeling. His infant title of King of Rome was replaced by the thoroughly Germanic one of the Duke of Reichstadt. His father's name Napoleon was exchanged for his grandfather's name, Francis; he was henceforth known as Franz. His origins – the identity of his father and his years as the King of Rome – were shrouded in mystery.

By the time he was old enough to appreciate fully the significance of his birth and inheritance, it was too late to do anything about it; Napoleon's son was already suffering from the consumption that was to kill him at the age of twenty-one.

While the King of Rome languished in his gilded cage in Vienna, several members of the Bonaparte family were living in Rome. Banished from France, they transferred what assets they could and took up residence in Italy. The colony of exiles was headed by Madame Mère. Older, sadder, but no less of a martinet, she bought herself a magnificent *palazzo* and crammed it with souvenirs of her son's Empire.

Living in an equally magnificent *palazzo* but in a far more extravagant fashion was her daughter Pauline, Princess Borghese. Now in her late thirties, Pauline was beginning to lose her celebrated looks; visitors began to talk in terms of the 'traces of her former beauty'. But the care and adornment of her body remained her overriding passion and guests might still be treated to the sight of a page devoting a couple of hours to the washing, creaming, perfuming and manicuring of her lovely feet. She and Prince Borghese, who had lived apart for many years, were finally legally separated at this time.

Also in Rome was the third Bonaparte son, the unpredictable Lucien, whom the Pope had long ago granted the title of Prince of Canino. By finally throwing in his lot with Napoleon after his brother's return from Elba, Lucien had forfeited the goodwill gained by his long years of exile during the Empire, and he was now mistrusted by the Allied powers. But the Pope remained a good friend and Lucien was able to resume his sybaritic life.

Living a very different sort of life in Rome was the fourth Bonaparte son, the surly Louis, ex-King of Holland. To his chief preoccupation – his health – was now added another. After years of unsuccessful demands, he finally managed to gain control of his eldest son by Hortense, Napoleon Louis. This gave him every opportunity to play the heavy-handed father. The boy was subjected to so rigorous a course of instruction that when, after several years, he was allowed to visit his mother, Hortense hardly knew him. His appearance strengthened her resolve never to part from her youngest son, Charles Louis Napoleon.

The rest of the family, with the exception of Joseph, ex-King of Spain, were in Trieste. At the fall of the Empire, the profligate Jerome, ex-King of Westphalia, had joined his wife Catherine in her father's kingdom of Württemberg. They remained there for two years, more or less prisoners, while Catherine's father repeatedly begged her to divorce the worthless Jerome. She refused. Unable to break her resolution, the King of Württemberg gave way and Jerome and Catherine were allowed to leave Württemberg. They moved, in 1817, to Trieste, where, on borrowed money, Jerome insisted on living in semi-regal state.

Caroline, ex-Queen of Naples, with her four children, had also taken up residence in Trieste. Her husband, the swashbuckling Joachim Murat, was dead. Having decided to stage his own return from Elba – by setting off from Corsica to recapture his old kingdom of Naples which he had lost in 1815 – he had dressed himself in one of his flashy uniforms and landed on the Neapolitan coast. The adventure had been a complete fiasco. Murat had been arrested, tried and shot. The last words of this vain and valiant warrior had been characteristic. The firing squad, he shouted, were to spare his face.

The last of the Bonapartes living in Trieste was Elisa. Her days of greatness, as the Grand Duchess of Tuscany, over, she devoted herself to the nursing of her considerable fortune and to her self-conscious fostering of the arts. Her husband, Bacciochi, seems to have played no more active a part in these sunset years than he had in their high noon in Tuscany.

Joseph, ex-King of Spain, was in America. He, too, had managed to hold on to his fortune and was living in a mansion near Bordentown, New Jersey. Here the cultivated ex-monarch was able to establish something not unlike a court; surrounded, as one entranced guest put it, 'by all the souvenirs and luxuries of his early life.' His wife Julie and their two daughters had remained in Europe.

But of all Napoleon's relations, the one who weathered the storm best was Josephine's son, Eugène de Beauharnais. Through the influence of Josephine's champion, Tsar Alexander, Eugène had been able to retain, not only his money, but also his property in France and Italy. Sheltered under the wing of his father-in-law, the King of Bavaria, and adored by his wife and children, Eugène was far more content now than ever he had been in his days as Napoleon's viceroy. Life in a small German court suited the good-natured Eugène very well; he even accepted a new German title, the Duke of Leuchtenberg.

It was due to Eugène's influence that his sister, Hortense, was able to set up house in Augsburg in Bavaria. Grateful for this place of refuge, Hortense gathered together such possessions as she had been able to save and settled down to the quiet life she loved so well.

Her chief comfort during these years was her second son, Charles Louis Napoleon, who – confusingly and in spite of his older brother being called Napoleon Louis – was generally known as Louis Napoleon. With her eldest son in the care of his father in Rome, Hortense found herself drawn more and more towards this youngest child. He was well worthy of her affection. Dreamy, kindly, sensitive, sentimental, full of loving gestures and disarming observations, he was a true Beauharnais, very much the Empress Josephine's grandson.

But gradually, as he matured, so did young Louis Napoleon's

somewhat flaccid personality begin to take shape. His mother's anecdotes of life in the palaces of France and his Uncle Eugène's tales of brave deeds on the battlefield began to fire his fertile imagination. Behind those pale blue, heavy-lidded eyes, an obsession – to restore the Empire – was beginning to take root.

While the new Emperor was growing up in Augsburg, the old one was dying on Saint Helena.

Much of Napoleon's five-and-a-half-year-long exile on Saint Helena had been spent in what he once described as the accomplishing of his destiny: the setting down of the story of his past with an eye fixed firmly on the future. By the presentation of his achievements and aspirations in the best possible light, he hoped to prepare the way for his son's eventual return to the imperial throne. And it is for this fashioning of the Napoleonic legend (which would, indeed, contribute to the restoration of his empire) that Napoleon's exile on Saint Helena is chiefly significant.

Napoleon, for all his protests against the inadequate accommodation, the humiliating restrictions, the lack of due respect to his person, was astute enough to appreciate the dramatic possibilities of his exile. What more suitable place to inaugurate a creed than on this lonely, wave-lashed, wind-swept rock? It was better for his son, he once admitted, that he should be on Saint Helena; his 'martyrdom' would win his son the crown.

Rewriting his history suited Napoleon very well. Always a great talker, he could now talk to his heart's content while his companions-in-exile – Count Bertrand, Count de Las Cases, Count de Montholon and Baron Gourgaud – tried to keep pace with the torrent that came tumbling from their master's lips. Up and down the small, hot, ill-furnished rooms of Longwood House he would strut, his followers setting down his words frantically, always two or three sentences behind. He would think nothing of sending for one of his officers at four in the morning and of subjecting the sleep-bemused man to a whirlwind of dictated reminiscences lasting well into the day. And at night, when all the house, when all the island – except for the ever-vigilant sentries – was asleep, there would come the ceaseless churning of that voice and the scratch of some swiftly moving pen.

Although the need to prepare the ground for the return of his dynasty coloured much of his reminiscing, it by no means coloured it all. When he was not dictating, he would be discussing every topic under the sun. The journals kept by his companions contain Napoleon's views on a bewildering variety of subjects. Among them were his characteristically frank and often indelicately expressed opinions of his relations. He was seldom complimentary.

And of all the members of his family, it was to Josephine that his thoughts seemed to revert most frequently. In these sunset years of his career memories of this woman whom he had loved in the days of his dawning greatness came flowing back. Perhaps there was something in the quality of the seductively warm, starlit evenings that reminded him of her; perhaps, surrounded by a bitter, bickering, dowdy, dissatisfied household, he had come to appreciate anew her kindness, her calm, her chic, her sympathy. 'She was really an amiable woman – elegant, charming and affable...,' he said to his doctor one day. 'She was the goddess of fashion; everything she put on appeared elegant; and she was so kind, so humane – she was the best woman in France.'[5] He assured Count Bertrand that he had really loved her; she had a certain something, he did not know what, that attracted him. Her little bottom, he mused, was the sweetest in the world.

One night, during Napoleon's final illness, he suddenly woke and turning to Count de Montholon, who was keeping watch by his bedside, said 'with extraordinary emotion,' 'I have just seen my good Josephine, but she didn't want to kiss me. She slipped away the moment I wanted to take her in my arms. She was sitting there; it was as if I had last seen her only the night before. She hadn't changed – always the same, still completely devoted to me. She told me we were going to see each other again and never again leave each other. She has promised me. Did you see her?'[6]

And when Napoleon died, on 5 May 1821, at the age of fifty-two, it was – again according to Montholon – with the name of Josephine on his lips. But Montholon's testimony is suspect. Not only was he the sole witness in that crowded death chamber to mention it but his account was written in the 1840s, at a time when Montholon was championing the cause of the new Bonaparte pretender, Josephine's grandson, Louis Napoleon.

It is, apparently, about Montholon that a far more serious allegation has been made in recent years. Although all the doctors present at Napoleon's autopsy agreed that the Emperor died of cancer of the stomach, a theory has since been propounded that Napoleon had been poisoned. His symptoms very much resemble those of arsenic poisoning; and his body showed none of the wasting away typical of cancer patients. His assassin, it is suggested, was a member of his suite in the pay of the restored Bourbons. The theory might well be correct.[7]

With the British authorities on Saint Helena having been given orders that Napoleon was to be buried on the island, his body – encased in four coffins – was laid to rest in a beautiful, steep-sided setting known as Geranium Valley. Because the governor, as an ultimate insult, had insisted that the name Bonaparte be added to Napoleon on the gravestone, the Emperor's companions had decided that, as an ultimate compliment, the stone should remain bare.

For almost twenty years Napoleon's body lay buried under the willow trees in Geranium Valley. But by then, the reigning French monarch, King Louis Philippe, had decided that, in the hope of bringing a little glitter to his own lack-lustre regime, he must identify himself more closely with the vanished glories of Napoleon's Empire. The Emperor's statue was once more hoisted atop the Vendôme column, his Arc de Triomphe was completed, the imperial battle pictures were put on show in the palace of Versailles. And, as a crowning gesture, it was decreed that Napoleon's body must be brought back from Saint Helena for burial in the French capital.

On 15 December 1840 the body reached Paris. At dawn that day, in the presence of a vast concourse of people, the coffin passed under the Arc de Triomphe and down the Champs-Elysées for burial in the Hôtel des Invalides. Nothing that could be achieved by paper, paint and plaster had been spared to welcome it. An immense hearse, needing every one of those sixteen richly capari-soned horses to drag it, lumbered between rows of mock-marble figures, eagle-crowned columns, vast funeral urns and outsize calico tricolours. It reached Les Invalides late in the afternoon and, after a long and tedious service, the remains were laid to rest.

Napoleon's wish, ringingly expressed in his will, that his ashes should 'repose on the banks of the Seine, in the midst of the French people whom I have loved so dearly', had finally been granted.

EPILOGUE

In Death Divided

THE settings in which the bodies of Napoleon and Josephine lie buried today, within ten miles of each other in Paris, are very different.

'Napoleon's Tomb' is now one of the great sights of the French capital. The Place Vauban and the surrounding avenues are thick with tourist buses as the crowds, in their thousands, pour daily into the hushed interior of the Dôme des Invalides. Reverently they tramp around the rim of the vast circular well at the bottom of which – surrounded by giant-sized statuary – lies Napoleon's huge porphyry sarcophagus. Everything is massive, heroic, larger-than-life; the air is solemn, almost religious. 'And why not?' as the watching Thackeray commented at the time of the Emperor's grandiose reburial, 'Who is God here but Napoleon?'[1]

To visit Josephine's tomb is a less easily accomplished undertaking. Enquiries as to its whereabouts are met, not only from the townspeople but from the gendarmerie of Rueil, by a shrug. In fact, the unremarkable little church in which Josephine is buried stands in a busy square in the heart of the town; outside, there is nothing to indicate that it houses the body of Napoleon's consort, the Empress of the French.

The interior of the church is no more distinctive. The light is dim, the atmosphere dingy. To the right as one faces the altar is Josephine's monument; to the left, is one to Hortense. The Empress's tomb is in the form of a graceful marble statue by Cartellier – based on David's painting of Napoleon's coronation – in which she is pictured kneeling at a prie-dieu. It was erected, over ten years after her death, at the instigation of Eugène and Hortense.

Opposite, in almost identical pose, is the statue marking the tomb of Queen Hortense, who died in 1837. It was erected by Hortense's only surviving son, after he had ascended the throne as the Emperor Napoleon III.

'A child by Josephine is what I needed,' Napoleon once said on Saint Helena, 'and would have served me best – not merely from the point of view of political significance but from that of my own personal happiness, my private life.'[2]

So it was one of the ironies of history that Napoleon's dynasty should have been continued and his Empire briefly but brilliantly restored, not by Marie Louise's son – the sickly young man who died in Vienna aged twenty-one in 1832 – but by the grandson of the woman whom he had sacrificed for the sake of his dynasty and Empire: the woman whom he had always loved the most, Josephine.

Notes

PROLOGUE

1 Hortense, *Mémoires*
2 *Ibid*

CHAPTER ONE

1 Bourgeat, *Lettres*
2 Rémusat, *Mémoires*
3 Carrington, *Napoleon*
4 *Ibid*
5 Las Cases, *Mémorial*
6 Bertrand, *Cahiers*
7 Bonaparte, Joseph, *Mémoires*

CHAPTER TWO

1 Hanoteau, *Ménage*
2 *Ibid*
3 *Ibid*
4 Masson, *Impératrice*
5 Chuquet, *La Jeunesse*
6 Masson, *Inconnu*
7 Las Cases, *Mémorial*
8 Masson, *Inconnu*
9 *Ibid*
10 Abrantès, *Mémoires*
11 Bonaparte, Joseph, *Mémoires*

CHAPTER THREE

1 Bouillé, *Souvenirs*
2 Beauharnais, *Mémoires*
3 Masson, *Josephine de Beauharnais*
4 *Ibid*
5 Bigard, *Josephine*
6 Hortense, *Mémoires*
7 Elliot, *Journal*
8 Ducrest, *Mémoires*
9 *Ibid*
10 Chuquet, *La Jeunesse*
11 Las Cases, *Mémorial*
12 Napoleon, *Correspondance*
13 Bonaparte, Joseph, *Mémoires*
14 Napoleon, *Correspondance*
15 Bonaparte, Joseph, *Mémoires*
16 *Ibid*

CHAPTER FOUR

1 Masson, *Inconnu*
2 *Ibid*
3 *Ibid*
4 *Ibid*
5 *Ibid*
6 Abrantès, *Mémoires*
7 *Revue des Deux Mondes*, Nov. 1939
8 Abrantès, *Mémoires*

CHAPTER FIVE

1 Quoted in Knapton, *Josephine*
2 Mossiker, *Napoleon*
3 D'Almeras, *Barras*
4 Pasquier, *Histoire*
5 Arnault, *Souvenirs*
6 Napoleon, *Correspondance*
7 Stendhal, *Mémoires*
8 Gourgaud, *Journal*
9 *Ibid*
10 Barras, *Mémoires*
11 Bourgeat, *Lettres*
12 *Ibid*
13 Gourgaud, *Journal*
14 Hortense, *Mémoires*
15 Bourgeat, *Lettres*

CHAPTER SIX

1 Creston, *In Search*
2 *Ibid*
3 Marmont, *Mémoires*
4 Gourgaud, *Journal*
5 Bourgeat, *Lettres*
6 Gourgaud, *Journal*
7 Bourgeat, *Lettres*
8 Masson, *Josephine de Beauharnais*
9 *Ibid*
10 Hortense, *Mémoires*
11 Bourrienne, *Mémoires*
12 Arnault, *Souvenirs*
13 Hortense, *Mémoires*
14 Bourgeat, *Lettres*

CHAPTER SEVEN

1 Las Cases, *Mémorial*
2 Marmont, *Mémoires*
3 Bourgeat, *Lettres*
4 *Ibid*
5 *Ibid*
6 *Ibid*
7 *Ibid*
8 Arnault, *Souvenirs*
9 Rémusat, *Mémoires*
10 Bourgeat, *Lettres*
11 Rémusat, *Mémoires*
12 Bourgeat, *Lettres*

13 *Ibid*
14 Masson, *Madame Bonaparte*
15 Bourgeat, *Lettres*
16 *Ibid*
17 *Ibid*
18 *Ibid*

CHAPTER EIGHT

1 Bourgeat, *Lettres*
2. *Ibid*
3 Mérimée, *Correspondance*
4 Abrantès, *Mémoires*
5 Miot, *Mémoires*
6 Bourgeat, *Lettres*
7 Masson, *Madame Bonaparte*
8 Aubenas, *Josephine*
9 Arnault, *Souvenirs*
10 Rémusat, *Mémoires*
11 Arnault, *Souvenirs*
12 Bourrienne, *Mémoires*

CHAPTER NINE

1 Masson, *Madame Bonaparte*
2 Bourrienne, *Mémoires*
3 Herold, *Mistress*
4 Lacour-Gayet, *Talleyrand*
5 Hastier, *Le Grand Amour*
6 *Ibid*
7 Bourrienne, *Mémoires*
8 Arnault, *Souvenirs*
9 Masson, *Madame Bonaparte*
10 *Ibid*
11 Bourrienne, *Mémoires*
12 Masson, *Madame Bonaparte*
13 Masson, *Les Femmes*
14 Bonaparte, Joseph, *Mémoires*
15 Hastier, *Le Grand Amour*
16 Hortense, *Mémoires*
17 Rémusat, *Mémoires*
18 Masson, *Madame Bonaparte*
19 Hanoteau, *Ménage*

CHAPTER TEN

1 Gohier, *Mémoires*
2 Abrantès, *Mémoires*
3 Rémusat, *Mémoires*
4 Bourrienne, *Mémoires*

5 Rémusat, *Mémoires*
6 Abrantès, *Mémoires*
7 Villefosse, *L'Opposition*
8 Ségur, *Mémoires*
9 Arnault, *Souvenirs*
10 Bourgeat, *Lettres*
11 Bourrienne, *Mémoires*
12 *Ibid*

CHAPTER ELEVEN

1 Constant, *Mémoires*
2 Burney, *Diary*
3 Bourrienne, *Mémoires*
4 Hortense, *Mémoires*
5 Constant, *Mémoires*
6 Rémusat, *Mémoires*
7 Bourrienne, *Mémoires*
8 Hortense, *Mémoires*
9 *Ibid*
10 Bourrienne, *Mémoires*
11 Gourgaud, *Journal*
12 Constant, *Mémoires*
13 Gourgaud, *Journal*
14 Hortense, *Mémoires*
15 Rémusat, *Mémoires*
16 Hortense, *Mémoires*
17 Abrantès, *Mémoires*
18 Rémusat, *Mémoires*
19 Creston, *In Search*
20 Bourrienne, *Mémoires*
21 Abrantès, *Mémoires*
22 Bourrienne, *Mémoires*

CHAPTER TWELVE

1 Bourgeat, *Lettres*
2 Hortense, *Mémoires*
3 *Ibid*
4 *Ibid*
5 Bourrienne, *Mémoires*
6 Masson, *Madame Bonaparte*
7 Girardin, *Journal*
8 Constant, *Mémoires*
9 Quoted in Knapton, *Josephine*
10 Las Cases, *Mémorial*
11 Rémusat, *Mémoires*
12 Quoted in Knapton, *Josephine*
13 Masson, *Madame Bonaparte*

14 *Ibid*
15 Bourrienne, *Mémoires*
16 Abrantès, *Mémoires*
17 Bourrienne, *Mémoires*
18 d'Arjuzon, *Madame Louis*
19 Hortense, *Mémoires*

CHAPTER THIRTEEN

1 Bourrienne, *Mémoires*
2 Roederer, *Mémoires*
3 Bourrienne, *Mémoires*
4 Masson, *Madame Bonaparte*
5 Bourrienne, *Mémoires*
6 Bourgeat, *Lettres*
7 Girardin, *Journal*
8 Bourrienne, *Mémoires*
9 Hortense, *Mémoires*
10 *Ibid*
11 *Ibid*
12 *Ibid*
13 Rémusat, *Mémoires*
14 *Ibid*
15 Hortense, *Mémoires*
16 *Ibid*
17 Rémusat, *Mémoires*
18 *Ibid*

CHAPTER FOURTEEN

1 Rémusat, *Mémoires*
2 *Ibid*
3 *Ibid*
4 *Ibid*
5 Constant, *Mémoires*
6 Rémusat, *Mémoires*
7 Stendhal, *Vie de Napoleon*
8 Saunders, *Napoleon*
9 Viel-Castel, *Mémoires*
10 Caulaincourt, *Mémoires*
11 Constant, *Mémoires*
12 Richardson, *Bisexual*
13 Bertrand, *Cahiers*
14 Richardson, *Bisexual*
15 Kemble, *Immortal*
16 Antommarchi, *Last Days*
17 Caulaincourt, *Mémoires*
18 Ségur, *Mémoires*
19 Caulaincourt, *Mémoires*

20 Bourgeat, *Lettres*
21 Méneval, *Mémoires*
22 Constant, *Mémoires*
23 Marbot, *Mémoires*
24 Méneval, *Mémoires*
25 Kemble, *Immortal*
26 Henry, *Events*
27 Quoted in Richardson, *Bisexual*
28 *Ibid*

CHAPTER FIFTEEN

1 Bonaparte, Lucien, *Mémoires*
2 Rémusat, *Mémoires*
3 *Ibid*
4 Napoleon, *Lettres*
5 Bourrienne, *Mémoires*
6 Rémusat, *Mémoires*
7 Bourrienne, *Mémoires*
8 Masson, *Madame Bonaparte*
9 Quoted in Bryant, *Years*
10 Hortense, *Mémoires*
11 Rémusat, *Mémoires*
12 Constant, *Mémoires*
13 Bertrand, *Cahiers*
14 Rémusat, *Mémoires*
15 Napoleon, *Correspondance*
16 Rémusat, *Mémoires*

CHAPTER SIXTEEN

1 Hortense, *Mémoires*
2 Rémusat, *Mémoires*
3 Hortense, *Mémoires*
4 Rémusat, *Mémoires*
5 Hortense, *Mémoires*
6 Savant, *Lettres*
7 Rémusat, *Mémoires*
8 *Ibid*
9 *Ibid*
10 *Ibid*
11 Roederer, *Journal*
12 Le Normand, *Secret Memoirs*
12 Napoleon, *Correspondance*
14 Abrantès, *Mémoires*
15 Rémusat, *Mémoires*
16 Abrantès, *Mémoires*
17 Rémusat, *Mémoires*
18 Bertrand, *Cahiers*

CHAPTER SEVENTEEN

1 Rémusat, *Mémoires*
2 *Ibid*
3 *Ibid*
4 *Ibid*
5 Constant, *Mémoires*
6 Hortense, *Mémoires*
7 *Ibid*
8 Constant, *Mémoires*
9 Méneval, *Mémoires*
10 Napoleon, *Correspondance*
11 Rémusat, *Mémoires*

CHAPTER EIGHTEEN

1 Constant, *Mémoires*
2 Rémusat, *Mémoires*
3 Constant, *Mémoires*
4 Rémusat, *Mémoires*
5 *Ibid*
6 *Ibid*
7 Constant, *Mémoires*
8 Rémusat, *Mémoires*
9 *Ibid*
10 Constant, *Mémoires*
11 *Ibid*
12 Rémusat, *Mémoires*
13 Mansel, *Eagle*
14 Napoleon, *Correspondance*
15 Rémusat, *Mémoires*
16 *Ibid*
17 *Ibid*
18 Ducrest, *Mémoires*
19 Rémusat, *Mémoires*
20 Quoted in Cronin, *Napoleon*
21 Metternich, *Mémoires*

CHAPTER NINETEEN

1 Rémusat, *Mémoires*
2 *Ibid*
3 Watson, *Carnot*
4 Rémusat, *Mémoires*
5 *Ibid*
6 *Ibid*
7 *Ibid*
8 *Ibid*
9 Avrillon, *Mémoires*

10 Rémusat, *Mémoires*
11 Masson, *Impératrice*
12 Avrillon, *Mémoires*
13 Abrantès *Mémoires*

CHAPTER TWENTY

1 Rémusat, *Mémoires*
2 Rémusat, *Lettres*
3 Bourgeat, *Lettres*
4 *Ibid*
5 *Ibid*
6 *Ibid*
7 Sutherland, *Walewska*
8 *Ibid*
9 Bourgeat, *Lettres*
10 Constant, *Mémoires*
11 Lefebvre, *Napoleon*
12 Bourgeat, *Lettres*
13 Rémusat, *Mémoires*
14 Bourgeat, *Lettres*
15 *Ibid*
16 *Ibid*
17 *Ibid*
18 *Ibid*
19 *Ibid*
20 Barnett, *Bonaparte*
21 Molé, *Life*
22 Geyl, *Napoleon*
23 Rémusat, *Mémoires*
24 Hortense, *Mémoires*

CHAPTER TWENTY-ONE

1 La Tour, *Duroc*
2 Rémusat, *Mémoires*
3 *Ibid*
4 *Ibid*
5 *Ibid*
6 Abrantès, *Mémoires*
7 Hanoteau, *l'Empereur*
8 Rémusat, *Mémoires*
9 *Ibid*
10 Talleyrand, *Mémoires*
11 Champagny, *Souvenirs*
12 Hanoteau, *l'Empereur*
13 Rémusat, *Mémoires*
14 Masson, *Inconnu*
15 Quoted in Cronin, *Napoleon*

16 Constant, *Mémoires*
17 Quoted in Cronin, *Napoleon*
18 Ventenat, *Jardin*
19 Napoleon, *Lettres*
20 Abrantès, *Mémoires*

CHAPTER TWENTY-TWO

1 Bertrand, *Cahiers*
2 Masson, *Famille*
3 Hanoteau, *l'Empereur*
4 Méneval, *Mémoires*
5 Rémusat, *Mémoires*
6 Hortense, *Mémoires*
7 Rapp, *Mémoires*
8 Napoleon, *Correspondance*
9 Hortense, *Mémoires*
10 Avrillon, *Mémoires*

CHAPTER TWENTY-THREE

1 Hortense, *Mémoires*
2 *Ibid*
3 Avrillon, *Mémoires*
4 *Ibid*
5 Méneval, *Mémoires*
6 Hortense, *Mémoires*
7 Bausset, *Mémoires*
8 Hortense, *Mémoires*
9 Rémusat, *Mémoires*
10 Hortense, *Mémoires*
11 *Ibid*
12 Masson, *Répudiée*
13 *Ibid*
14 Hortense, *Mémoires*
15 Constant, *Mémoires*
16 *Ibid*
17 Hortense, *Mémoires*

CHAPTER TWENTY-FOUR

1 Bourgeat, *Lettres*
2 Hortense, *Mémoires*
3 Avrillon, *Mémoires*
4 Hortense, *Mémoires*
5 Bourgeat, *Lettres*
6 Rémusat, *Lettres*
7 Abrantès, *Mémoires*
8 Bourgeat, *Lettres*

9 Lenôtre, *Napoleon*
10 Napoleon, *Lettres*
11 Bertrand, *Cahiers*
12 Metternich, *Mémoires*
13 Constant, *Mémoires*
14 Gourgaud, *Journal*
15 Rémusat, *Lettres*
16 Hanoteau, *l'Empereur*

CHAPTER TWENTY-FIVE

1 Napoleon, *Lettres*
2 Rémusat, *Lettres*
3 Mossiker, *Napoleon*
4 Bourgeat, *Lettres*
5 *Ibid*
6 Hanoteau, *l'Empereur*
7 Hortense, *Mémoires*
8 Ducrest, *Mémoires*
9 Hortense, *Mémoires*
10 *Ibid*
11 Avrillon, *Mémoires*
12 Bourgeat, *Lettres*
13 Caulaincourt, *Mémoires*
14 Castelot, *King of Rome*
15 Prokesch-Osten, *Les Témoins*

CHAPTER TWENTY-SIX

1 Hanoteau, *l'Empereur*
2 Caulaincourt, *Mémoires*
3 Quoted in Markham, *Napoleon*
4 Hortense, *Mémoires*
5 Hanoteau, *l'Empereur*
6 Avrillon, *Mémoires*
7 Masson, *Répudiée*
8 *Ibid*
9 *Ibid*

10 Avrillon, *Mémoires*
11 Hortense, *Mémoires*
12 Hanoteau, *l'Empereur*
13 Hortense, *Mémoires*
14 Caulaincourt, *Mémoires*
15 *Ibid*
16 Napoleon, *Correspondance*
17 Bourgeat, *Lettres*

CHAPTER TWENTY-SEVEN

1 Hanoteau, *l'Empereur*
2 Quoted in Knapton, *Josephine*
3 Knapton, *Josephine*
4 Ducrest, *Mémoires*
5 Avrillon, *Mémoires*
6 Oudinot, *Mémoires*
7 Masson, *Répudiée*
8 Cochelet, *Mémoires*
9 Rémusat, *Mémoires*
10 Beauharnais, *Mémoires*
11 Masson, *Répudiée*

CHAPTER TWENTY-EIGHT

1 Hortense, *Mémoires*
2 *Ibid*
3 *Ibid*
4 *Ibid*
5 Antommarchi, *Last Days*
6 Montholon, *Récits*
7 Forshufund, *Who killed Napoleon?*

EPILOGUE

1 Thackeray, *Funeral*
2 Gourgaud, *Journal*

Bibliography

Abrantès, Duchesse d', *Mémoires*, 4 vols, Paris, 1832

Antommarchi, Francesco, *The Last Days of Napoleon*, 2 vols, London, 1826

d'Arjuzon, Caroline, *Madame Louis Bonaparte*, Paris, 1901

——*Josephine contre Beauharnais*, Paris, 1906

Arnault, Antoine, *Souvenirs d'un sexagénaire*, Paris, 1833

Arnott, Archibald, *An Account of the Last Illness, Disease and Post-mortem Appearance of Napoleon Bonaparte*, London, 1822

Aubenas, Joseph, *Histoire de l'Impératrice Josephine*, 2 vols, Paris, 1857

Avrillon, Mademoiselle (pseud. Catharine de Villemarest), *Mémoires sur la vie privée de Josephine*, Paris, 1835

Baring-Gould, Sabine, *The Life of Napoleon Bonaparte*, London, 1897

Barnett, Corelli, *Bonaparte*, London, 1978

Barras, Paul, Vicomte de, *Mémoires de Barras*, 4 vols, Paris, 1895–6

Bausset, L. F. J. de, *Mémoires anecdotiques*, 5 vols, Brussels, 1827–9

Beauharnais, Eugène de, *Mémoires du Prince Eugène*, Paris, 1858

Bertrand, Henri-Gratien, General, *Cahiers de Sainte-Hélène*, 3 vols, Paris, 1949–59

Besnard, François, *Souvenirs d'un nonagénaire*, 2 vols, Paris, 1880

Bigard, L., *Josephine de Beauharnais à Croissy*, Revue des études napoleoniennes, Paris, 1926

Billiet, Joseph, *Malmaison. Les appartements de Josephine*, Paris, 1951

Bonaparte, Joseph, *Mémoires et correspondance politique et militaire*, Paris, 1855

Bonaparte, Lucien, *Lucien Bonaparte et ses mémoires* (Editor: Théodore Iung), Paris, 1882–3

Bouillé, Louis Joseph de, *Souvenirs et fragments*, 3 vols, Paris, 1906–11

Bourgeat, Jacques, *Napoleon, lettres à Josephine*, Paris, 1941

Bourrienne, L. A. F. de, *Mémoires*, 4 vols, Paris, 1830

Bryant, Sir Arthur, *Years of Victory*, London, 1944

Burney, Fanny, *Diary and Letters*, London, 1846

Campan, Madame, *Correspondance avec la Reine Hortense*, 2 vols, Paris, 1836

Carrington, Dorothy, *Napoleon and his Parents*, London, 1988

Castelot, André, *The King of Rome*, London, 1960

Caulaincourt, A. A. L. de, *Mémoires*, 2 vols, Paris, 1933

Champagny, Jean-Baptiste, Comte de, *Souvenirs*, Paris, 1846

Chuquet, Arthur, *La Jeunesse de Napoleon*, 3 vols, Paris, 1897–8

Cochelet, Louise, *Mémoires sur la Reine Hortense*, 2 vols, Paris, 1836

Cole, Hubert, *Josephine*, London, 1962

Constant (Louis-Constant Wairy), *Mémoires de Constant*, 4 vols, Paris, 1830

Creston, Dormer, *In Search of Two Characters*, London, 1945

Cronin, Vincent, *Napoleon*, London, 1971

D'Almeras, H., *Barras et son temps*, Paris, 1930

Decaux, Alain, *Napoleon's Mother*, London, 1962

Delderfield, R. F., *Napoleon in Love*, London, 1959

Ducrest, Georgette, *Mémoires sur l'Impératrice Josephine*, 3 vols, Paris, 1828

Durand, Sophie, *Anecdotes of the Court and Family of Napoleon Bonaparte*, London, 1818

Elliot, Grace Dalrymple, *Journal of My Life during the French Revolution*, London, 1859

Bibliography

Fain, Baron Agathon, *Mémoires*, 2 vols, Paris, 1908

Fleischmann, Hector, *Josephine Infidèle*, Paris, 1910

Forester, C. S., *Josephine, Napoleon's Empress*, London, 1925

Forshufund, Ster, *Who killed Napoleon?*, London, 1962

Fouché, Joseph, *Mémoires*, Paris, 1945

Garros, Louis, *Itinéraire de Napoleon Bonaparte*, Paris, 1947

Gavorty,A., *Josephine, Hoche et Bonaparte*, Revue des Deux Mondes, April, 1958

Geer, Walter, *Napoleon and Josephine*, New York, 1924

George, Marguerite, *A Favourite of Napoleon: Memoirs of Mlle George*, London, 1909

Geyl, Pieter, *Napoleon: For and Against*, London, 1964

Girardin, S. G. de, *Journal et Souvenirs, Discours et Opinions*, 4 vols, Paris, 1828

Gohier, Louis-Jerome, *Mémoires*, Paris, 1824

Gourgaud, Gaspard Baron, *Sainte-Hélène: Journal inédité de 1815 à 1818*, Paris, 1899

Gunn, Peter, *Napoleon's 'Little Pest'*, London, 1979

Hanoteau, Jean, *Le Ménage Beauharnais: Josephine avant Napoleon*, Paris, 1935

——*Les Beauharnais et l'Empereur: lettres de l'Impératrice Josephine et de la Reine Hortense au Prince Eugène*, Paris, 1936

Hastier, Louis, *Le Grand Amour de Josephine*, Paris, 1955

Henry, Walter, *Events of a Military Life*, London, 1843

Herold, Christopher, *Mistress to an Age*, London, 1958

——*The Mind of Napoleon*, London, 1961

Hortense, Queen, *Mémoires de la Reine Hortense*, 3 vols, Paris, 1927

Howard, J. E. (Edit), *The Rise to Power: Letters and Documents of Napoleon*, New York, 1961

Hue, François, Baron, *Souvenirs du Baron Hue*, Paris, 1903

Kemble, James, *Napoleon Immortal*, London, 1959

Knapton, Ernest John, *Empress Josephine*, London, 1964

Lacour-Gayet, L., *Talleyrand 1754–1838*, 3 vols, Paris, 1928–34

Laing, Margaret, *Josephine and Napoleon*, London, 1973

Larrey, Hippolyte, *Madame Mère*, Paris, 1892

Las Cases, Le Comte de, *Mémorial de Sainte-Hélène*, 4 vols, Paris, 1823

La Tour, Jean de, *Duroc, Grand Maréchal du Palais Imperiale*, Paris, 1907

Lavalette, Antoine de, *Mémoires et Souvenirs*, Paris, 1831

Lefebvre, George, *Napoleon 1799–1807*, London, 1969

Le Normand, M. A., *The Historical and Secret Memoirs of the Empress Josephine*, 2 vols, London, 1895

Lenôtre, G., *Napoleon*, Paris, 1933

Levy, Arthur, *Napoleon Intime*, Paris, 1898

Lumbrosos, Alberto, *Miscellanea Napoleonica, Serie V*, Rome, 1898

Mansel, Philip, *The Eagle in Splendour*, London, 1987

Marbot, Antoine, *Mémoires*, Paris, 1892

Marchand, L. N., *Mémoires*, 2 vols, Paris, 1953–5

Markham, Felix, *Napoleon*, London, 1963

Marmont, A. F. L., *Mémoires du Duc de Raguse*, 9 vols, Paris, 1857

Martineau, Gilbert, *Napoleon's Mother*, London, 1977

Masson, Frédéric, *Napoleon chez lui: La Journée de l'Empereur aux Tuileries*, Paris, 1884

——*Napoleon et les Femmes*, Paris, 1894

——*Napoleon Inconnu: Papiers Inédités*, Paris, 1895

——*Josephine de Beauharnais, 1763–1796*, Paris, 1898

——*Josephine, impératrice et reine, 1804–1809*, Paris, 1899

——*Josephine répudiée, 1809–1814*, Paris, 1900

——*Napoleon et sa Famille*, 15 vols, Paris, 1908–19

——*Madame Bonaparte, 1796–1804*, Paris, 1920

Méneval, C. F., Baron, *Mémoires*, Paris, 1894

Mérimée, Prosper, *Correspondance Générale*, Paris, 1955

Metternich, Prince, *Mémoires, documents et écrits divers*, Paris, 1880

Miot de Melito, André-François, *Mémoires*, Paris, 1873

Molé, Louis, Comte, *Life and Memoirs*, London, 1923

Montholon, C. J. F. T., Comte de, *Récits de la capitivité de l'Empereur Napoleon à Sainte-Hélène*, Paris, 1847

Mossiker, Frances, *Napoleon and Josephine*, London, 1965

Napoleon I, Emperor, *Lettres de Napoleon à Josephine; et lettres de Josephine à Napoleon et à sa fille*, 2 vols, Paris, 1833

Bibliography

——*Correspondance de Napoleon Ier*, 32 vols, Paris, 1853–69

Ober, F. A., *Josephine, Empress of the French*, London, 1901
Oman, Carola, *Napoleon's Viceroy*, London, 1966
O'Meara, Barry, *Observations upon the authenticity of Bourrienne's Memoirs of Napoleon*, London, 1831
d'Ornano, Comte, *Marie Walewska, l'épouse polonaise de Napoleon*, Paris n.d.
Oudinot, le maréchal Nicolas, Duc de Reggio, *Mémoires*, Paris, 1895
Ouvard, G. J., *Mémoires*, Paris, 1826

Palmer, Alan, *Alexander I, Tsar of War and Peace*, London, 1974
Pasquier, Etienne-Denis, Duc de, *Histoire de mon Temps*, 3 vols, Paris, 1893–5
Pichevin, René, *Impératrice Josephine*, Paris, 1909
Prokesch-Osten, Comte de, *Les Témoins de l'Epopée*, Paris, 1934

Rapp, Jean, Comte, *Mémoires du General Rapp*, Paris, 1822
Rémusat, Claire de, *Mémoires*, 2 vols, Paris, 1880
——*Lettres*, Paris, 1881
Richardson, Frank, *Napoleon: Bisexual Emperor*, London, 1972
Roederer, Pierre-Louis, Comte de, *Journal*, Paris, 1909
——*Mémoires de la Revolution, le Consulat et l'Empire*, Paris, 1942
Rose, J. Holland, *The Personality of Napoleon*, London, 1912

Saint-Denis, Louis Etienne, *Souvenirs du Mamelouck Ali*, Paris, 1926
Saunders, Edith, *Napoleon and Mademoiselle George*, London, 1958
Savant, Jean (Edit), *Napoleon et Josephine. Première édition intégrale ... des lettres de Napoleon à Josephine*, Paris, 1955
——*Napoleon et Josephine, leur roman*, Paris, 1960
Ségur, Philippe-Paul, Comte de, *Mémoires*, 2 vols, Paris, 1894–5
Sergeant, Philip W., *The Empress Josephine: Napoleon's Enchantress*, New York, 1909
Sloane, W. M., *Life of Napoleon Bonaparte*, 4 vols, London, 1901
Stendhal, H. B., *Vie de Napoleon*, Paris, 1876
——*Mémoires sur Napoleon*, Paris, 1930
Sutherland, Christine, *Marie Walewska*, London, 1979

Talleyrand-Périgord, Charles-Maurice de, *Mémoires*, Paris, 1892

Thackeray, W. M., *The Second Funeral of Napoleon*, London, 1882

Tschudi, Clara, *Napoleon's Mother*, London, 1900

Turquan, Joseph, *Impératrice Josephine*, Paris, 1896

——*The Love Affairs of Napoleon*, London, 1909

Ventenat, E. P., *Jardin de la Malmaison*, Paris, 1803

Viel-Castel, H., Comte, *Mémoires*, Paris, 1884

Villefosse, Louis de, and Bouissounouse, Janine, *L'Opposition à Napoleon*, Paris 1969

Watson, S. J., *Carnot, 1753–1823*, London, 1954

Welschinger, Henri, *Le Divorce de Napoleon*, Paris, 1889

Wertheimer, Edward de, *The Duke of Reichstadt*, London, 1906

Wright, Constance, *Daughter to Napoleon*, London, 1961

Index